PAKISTAN
at knife's edge

OTHER LOTUS TITLES

Ajit Bhattacharjea	*Sheikh Mohammad Abdullah: Tragic Hero cf Kashmir*
Anil Dharker	*Icons: Men & Women Who Shaped Today's India*
Aitzaz Ahsan	*The Indus Saga: The Making of Pakistan*
Alam Srinivas & TR Vivek	*IPL: The Inside Story*
Amir Mir	*The True Face of Jehadis: Inside Pakistan's Terror Networks*
Ashok Mitra	*The Starkness of It*
Dr Humanyun Khan & G. Parthasarthy	*Diplomatic Divide*
Gyanendra Pandey & Yunus Samad	*Faultlines of Nationhood*
H.L.O. Garrett	*The Trial of Bahadur Shah Zafar*
M.J. Akbar	*India: The Siege Within*
M.J. Akbar	*Kashmir: Behind the Vale*
M.J. Akbar	*The Shade of Swords*
M.J. Akbar	*Byline*
M.J. Akbar	*Blood Brothers: A Family Saga*
Maj. General Ian Cardozo	*Param Vir: Our Heroes in Battle*
Maj. General Ian Cardozo	*The Sinking of INS Khukri: What Happened in 1971*
Madhu Trehan	*Tehelka as Metaphor*
Mushirul Hasan	*India Partitioned. 2 Vols*
Mushirul Hasan	*John Company to the Republic*
Mushirul Hasan	*Knowledge, Power and Politics*
Nayantara Sahgal (ed.)	*Before Freedom: Nehru's Letters to His Sister*
Nilima Lambah	*A Life Across Three Continents*
Sharmishta Gooptu and Boria Majumdar (eds)	*Revisiting 1857: Myth, Memory, History*
Shashi Joshi	*The Last Durbar*
Shashi Tharoor & Shaharyar M. Khan	*Shadows across the Playing Field*
Shrabani Basu	*Spy Princess: The Life of Noor Inayat Khan*
Shyam Bhatia	*Goodbye Shahzadi: A Political Biography*

FORTHCOMING TITLES

Amir Mir	*Fluttering Flag of Jehad*
M.J. Akbar	*Have Pen, Will Travel*

PAKISTAN at knife's edge

M.B. Naqvi

LOTUS COLLECTION
ROLI BOOKS

Lotus Collection

First published in India in 2010
The Lotus Collection
An imprint of
Roli Books Pvt. Ltd.
M-75, G.K. II Market, New Delhi 110 048
Phones: ++91 (011) 40682000
Fax: ++91 (011) 2921 7185
E-mail: info@rolibooks.com
Website: www.rolibooks.com
Also at Bangalore, Chennai, Jaipur, Kolkata,
Mumbai & Varanasi

Cover Design: Supriya Saran

ISBN: 978-81-7436-790-7

Typeset in Adobe Jenson Pro by Roli Books Pvt. Ltd.
and printed and bound at Replika Press Private Limited

Dedication

I dedicate this book to the lawyers of Pakistan and its superior judiciary, who have shown by their recent brave conduct that they mean to remain in the forefront of democratic forces in this overly militarized country.

This movement started almost by a typical incident when an unaccountable military dictator, General Pervez Musharraf, secure in his powers over every segment of the government, demanded the resignation of the Chief Justice of Pakistan (CJP), Justice Iftikhar Muhammad Chaudhry, who refused. This was a magical moment of history and a whole chain of events started. This judge had been on good personal terms with Musharraf but over the years his judicial activism and bold independence had so frustrated the dictator as to make him go over the top and decided to sack him, if he did not tamely resign on demand. Justice Chaudhry stood his ground and challenged him to try him in an open court of law, if he had done anything illegal.

That no to Musharraf was followed by Justice Chaudhry's arrest, maltreatment and harassment. It electrified the legal fraternity and the rest of the people. It is over two years since. Many shameful and illegal acts by the dictator followed, including the sacking of as many as sixty-two judges of Supreme and High courts and keeping many of them locked up in their homes. But the lawyers' movement was only strengthened. Although Musharraf's successors have managed to tempt, browbeat or threaten many of these judges into seeking re-employment into their old jobs some remained unbending. This lawyers' movement has shaped the substance of politics by ensuring that democracy will take roots in the soil and that the generals had better remain confined to their military jobs. One usurper has been sent home largely as a result of the soul-lifting way the sacked judges had to be restored to their offices. It was a grand victory of the people, though curiously Pakistan Peoples Party boys who prevented people from Sindh and Balochistan to join the people of Punjab, specifically of Lahore and Gujranwala. A salute to the leadership of Mian Nawaz Sharif of Raiwind, who inspired and mobilized these people, is also called for.

The fight for Pakistanis' human rights is far from being over, though a framework for that however exists. Lawyers and the rest of civil society have to make sure that the empty shells of democracy's institutions do not remain without the soul and substance of democracy: equal human rights for all enshrined in law and respected by those who govern.

Contents

Preface

This is not a treatise or a work of research; it is just a glance at troubled Pakistan as it is today and how it is likely to develop, identifying the forces at work in transforming it.

An effort, however, has been made to look at the issues in perspective. I, as a writer, do not live in an ivory tower; I am a human rights activist and a fervent supporter of the liberal democratic dispensation. Therefore, my prejudices and prepossessions can easily be noted by readers.

I do hope that my readers will take meaningful interest in problems that the people of Pakistan face. Our democratic struggle will be reinforced by their support.

One-Man Rule: Compulsions

Although one or even a few individuals cannot radically change the fortunes of a whole people, in Pakistan's case, one is forced to be individual-centric in describing history or writing scenarios for its near future. The question here is: what is to be expected in Pakistan? After a brief historical outline has been sketched out, the reality is that, in the place of a political class and organized governance, what Pakistan now has is one-man rule despite the resignation of General Pervez Musharraf. In all essentials, only General Musharraf, the chief of army staff, who also wore the additional hat of the president of the Islamic Republic, mattered until August 2008; and now, the new president, Asif Ali Zardari, also co-chairman of Pakistan Peoples Party (PPP), is who counts. Everyone, from the prime minister down to the bureaucracy as well as intelligence services and subordinate departments, take their cue from the policy decisions the president takes. Nobody else matters. There is supposed to be a Parliament with all the usual appurtenances, but what counts is the will of this man at the top.

True, the president has advisers. But who are they? Apart from the advice of international financial institutions – WTO, World Bank, IMF, Paris Club, Asian Development Bank, American Treasury et al – on economic matters, the prime minister and coterie of advisers seem to take decisions more or less autonomously. Even here broad outlines of business as usual goes on. What the boss desires is the ideal. It is really a coterie of a few ministers and officials who manage both finance and development. This coterie runs the economy, insofar as it is possible, in accordance with the economic paradigm of globalization. Pakistan started acting on the IMF's Structural Adjustments Programme way back in the 1970s and 1980s; globalization being an amplification of those adjustments. As for politics, Musharraf's real advisers constituted a sort of Parliament of top generals who assembled every month to review the political and security situation. They took the policy decisions; although the generals gave their input, Musharraf was a primus inter pares. Execution was the business of the civil bureaucracy and even the government as such was an obedient tool; true, a few bureaucrats did become second-rank advisers. For dealing with the Parliament and other parties, President Musharraf consulted primarily two individuals: Chaudhry Shujaat Hussain, the president of the governing Pakistan Muslim League (Qaid-e-Azam) [PML (Q)] and his cousin, Chaudhry Pervez Elahi, the chief minister of Punjab, the key province of Pakistan. The president had identified himself with the Q League and was already in election mode, campaigning primarily for the party in preparation for the elections that were due late in 2007. Other allied parties continued to support him in the hope of sharing office, even if power eluded them – largely because they had no alternative course – while the Opposition claimed that Parliament is nothing more than a rubber stamp since no major decision was taken in it and no substantive legislation was passed by its members. The will of one man prevailed and that was the supreme law, in practice.

After the resignation of General Musharraf on 18 August 2008, Asif Ali Zardari was elected virtually unanimously. He, at first, appeared to have considerable moral authority due to an unusual amount of support from Parliament. But it soon became evident that Zardari's priority was to consolidate his own power rather than implementing the programme of basic legislation of amending from the Constitution all the obnoxious changes that various dictators had forced different Parliaments to put in. Zardari chose to lose the support of the second largest party in the new Parliament, Pakistan Muslim Leaque (Nawaz) [PML (N)], that was elected on 18 February 2008, and which supports all the reform measures to make Pakistan a normal democracy of the parliamentary type and with which PPP's original leader, charismatic Benazir Bhutto and Zardari himself were signatories to various documents: Charter of Democracy, Bhurban Declaration and a later two written agreements between the PPP and PML (N). Zardari has remained adamant not to implement those agreements and other urgent demands of opposition parties through dilatory tactics and, indeed, chicanery. Specifically about the matter regarding undoing of the mischief Musharraf made on 3 November 2007, where he virtually sacked all the High and Supreme courts judges who refused to take a fresh oath on the Musharraf-amended Constitution in pursuit of his struggle and held the stand taken by the chief justice of Pakistan, Justice Iftikhar Muhammad Chaudhry throughout. The long and epic struggle the latter waged against the former began on 9 March and ended in sixty-two superior court judges being sent home as a result of Musharraf's infamous Emergency of 3 November 2007. It is still a cause celebre in which all democrats want a clear and quick reversal of that declaration which was quickly adjudicated as invalid in law by the old Supreme Courts before most of its members were locked up in their homes.

When an individual reigns, such as in the absolutist monarchy of King Gyanendra of Nepal, sovereignty and the source of all legislation is the will of that person. An individual, however, is always vulnerable to political pressures, as evidenced by the uncertain fate of King Gyanendra, showing that one-man rule is much more vulnerable and weaker than a democratic government. This also applies to Pakistan. Examples are galore: the way Musharraf took an about turn on his Afghanistan policy in 2001: a mere phone call from an American general was all it took for him to reverse Pakistan's fifty-year-old policy on Afghanistan of acquiring suzerainty-like influence over it, when he rounded on Pakistan's erstwhile protégés, the Taliban, who were ruling Kabul at the time. Such a sudden change is only possible when one man alone wields power – who is not backed by his nation. The political troubles of recent years seem worsened for the same reason. They are largely the result of one-man rule.

At a Knife's Edge

Pakistan still presents a picture of strange lack of harmony between the government and its people despite an elected Parliament, governments and also an elected president. The polity's basic problems are discussed later in this book, but here, a few symptoms that are still apparent to most Pakistanis, are being identified. Much of it was written before Pervez Musharraf was forced to resign on 8 August 2008. Since no material changes have taken place; one leaves it untouched.

CIVIL SOCIETY VERSUS MILITARY GOVERNMENT

A dictatorship is still in full control in Pakistan and the people are disgruntled; feeling amongst a growing number of people is that they are at war with the non-democratic regime; it has been growing. Since General Pervez Musharraf made his putsch in 1999 and he had resigned in 2008; but that feeling has not gone away even when a PPP-led elected government is being run by President Asif Ali Zardari. Lawyers throughout the country had agitated against Musharraf's and Zardari's governments over the sacking of Justice Iftikhar Muhammad Chaudhry, sitting chief justice of the Supreme Court, by General Pervez Musharraf. The general was the chief of the army staff, but had also proclaimed himself president ten years ago, without the qualification of being elected under the Constitution. What he could have done as president in this case was to send a reference to the Supreme Judicial Council against the chief justice, which he did, although he lacked the legitimacy of a properly-elected president. But he also went on to do something else: he had him arrested on 9 March 2007 after Justice Chaudhry refused to resign as demanded by the general-president, and kept him confined in the Army House for six hours. Musharraf had summoned the chief justice to confront him with a charge sheet alleging 'misuse of office'. The chief justice, Iftikhar Muhammad Chaudhry, refused to resign, saying that he would fight the Reference in open hearings. He was prevented from returning to his chambers by men in police uniform, whom the public mistook to be law-enforcing personnel, and was manhandled and 'escorted' to his house, which was quickly surrounded and barricaded. The chief justice was not only detained and kept incommunicado between 9 and 13 March; he was prevented from reading newspapers and using the telephone and television, supposedly by law-enforcing agents. Even his children were not allowed to go to school or meet friends in the house. The panel of lawyers defending him could not meet him until the first hearing by the Supreme Judicial Council (which hears complaints against senior judiciary on References by the president, upon the recommendation of the chief justice concerned) on 13 March. The legal fraternity soon began demanding the withdrawal of the Reference, that the proceedings be openly held – not in camera as the government wanted – while the case goes on. All the political parties in the Opposition, human rights organizations and journalists demanded that the chief justice be reinstated and given maximum facilities to defend himself.

The lawyers' agitation that began in March 2007 and continued till 16 March 2009 has changed Pakistan's politics in great many ways. The support for the lawyers comes from the middle class across parties. In fact, there was an upsurge of popular support for the lawyers that forced many parties – PPP, PML (N), MMA, particularly Jamaat-e-Islami, and of course, various small parties of the country – to join the lawyers' movement in varying degrees. One of the tactics adopted by the lawyers' leaders – Barrister Aitzaz Ahsan, Munir A. Malik, Hamid Khan and Ali Ahmed Kurd – was to make the suspended chief justice of Pakistan address various bar associations, particularly in Hyderabad, Peshawar, Lahore and many smaller places. While the general-president had begun by confining the CJP to his house and keeping him incommunicado, he had to allow him to go to the Supreme Court for the hearing of the Reference he had filed. The kind of uproar that took place in the country over this case was of a kind that he was forced to relax the confinement of the CJP to some extent. It was quickly announced that he was not under arrest, though the CJP was first called 'non-functional', then 'suspended' and finally 'on forced leave' – all odd and illegal in the case of the chief justice of Pakistan. The journey that he undertook from Islamabad to Lahore by road in May 2007 lasted, instead of the usual 3-4 hours, 27 long hours and the entire route was dotted by clusters of thousands of Pakistani villagers who just wanted to see their chief justice, touch his car or him – a brave man who could defy the all powerful dictator and say 'no' to his suggestion. The chief justice made no political speeches whatsoever after his order. The CJP has been talking, of course, of rule of law, what the Constitution says, or the importance of Constitution, independence of judiciary and separation of powers. Only these and no politics was included in his speeches-cum-lectures.

It is true most political parties have skeletons in their cupboards on the issue of the judiciary's independence. PPP, when last in office, had had legal fracas, though much less severe, with chief justice of its days. The PML (N) had a similar spat with the same chief justice, and indeed had organized a physical attack by goons on the Supreme Court, which the ministers led. Among the ministers, Mushahid Hussain Sayed, who later became the eminent rouges of Musharraf's government and is now secretary general of the PML (Q), is known to have been the leader. Their Lordships had to save themselves by leaving their courts and hiding in their chambers. No leadership of any party, it appears, was wholeheartedly supporting the cause of the lawyers, perhaps, none of them really wanted a truly independent judiciary. While in power each party tends to want to do things that it does not like the Supreme Court to look too closely into. This is an unfortunate situation that characterizes most political parties of the country, except the smaller nationalist parties, none of which ever came to power or was tested in office.

And yet, every section of the civil society came out in support of the lawyers. While the masses were not being mobilized simply because after the 3 November counter attack by the Musharraf regime, the country was virtually under martial law – in the name of Emergency. Dissent and agitation of all kinds were being suppressed brutally. But events were moving fast because a US-brokered secret deal between President Musharraf and PPP's Life-Chairperson Benazir Bhutto was announced. The PPP was won over to support. Musharraf's design for staying on as president for another five-year-term, in lieu of taking off general's uniform, holding a free election and most importantly dropping various corruption cases against Benazir Bhutto and her husband Asif Ali Zardari, otherwise known as Mr Ten Per Cent. Both sides delivered on their promises. The atmosphere changed rapidly after Benazir returned on 18 October 2007 to campaign for the coming election, and the momentum of freer political activity could not be dampened even by the tragic murder of Benazir in December 2007. That remains a mystery. PPP tried to cash in on it electorally and emerged the largest party in the National Assembly and went on to form a coalition government in March with Mian Nawaz Sharif's PML (N) that broke down two months later in May 2008 though a mostly verbal coalition survives because of two factors: First, PML (N) seems to be under some unacknowledged pressure or a secret deal through the Saudi royal family and the US diplomacy. The other, and more prosaic, factor may be that although PML (N) withdrew from the federal government, it wanted to retain this coalition in the Punjab Assembly. Interestingly, PML (N) could manage a comfortable simple majority and felt no need for allies to keep the government intact. This suggests a mastermind that wants the larger parties to remain in a multicoloured coalition. People have instinctively seen it as a US design: let Musharraf remain president and lead a rainbow coalition government in the War on (Islamic) Terror.

The civil society nevertheless was evolving new tactics during the lawyers' movement. NGOs, professional groups and many others started assembling at unannounced places, demonstrate briefly and disperse before the police could muster themselves to break the crowd or make arrests. Journalists joined the fray and they have been protesting against the counter measures of 3 November 2007 by General Musharraf, in which electronic media and press were also put under new restrictions. The journalists' agitation continued in tandem with lawyers'. However, the fact must be noted that the main political parties mostly paid lip service to these two agitations, without getting themselves involved too deeply or too actively. Moreover, as said before, most party leaderships are as wary of journalists, as of the lawyers or superior judiciary, that is truly independent. Independent professionals cannot be influenced easily. Both agitations are continuing after a fashion and the parties dutifully support both campaigns without much conviction. And yet, they dare not say anything specific against these movements, except perhaps PML (N) that has opted to support the lawyers' and judges' causes for strategic purposes of its own – and has even achieved it cheaply. That unfortunate circumstance is also a fact of life.

A certain pattern has emerged: people's response, particularly in Punjab, for both agitations is far more strident and clear-cut than in the other provinces, including Sindh, otherwise a hotbed of dissent and restiveness. This is due to a profound change in Punjab. Time was when Punjab was always with the Pakistan Army and the explanation was simple: 65 per cent or more of the army always comprised Punjabis. Whenever the military took over, Punjabis had the least trouble in finding a way of approaching a soldier, NCO or officer to redress some of their grievances. That was not true of other provinces, namely, Sindh and Balochistan; although the Pushtoons and other NWFP residents had the same opportunity as Punjabis, to a lesser extent however, because they also had a notable representation in the army. But the general climate of opinion in NWFP was never pro-Army.

However, Punjab was different; it identified with the army – which could take Punjab's support for granted. Punjab now seems to have changed greatly. Partly, there is the growth of civil society organizations and people are now becoming conscious of the taunts they used to hear – that Punjabis are not wholehearted in their opposition to military dictatorship. Some even claim that military today is being far more stridently opposed in Punjab than elsewhere. All this is not without an element of truth. One explanation for this is the relatively greater spread of education in Punjab than elsewhere. Punjab has done much better economically as compared to other provinces. A Marxist thinker, Abdul Khaliq Junejo, wrote in the daily newspaper *Dawn* that the explanation lies in the fact that Punjab is now more industrialized than any other province of Pakistan, and it has thrown up a middle class comprising commercial, technological, professional and business people who are economically better off. Like all true middle classes it also needs freer conditions, more opportunities for self-expression and needs the removal of the dead weight of an unthinking feudal-minded, inefficient, military or military-favoured regime. Whatever the explanation, Punjab was in the forefront of opposition to Musharraf and hopefully will remain so against future dictators as well, if any.

MUSHARRAF'S LEGITIMACY

This is but one aspect of the many-sided struggles that are going on. The real demand of the lawyers, opposition parties and the rest of the civil society was that, the then forthcoming election in the autumn of 2007 (that had to be postponed to February 2008) be transparent, free and fair, and meddling by the intelligence agencies, both civil and military, be prevented. There should, in fact, be a truly neutral caretaker government under whose auspices the election should be held, as indeed a practice has grown since 1988. But appointing neutral caretakers was unlikely. Who will appoint the caretakers? The same president who is calling the shots and formulating all the policies. In the end, it was General Musharraf who appointed caretaker governments both at the Centre and in the provinces in November 2007. One look at those caretakers and the country found them to be Musharraf's friends and not at all neutral – as required to carry conviction that they would hold fair elections. The government apparatus, especially the intelligence agencies, was still taking orders not so much from the Government of Pakistan as from General Musharraf, the army chief, who was also occupying the office of the president. He formally did retire from the army, but only in November 2007, handing over the reign of the army to a long-time friend and confidante who was running the dreaded outfit, ISI. People think that whatever happens in Pakistan does so because the army chief wills it. Since Musharraf had the backing of the army he could declare himself the president without having been elected in proper constitutional way.

Most people found his description of being an elected president until October 2007 convoluted. He was only the serving army chief and remained so until nearly the end of 2007. He had not stood in any presidential election, but had simply sent a constitutionally-elected president home, and occupied the President House himself. Subsequently, he held a laughable Referendum in April 2002 that 'elected' him the president. Later in 2002, general elections were held under his auspices after he had promulgated a Provisional Constitution Order (PCO), now supposedly a part of the Constitution, without possessing any constitutional power to do so and the elections were held under his thumb. Earlier, soon after the October 1999 military coup, he formed a government after 'manufacturing' a wholly new party called the Pakistan Muslim League (Quaid-e-Azam), that comprises almost all turncoats, mainly of the opposition party, PML (N) of Mian Nawaz Sharif, the former prime minister, and some from the Pakistan Peoples Party, presided over by Benazir Bhutto, another former prime minister.

The most interesting part is that the third nominal opposition party, an alliance of six religious parties called Muttaheda Majlis Amal (MMA), voted for the PCO to be incorporated into the Constitution. Later, the 2002 National Assembly passed an Act expressing confidence in Musharraf. This is how the president acquired whatever legitimacy he has been claiming from the 2002 assemblies that were held under his supervision – in which, by common consent, the intelligence agencies are believed to have queered the pitch against the larger parties, the PPP and PML (N). The legitimacy of these assemblies has been questioned by almost the entire civil society and the opposition parties. Musharraf's legitimacy has never been accepted by any major party except his own, the PML (Q). It has not been accepted even after the presidential election held in October 2007.

He did go through all the motions of polling – the Electoral College, for instance – prescribed by the Constitution, but this made no significant addition to his legitimacy. Many reasons are cited. First, the assemblies elected in 2002 themselves lacked legitimacy: they were tainted by the main winning party, the PML (Q) which was formed just a few months before the election by none other than Musharraf and ISI, and which comprised mostly of turncoats and defectors from PML (N) and PPP. Then, he was challenged by a retired Supreme Court judge, Wajeehuddin Ahmad in the apex Court, for being ineligible to run for any elective office because he was a serving government servant drawing a salary. No further argument was necessary: the Constitution barred all government servants from all elective offices, unless they have spent two years after leaving that service. Supreme Court took time to decide but before it could pronounce Musharraf struck his promised 'last punch': he imposed an Emergency by virtue of being army chief in November 2007, along with a Provisional Constitution Order under which he sacked over sixty-two judges of the High and Supreme courts, by the simple device of not inviting them to take a fresh oath by the PCO-amended Constitution.

STRUGGLES

The overall picture is one of a splintered polity, marked by several ongoing battles or struggles over various issues. The regime first began fighting 'foreign' Islamic militants in Pakistan, as an ally of the US and the 'Coalition of the Willing' (the countries that supported the US in its 2003 invasion of Iraq mostly) that it had assembled. Those who are described as foreign Islamic militants have been living in Pakistan for over two decades in the Federally Administered Tribal Agencies (FATA) of the North West Frontier Province (NWFP). They are a leftover of 1980s' jihad against the Soviets in Afghanistan because they simply could not return to their homes for fear of being killed. The 'militants' are by no means the only 'foreigners'; it soon became clear that most of them were local residents in affected areas in FATA. Earlier the war was fitful (that is, until about 2004); whenever criticism of President Musharraf became too strong in the American and Western media, a fight was arranged, usually in FATA, in which many people, including Pakistani soldiers and Islamic militants, usually died. This happened many times.

The Islamic militants are now fighting the Musharraf regime in their own way: after the Soviet withdrawal from Afghanistan, they, under ISI tutelage, trained their guns on Indian-controlled Kashmir in order to please the Pakistan Army – so as not to be prevented from stabilizing their local influence in FATA. The militants and the army got what they were after. This was after 1989, when a spontaneous political agitation that had begun in Indian-controlled Kashmir, the movement was originally spontaneous, secular, democratic, and was conducted mainly by the Kashmiris themselves, quite non-violently against the rigging of 1987 elections in Kashmir. Pakistan's military wanted to convert this protest movement into a jihad against India's infidel Army and the militants obliged. But first a word about a certain circumstance towards the end of 1980s.

That was the time when Pakistan had sparked a global suspicion of having become a nuclear power. There certainly was overconfidence among the Pakistani generals; their chief, General Mirza Aslam Beg, was under the impression that Pakistan's defences have already become unassailable by this putative deterrent. The generals in Pakistan arrogantly thought they could now do anything with impunity and decided on a war of a thousand cuts against India, with the help of these militants. These jihadis in their zeal attacked Indian soldiers, and along the way managed to convert the non-violent, secular democratic movement of the Kashmiris into a jihad against infidels, changing the secular characteristics of the indigenous movement. The basic understanding was that the proxy war against India was refutable at the diplomatic level and that, anyway, it was not a proper war under ordinary definition of war. The Indians suffered many casualties; 7,000 or 8,000 soldiers are said to have been killed. But most of the casualties were borne by the Kashmiris who became the main targets of the Indian Army. The Indian Army concedes over 40,000 dead among the Kashmiris, in addition to an unknown number of extra-judicial killings, preceded by the disappearance of suspects. The Kashmiri leadership, represented in All Parties Hurriyat Conference, claims 80,000 or more.

The Indians could have been tempted to go to war against Pakistan, but stayed deterred by the much discussed 'bomb' that Pakistan had secretly acquired. The Indian military was again tempted to go to war in 1999 as a result of the Kargil semi-war, and later in 2002, when India threatened a grand ground invasion of Pakistan because it was encouraging terrorist attacks on the Indian mainland as well as Kashmir. At the height of the 2002 crisis, President Musharraf gave certain assurances that Pakistan would not assist the jihadis to fight in Kashmir. Apparently the assurances, as well as the diplomatic action by the go-betweens, mainly the United States, satisfied the Indian government that called off the intended invasion by sending the army back from the ten-month long sojourn on Pakistan's borders.

Reasons of Indian restraint or what deterred them are not relevant here. The subsequent behaviour of the jihadis, however, is of far more interest. After the Pakistan-inspired Kashmir jihad ended, the Taliban turned their guns on the Musharraf regime after his 'betrayal' of the Taliban in Afghanistan after 9/11. The Taliban story actually began in 1994 when the Pakistani military brought its 'secret' weapon, the Taliban, into action. This group of young Islamic fundamentalists went on to conquer much of Afghanistan when the country was marked by chaos and civil wars – when the state had disappeared a few brief years after the killing of the last Soviet-backed president of Afghanistan, Dr Mohammad Najibullah, and a brief period of rule by the seven religious parties that had carried on the 1980s jihad against the Soviet Army in Afghanistan.

At most times, Afghanistan used to reap rich harvests of opium and reportedly, during the jihad years of 1980s, the CIA had helped organize a roaring drug trade under American and Pakistani tutelage. This partly financed the jihad and later enriched Taliban and Pakistani generals. Later still, the Taliban regime's mainstay for resources was cannabis and heroin. Many laboratories had originally been set up to process opium into heroin that was exported through Pakistan. Later, this trade developed further and became far more sophisticated. Much of the opium is now exported either through Central Asia or India, although the Pakistan route is still in occasional use. Pakistan had come to acquire a suzerain-like power vis-à-vis Afghanistan after the induction of post-Najibullah governments. But these very governments had begun resenting Pakistan's overlordship and had also stumbled into a civil war of all against all, that was their undoing and yielded place to so many warlords. It was at this time that Pakistan introduced its new weapon, the Taliban. They were devout madrassa (religious school) students, mostly Afghan refugees, some of whom were armed, while most displayed a

Quran over their heads as they invaded the cities one by one, winning them without a fight – claiming they are interested only in eliminating evil through enforcing the Shariah.

They could also fight, make no mistake; what with Pakistan's strategic support in the form of troops and armaments, and their own earlier military training and arming by ISI. But the Taliban forces conquered mainly through trickery, proclaiming that they were interested in wiping out sin and establishing God's will while entering a city or any area. All the cities fell like nine pins also because the Pakistani military had established links with various commanders, since the ISI was the conduit through which these commanders received armaments and money provided by America and the Arabs in the 1980s. Thus most of Afghanistan could be conquered by 1996, although the Taliban had entered the scene only in 1994. Military-controlled Pakistan was the obvious beneficiary of Afghanistan's political transformation into a virtual satellite of Pakistan – which itself was, and is, a satellite of America. But the Taliban were also wilful people, being Islamic fanatics. They did not always obey Pakistan, although largely remaining under Pakistan's guidance.

The Taliban constitutes the heart of Islamic extremists operating in Pakistan today. They are now like a new state, gradually emerging for the specific purpose of replacing the old formal state structures in FATA and elsewhere. The Taliban command the confidence and support of the common, gullible people of tribal areas who are extremely conscious of their cultural identity, both Islamic and Pushtoon, that they share with other Pushtoons in Pakistan and Afghanistan. The Pushtoons regard the Taliban as their own kith and kin, and admire their Islamic zeal and austerity. They fall for the Taliban's talk of the Quran, Islam, God and the morality that has been enjoined by the Prophet. Now, of course, Pakistan's Army is hard put to counter or lessen the influence of these fanatics in FATA and the rest of NWFP. The Americans are also finding the going rather rough in Afghanistan because the resurgent Taliban have regrouped and rearmed in Pakistan – the only place they could have gone to after the destruction of their regime in Afghanistan, that they claimed was the Islamic Caliphate.

Few know the sources of their funding and who is really

masterminding their rearmament. But the hard fact is that this has taken place and has happened on Pakistani territory, and probably is an ongoing process. Most foreigners believe that the Pakistani military cannot be entirely innocent of what has been happening, though it will be preposterous to think Pakistan has rearmed and funded the Taliban after 2001, or that it was mainly done by others. But the Taliban is everywhere in FATA today, and their influence is spreading to the settled areas of NWFP. They are obviously becoming new centres of power within the state, executing government informers, attacking and ambushing army convoys and other targets, not to mention government offices and personnel. But the fact is that earlier they could get away with any crime simply because they had popular support and in most cases, authority was not too tough with them for fear of a local uprising.

What was only a cloud no bigger than a man's hand, is now a big dark cloud ominously lowering. Pakistan Army has been worsted in several areas, losing control of stretches in both North and South Waziristan, and much of Swat district in the Malakand Division. Pakistani Army has had to fight village-by-village, suffering casualties and inflicting probably even more casualties. It so happens that on both sides the fighting personnel are Pushtoons and the secular nationalist Pushtoons, the progeny of Red Shirts of Frontier Gandhi of 1920s, and victors in the 2008 elections, are noting that it is a tragedy that Pushtoons are being made to fight Pushtoons and the intentions of the rulers of Pakistan and America are not honest. What has been proved is that a post 2002 provincial government in NWFP that comprised MMA parties was a Taliban-friendly force that, on the one side, encouraged the Taliban and other militants and had hassle-free relations with Musharraf, on the other side. The leader of the Jamiate Ulmai Islam (JUI), the supremo of the largest MMA party and also the godfather of most of the Taliban, Maulana Fazlur Rehman, has been proclaiming from housetops 'if a peace in this area or even in Afghanistan is desired, please come to me and seek my intercession'. Many local pacts that Pakistan Army made with the Islamic militants, Taliban or other, was mostly with the help of JUI leaders. They made an agreement in North Waziristan in 2005 that angered the Americans a great deal and the benefit of which lasted for only a few weeks. After which things went the way they had gone on earlier and most agreements broke down. Other agreements could not be signed in South Waziristan on more than one occasion and things remained fluid.

Pakistan authorities under American prodding have fought ferociously for a while and then they have usually sought peace. During this phase, terrible damage has visited upon Pakistan Army's morale and prestige. At one stage, Baitullah Mehsud's a few score men arrested over 264 Pakistani soldiers, all armed and in the company of five commissioned officers, without a shot being fired. How does a score or more Taliban can 'abduct' a properly armed convoy of 19 trucks with necessary defensive armaments? It beats the imagination. It looks like desertion to many, though the authorities had stuck to the story of these people having been misled, lost their way. It was only after two months that they were released and each person bringing with him Rs 500 as some kind of bakshish that puts paid to losing their way fiction. And this was not the only 'abduction'. It has been happening off and on.

Pakistani Army is split between two opinions: one that wants to have no dealings with Islamic extremists, Taliban and all the others; this approach is purely military under American goading and this school wishes to fight an all out war against Taliban – the umbrella term for all Islamic extremists who are many – though Baitullah Mehsud seems to have somehow united many of them under his leadership and calls himself the Amir of the Tehreek-e-Taliban, Pakistan. It is an 'embryo state' that he claims to have established. Whether Pakistan would fight it or make peace with it is the question. The peacemakers are timid in their approach because they do not want to go wholeheartedly into making peace, recognizing the loss of their own territory and authority over what has been the state of Pakistan, and annoy the Americans and even so want the Pakistani authorities to assert their supremacy – in fact, suppress all these militants.

Suppressing the Islamic terrorists in FATA and other areas of NWFP actually means a civil war. This would be a terrible thing for Pakistan. The area is vastly armed. Pakistan already has 100,000 troops or more in FATA mostly along the Afghanistan border. But this is not enough to plug all the holes that there are in the so-called Durand Line. The entire population is more or less armed, and the sympathies of the common people are decidedly with the militants and the Taliban. The militants are also employing guerrilla tactics that no regular Army has so far been able to counter successfully. Since their appeal is a potent mixture of Pushtoon nationalism, cultural traditionalism and an extra-austere Islam that is respected and obeyed, the Taliban is proving to be far too strong to be subdued. The entire Pakistani Army will have to fight for years and yet may remain entangled there.

The difficulty is that the Americans and the hardliners do not realize that there is no way that an ideology that has emerged, can be suppressed by purely military means, especially when it appeals to the simple and naive sentiments of local population. The number of volunteers for the Taliban and other extremists grow faster as the casualties suffered by the local population mount – the so-called collateral damage. It is the Taliban's collateral advantage. This is a dilemma that Musharraf's successors are facing because of rapidly growing hatred for pro-American policies.

LAL MASJID AND TALIBAN-MAKING

The Islamicist insurgency has acquired a new impetus recently. There was an incident in the heart of Islamabad where Lal Masjid (Red Mosque) stands. Lal Masjid had become a storm centre of Islamic zealotry. Two clerics, brothers Maulana Abdul Aziz and Abdul Rashid Ghazi, ran the complex which had two madrassas, one for boys called Jamia Faridia and another for girls, known as Jamia Hafsa. In addition to the usual Dars-i-Nizami, a centuries old curriculum of Islamic disciplines, they also seem to have taken the Islamic precept of 'fighting sin and promoting virtue' to a ridiculous height of intolerance by employing coercion and physical force to impose the doctrine. Until then it was understood in all the various Islamic schools of thought in the subcontinent that this injunction, being common to all Muslims, implies no coercion, because Quran has clearly laid down that there is no coercion in matters of faith and belief. Islam has an over one thousand-year-old domicile in what is the Indian subcontinent. No one had tried to go round the various localities and tried to impose virtue with the use of physical force, or prevent sin by similar means.

This is a new phenomenon associated with various Arab Islamic militant groups, like Hizbul Tehreer, and is associated with some of the followers of the Wahabi and Salafi schools of Saudi Aabia. This is a noble teaching that is to be implemented by moral suasion. The extremists' contribution is to make it a threat to all non-Muslims or minorities, and even Muslim women and girls. It has the potential of a gigantic blood bath among Muslim communities, wherever they happen to be. The girl students of Jamia Hafsa, covered head to foot in burqas, were armed with lathis (staffs) and went about terrorizing shopkeepers and 'arrested' three women on the charge of being engaged in immoral activities. It was reported that many of them were being trained as suicide bombers. Not all the stories in the press about what the two clerics could be relied upon because much of it was misinformation, fed by intelligence agencies and the government for their own propaganda. The government's propaganda aimed first at the appeasement of Islamic zealots and extremists for fear of sparking a general rebellion among the simple, gullible Muslims who make up over 95 per cent of Pakistan's population. On the other hand, there was tremendous pressure from the Americans that Pakistan should take strong military action against, not merely the Taliban but all Islamic extremists, and their madrassas must stop imparting militant teachings. A curricula reform was supposed to have been initiated ever since 2004, and there was a process of registration of all madrassas (said to number now about 20,000). Not much progress has been made – except the statistics of the registered madrassas announced by the government – after many relaxations and concessions in the original terms of registration. The process of registration of madrassas was by no means complete several years after it began or even now. Progress on the reforms of curricula is not even being discussed; MMA parties oppose it and volunteered to add computer science and a few other subjects on an ad hoc basis. The government's intention was apparently to control and reform the curricula and ensure that no extremist teachings were imparted. This apparently has not had much success.

What many madrassas in Pakistan are actually doing is obscure. However, it is now a historical fact that not merely the

Taliban, but many others have been trained in some madrassas to become militants – some fighters later went to India, after serving American purpose in Afghanistan in the 1980s. Many were Pakistanis, while Afghan boys made up a significant proportion of students in madrassas in all parts of Pakistan – because of the three million Afghan refugees in Pakistan. After all, these three million Afghans have been in Pakistan for over a generation and many have acquired Pakistani documents, such as identity cards and passports. Some have flourishing businesses in all cities of Pakistan. But it is well known that it is the children of poorer and unskilled Afghan labourers who flock to the madrassas. The same phenomenon occurs among the poorer sections in the NWFP and elsewhere – it is the poor who send their children to madrassas. These religious schools attract poor students because they are not only taught free, but are not required to pay for their boarding and lodging. They get healthy meals and undergo exercises to stay fit, many becoming semi-warriors by playing war-like games in some madrassas, under guidance from Pakistani military trainers who teach them the art and craft of guerrilla fighting.

Much of this training is not really known to outsiders because a madrassa is a closed world of its own, discouraging outsiders from peering in. It is firmly claimed by madrassa authorities, as well as their supporters, that the schools are peaceful institutions teaching a course in Islamic tenets (called Dars-i-Nizami) which is at least 800 years old, producing neither warriors nor guerrilla fighters. All this is true, but what is also a fact is that the Taliban has filtered out of the madrassas of Pakistan to Afghanistan to wage a war against a weak and squabbling Islamic regime early in the middle of 1990s, and conquered the country for Pakistan under the Pakistan Army's stewardship in two years. Their military training could only have come from military instructors of the army, possibly retired personnel.

Whatever the precise situation of the madrassas, the hard fact is that Islamic zealots of many descriptions are now battling the Pakistani state from their redoubts in the Frontier province, especially in FATA and Provincially Administered Tribal Agencies (areas under the governor's direct rule, as distinct from the constitutional Provincial Government). The battle has matured into a rebellion, mostly in attitude, but also in the shape of secret or semi-secret militant organizations after the Lal Masjid incident in which the Pakistan Army belatedly raided the Lal Masjid complex in Islamabad and killed a controversial number of students and Maulana Abdul Rashid Ghazi, one of the madrassa's directing cleric. The exact figures of killed is not really important, except that the gullible, pro-religion people were shocked and would not forget the incident. That has given a fillip to an insurgency-cum-rebellion in many Frontier areas. The Pakistani Army is now directly under attack from the Islamic zealots, and is being attacked by its own trainees.

PUBLIC OPINION

The citizenry in general presents a picture of apathy and cynicism. The attitude is one of despair and a sense of futility, seeming to say the Pakistani Army always intrudes and rules, so what is the point of politics and the struggle for democracy? The people find the situation daunting for many reasons: crime is rising dangerously in most parts of the country, and there seems to be a primary breakdown of the law enforcement apparatus, weighed down as it is by corruption; the social order is marked by gross injustices; and the economic condition of a vast majority is miserable, as persistent high inflation has made it hard for most citizens to make two ends meet, no matter what their income is. In the face of this disillusionment, the government is blithely singing songs of self-achievement with a case of 'Shining Pakistan' being projected raucously and consistently while the misery and disunity of the people is a harsh reality.

People are radically divided, thanks to the Taliban and its sister organizations – the sectarian terrorists (when they are not the same) or Taliban-like militants. The same people put on the face of the Taliban in the Pushtoon context but assume the identity of sectarian terrorists in the Pakistani context in general. This was garishly on display when Taliban commander Baitullah Mehsud released 264 or so soldiers with a bonus of Rs 500 to each released soldier as a gesture of goodwill, in the negotiations with the army. But those among the captured soldiers who were Shias were beheaded in the early days of their detention. Nothing illustrates the psychology of both al-Qaeda and the Taliban (who are primarily anti-Shia) better – feeling obliged to murder them all within the areas of their domination, while being highly motivated militants against non-Muslims. Ordinary Sunnis, of Barelvi, Deobandi and other schools have lived with Shias amicably for a thousand years throughout the subcontinent, but not now. Why? One explanation is Saudi money and influence have helped adopt, Salafi and Wahabi ideas. Saudi funds, easily available to most Deobandi schools, usually come with these medieval and intolerant ideas. These may be relevant to Saudi Arabia where no one ordinarily acknowledges the existence of Shias. They are highly disruptive in Muslim countries and where Muslims are in a minority as in India, China, Russia and now many European countries and the US, where they adopt a totally anti-Western and anti-modern attitude. It is incumbent on Muslims with a liberal outlook and tolerant faith to make their inclusive and tolerant faith the norm – and not the exception.

The Pakistani state is also engaged in a hectic arms race with India, that many question saying since there is not going to be a war, why go on preparing for it? The arms race covers both conventional weapons – tanks, heavy guns, aircrafts – and non-conventional atomic weapons and missiles. This releases excess money for circulation, bringing about high inflation rates and hardship for the masses. The private sector's greed comes in here, adding to economic problems – by hoarding (and profiteering) primary commodities (such as wheat) that become the safest activity for cornering excess money which is harder to employ in productive enterprises.

The second issue that divides the citizens is the question of the nature of the state of Pakistan – with differing opinions about what it should be. It is a highly centralized power structure, marked by one particular contradiction. The central government is in theory the master of the army, but the way centralization works in Pakistan, it is the army – far from being a subordinate arm of the government – that is the directing power for the rest of the government. The central government remains a monolith in either case. Many people are rebelling against it in the smaller provinces, because the domination of the army is seen as the domination of a single province, Punjab. How is this conclusion arrived at? It is simply because much of the army, the bureaucracy and the representatives of big businesses are Punjabis. When the army rules there are only a few in the civilian setup of the government that can come to the aid of any common Sindhi, Baloch or even Pushtoon in trouble. In provincial governments run by civilians, despite centralization, there is formal representation of politicians from smaller provinces who are accessible to their people, while during military rule Punjabi military officers and men run the show everywhere.

A picture of unrest in Pakistan emerges from smaller provinces. For instance, an irregular war in Balochistan is being fought by secular Baloch nationalists against the Pakistan Army and federal government, the aim being more autonomy and ultimately, perhaps independent Balochistan. Sabotage of gas pipelines and railway tracks, bomb explosions and frequent attacks on government institutions are the highlights of this war. In Sindh, another restive province, Sindhi nationalists are wholly disenchanted with Pakistan. They demand, like Baloch nationalists, more autonomy at the least, and ownership of the resources within the province. This is a recurrent theme in Balochistan and Sindh, also shared by the Frontier – that underground resources of the area belong to the province, which must decide who gets what.

There should be no confusion. True, the clamour about Islam is loudest in NWFP, where Islamic zealots are rebelling against the state with a determination that threatens to spread. But Islam is not a recent phenomenon; it is at least 1500 years old and consists of over a hundred sects. No sect can tolerate another in theory, with each sect considering itself as representing the real Islam, while all others are in grave error. There is, therefore, a lot of confusion and division within the ranks of Islamic extremists. In the NWFP, for example, a differentiation has to be made between two major subcontinental categories: the Deobandi version of the Sunnis' Hanafi Fiqah of Islam and the Barelvi version of the same Hanafi Sunni Fiqah of Islam. The country has many minority sects too, including Shias (the exact number of Shias is controversial, but is supposed to be somewhere between 17 to 22 per cent).

Meanwhile, the people of Pakistan are disenchanted and disheartened. They do not like what they see, but do not know what to do. The political parties are divided and major parties are crippled since their top leaders' exile was ensured by Musharraf and lasted long. The absence of true democracy means there is no rapport between the rulers and the ruled and the dominant corrosive feeling is that the country is being run for the benefit of the top capitalists and the United States of America.

Historical Notes

Before looking for what is likely to happen, it is necessary to keep the broad framework of Pakistan's history since Independence in focus. Indeed, it need not be so much a narrative as a bird's eye view. Anyhow, some facts from the past should be kept in mind for better understanding of the current situation.

Pakistan came into being as a result of the partition of India on 14 August 1947. It was to meet the demand of the All India Muslim League (AIML) led by Muhammad Ali Jinnah that had won the Central Assembly elections from Muslim seats throughout much of India in the February 1946 elections. On that basis, the Partition of the provinces of Bengal and Punjab took place, while Sindh opted for Pakistan. Since the NWFP had a Congress government that did not favour partitioning of India, a referendum was held, with votes going in favour of the Muslim League. Similarly, Assam was also divided and their Muslim-dominated parts became the eastern wing of Pakistan, which later came to be known as East Pakistan.

The Pakistan government was formed with Muhammad Ali Jinnah as the first governor-general and Liaquat Ali Khan, the general secretary of All India Muslim League, as the prime minister. It functioned as a parliamentary democracy under the Government of India Act passed by the British Parliament in 1935. This was one of several reform legislations to go some way towards meeting the demands of the Indians who were campaigning for independence from Britain's colonial yoke. The British response was to give instalments of what they called self-rule to train Indians for Dominion status (as an equivalent of independence). After a much-prepared Roundtable Conference in London on the future of India, a penultimate step towards Dominion Status, called the Government of India Act of 1935 was taken. Only the provincial part of this Act was implemented after an election in 1937. Indian Independence Act of 1947 completed the process by creating two Dominions of India and Pakistan, the latter adapting the same 1935 Act as its interim Constitution. That first Pakistan government lasted till 16 October 1951, the day when Prime Minister Liaquat Ali Khan was assassinated in Rawalpindi. The mystery of that murder has never been resolved despite many investigations. There was then the suspicion that this was a part of a complex international intrigue reportedly involving the US and United Kingdom, in different ways, as well as some members of the Pakistan government. This suspicion resulted from the fact that there were widespread telltale rumours of internal factionalism and dissension within the Muslim League ranks. But no evidence to bolster this or any other theory has so far emerged and rumours have never been put to rest.

Power thereafter shifted to a Punjab-dominated bureaucracy, typified by the new governor-general, General Ghulam Muhammad, who was a former bureaucrat. He assembled a coterie of senior bureaucrats, mostly Punjabis, and concentrated all power in his own hands. This process was remarkable: he began by dismissing, Prime Minister Khwaja Nazimuddin, the successor of Liaquat Ali Khan and a respected Bengal leader, just after the latter had the national budget passed by the Constituent Assembly (acting as Parliament), and commanded a majority of the otherwise faction-ridden Muslim League legislators. The governor-general soon followed it up, as a result of nonstop wrangling in constitution-making, by dismissing the Constituent Assembly. The Pakistan Federal Court, the top court of the day, upheld the governor-general's decision on what is called the Doctrine of State Necessity (a doctrine based on three maxims: what is otherwise unlawful becomes lawful because of necessity; the safety of the people is the supreme law; and the safety of the state is also a supreme law). This doctrine has been highly controversial. Every time a dictator from the army took over, someone went to the Supreme Court (earlier Federal Court) to challenge this violation of the Constitution of the day and to get him declared a usurper.

Out of four military coups, including the 1999 one, the Supreme Court used this principle to validate three otherwise illegal changes of government, except one in 1970s when it pronounced General Yahya Khan's coup of 1969 an usurpation. But that was long after Yahya Khan had been forced by other generals to hand over power to Zulfikar Ali Bhutto, and was put under protective custody in his own house by Bhutto. But repeated military takeovers led to a psychosis among politically conscious people that equates generals with anti-democratic ambitions and holds superior court judges as intellectual and moral cowards who are always ready to validate the grossest possible illegality – military coups d'état – for fear of losing jobs. Therefore, in a recent case in Supreme Court involving General Pervez Musharraf, the judges repeatedly asked lawyers, 'Please do not mention the Doctrine of State Necessity: it has become a term of abuse for us judges'.

This sensitivity was the result of the new climate of opinion created by the intelligentsia and media, later completed by the lawyers' 2007 agitation following the foolish attempt by General Musharraf to fire his own chief justice in March 2007. The judges, therefore, repeatedly observed in court during hearings of the CJP case that citing Justice Muhammad Munir – the top judge of Pakistan's Federal Court in 1950s who first invoked the Doctrine of State Necessity to validate totally unconstitutional and anti-democratic deeds of dictator Ayub Khan – has now become a term of abuse for senior judiciary. It was repeatedly said in court by several judges that 'Don't quote Supreme Court's earlier three judgements based on State Necessity; we have now buried it as unjust and wrong'. The stock of superior judiciary went up after its 2007 judgements and suo motu actions that made the actions of the current dictator judiciable. Its judgement in July 2007 restoring the ousted chief justice to his office was the first Supreme Court judgement against a ruling dictator and created an euphoria. But in reply, General Musharraf sacked over 60 Supreme and High Court judges for planning to thwart his schemes and actions on 3 November 2007, with the result that restoration of these judges to their courts became a major political demand of much of civil society and several parties made it a part of their programme.

However, to get back to mid 1950s, another Constituent Assembly was brought into being in 1955, incidentally after a delayed normal elections in East Bengal in 1954, while no new elections were held in other provinces – provincial elections were earlier held in West Pakistan provinces. But these were commonly seen to be unfair and rigged; the central government did not rely on them. By 1956 a new Constitution was framed on the basis of an unequal compromise: parity in representation between East Pakistan – which constituted the majority by itself – and all the provinces of West Pakistan – a minority taken together – that had been grouped into what was called One Unit, created by merging West Punjab, Sindh, NWFP, Balochistan and Bahawalpur, and other princely states. East Bengal leadership was desperate for normal democratic practices so as to have a voice in the central government, because the cornering of all powers by a bureaucratic coterie was perceived not only an abortion of democracy but an intended denial of human and political rights of East Bengalis. Judging the intentions of West Pakistan, arrayed behind the ruling bureaucracy, as anti-democratic, the new Bengali leadership – as a last resort concession to get a Constitution, democracy and new elections – agreed to give up their right to majority representation in national Parliament and remained content with having equal representation with West Pakistan. On this basis, the new Constituent Assembly was able to pass a new Constitution that came into force on 23 March 1956.

During the tenure of Ghulam Muhammad, power had resided mainly in the hands of the governor-general, that is, himself, but the old Constituent Assembly had attempted to curb some of these powers. It was because of this attempt that the governor-general sacked the first sovereign assembly (to which power had been transferred by the UK) in October 1954. The bureaucrats' cabal that included the Pakistani Army C-in-C, had bullied and cajoled the new East Pakistan leadership – Hussein Shaheed Suhrawardy being a major part of it – into accepting the twin proposals of Ghulam Muhammad: let East Bengal give up the privilege of being the majority province by accepting equal representation with West Pakistan; the second principle was to unite all West Pakistan provinces and princely states into One Unit. In the meantime, on the pretext of ill-health of the governor-general, Colonel Iskandar Mirza pushed Ghulam Muhammad out of the Governor General House. By the time a new Constituent Assembly could be convened, One Unit had come into being. Later it was Iskandar Mirza who presided over Pakistan's destiny while the first Constitution for the Islamic Republic of Pakistan was framed and came into force in March 1956.

The secret of the power of the bureaucratic coterie lay in the fact that one of its members, colonel, and later honorary major general, Iskandar Mirza, the defence secretary, was known to be the benefactor of C-in-C General Ayub Khan, and the latter was thought to be Mirza's man. Mirza became, first, the governor-general in September 1955 and later still, the first president of the Islamic Republic in March 1956. Later in October 1958 President Mirza sacked the Assembly and the government and proclaimed martial law with General Ayub Khan as the chief martial law administrator. Ayub Khan had allowed himself to be used by Mirza before, but as soon as Mirza declared martial law and made him its chief administrator, he took just twenty days to depose Mirza and proclaim himself the president, as well. Later Ayub imposed a new constitution of his own in 1962 that created the system called Basic Democracy: it involved direct elections to local village and neighbourhood councils, whose members constituted the Electoral College, comprising just 80,000 basic democrats, for electing provincial and central governments and the president. It was a presidential system of government but sans any checks and balances.

Ayub Khan ruled for eleven years, during which time he was seriously challenged only twice. The first time was in 1964 when he ran for presidential election a second time against Miss Fatima Jinnah, the sister of Quaid-e-Azam Muhammad Ali Jinnah. The atmosphere in the country became electric and every politically aware citizen wanted, and expected, Fatima Jinnah to win. But the system Ayub had enforced was tailor-made to return only to Ayub Khan, which is what happened. The secret was simple and effective: all members of local councils, also being members of the Electoral College, were entrusted with development work in their areas with funds, and these public funds were not audited by the accountant general's office. Ayub's survival in office ensured to Basic Democracy members many opportunities to benefit themselves. The second challenge was the raging and tearing protest campaign by nearly all political parties in the country from the autumn of 1968 to January 1969. Although Ayub had conceded all the demands of the opposition parties, the army prevented him from implementing the agreement. Ayub had to transfer power to another general, Yahya Khan.

Yahya Khan's brief rule, lasting two-and-a-half years, was deceptively calm, but ended with a traumatic result. Yahya Khan implemented the agreement that Ayub had entered into with opposition parties at a deliberately slow pace, but did hold a free national election in 1970, the first in Pakistan's twenty-four-year history. The result was that two clear winning parties emerged: the Awami League in East Pakistan and the Pakistan Peoples Party in West Pakistan, although there were other significant parties in two West Pakistan provinces that were restored by Yahya Khan. Yahya rejected the 1970 election results, and did not convene the newly elected Assembly to session, meant to draft a new constitution for the country within 120 days. This Assembly was never allowed to meet, much less frame a constitution in 120 days – the condition Yahya had laid down before the election. Despite agitated demands from the people of East Pakistan, he refused to convene the Assembly and on 25 March 1971, began a military crackdown that was, in fact, aimed at the people of East Pakistan. Bengalis exploded in anger, the result of which was a civil war between the army and, formally the Awami League-led rebels. That became a war of Pakistani Army (overwhelmingly West Pakistani) against Bengalis, who regarded it as genocide. At some stage, most Awami League leaders demanded complete independence for East Pakistan. Later, in the civil war, circa November that year, India intervened. A war between West Pakistan and India took place that ended with a decisive defeat of Pakistan and its dismemberment; East Pakistan became a separate independent state of Bangladesh.

The second phase of Pakistan history began after 1971 war with India, with the Pakistan Peoples Party, the largest winning party from West Pakistani seats in 1970 election, forming the government that lasted six years. It convened the West Pakistani rump of the Assembly and was able to write a proper Constitution for the first time in 1973 – an achievement that gave satisfaction to most parties, factions and groups at the time. But the PPP leader Zulfikar Ali Bhutto had a special talent for alienating most people who worked with him and as a result had to face a popular agitation that shook his regime because he had unnecessarily rigged the elections held in 1977. Bhutto was going to win these anyway, by most assessments. Why did he do it? He wanted to ensure a two-thirds majority in the assemblies. Thus weakened, he was overthrown by his own handpicked commander-in-chief, General Zia-ul-Haq, in July 1977. Zia-ul-Haq ruled for eleven years and, affecting to be a born-again Muslim, he tried to Islamize a predominantly Muslim Pakistan only to strengthen his own hold on power. He brought much misery to Pakistan as a result of colluding with the US and by conducting a proxy war against the Soviet Union on behalf of the United States. Zia perished in a mysterious air crash in 1988 and after his rule, Pakistan was never the same again.

The Pakistan Army, used to calling all the shots, this time round decided against continuing to rule openly. The reason seems to have been dissension among senior generals that forced it to allow sham democracy, strictly controlled by Army High Command. After 1988, the military retained ultimate power by utilizing changes in the Constitution effected by General Zia, known as the Eighth Amendment under which the powers that were meant for Zia who also wore the hat of the president. The president, constitutionally a rubber-stamp figure, was given powers of life and death over elected assemblies and governments, and was repeatedly pressurized by the army to dismiss the whole system of elected governments. The door of the Prime Minister House thus became a revolving one, again like the 1950s. Two prime ministers came in and went out four times. Five general elections took place in the space of eleven years, and all were programmed to return the party the army favoured. Ultimately, this controlled-democracy gave way to the open military regime of General Pervez Musharraf in 1999. He was still on the throne and threatened to remain in power indefinitely, while the going for him became too rough as a result of developments in the year

2007. Musharraf was tactfully forced to resign by the victors of February 2008 election in August 2008.

Power openly resides with the army. The Army High Command was initially rumoured to be faction-ridden but had, in fact, remained loyal to General Musharraf for long. They both clung to each other for fear of what the people of Pakistan might do. Musharraf had superficially preserved the façade of all the known institutions of a democracy. But an unwritten rule (the more real constitution) is still the will of the top general, General Musharraf, who followed the 1973 Constitution in letter, but not in spirit. In a supposedly parliamentary democracy, a civilian president co-chairs with the prime minister when major decisions are being taken, making it a 'democracy' of its own kind – in which the president is said to have cognizable powers along with the prime minister and the army chief: the troika of power.

For many years after the Muslim terrorists' aircraft attacks on the World Trade Towers in New York and the Pentagon in Washington, the Taliban were beaten and overthrown from Afghanistan by the Americans. They could only run away to Pakistan, and did so. But they brought with them the Taliban ideology and terrorist practices. Pakistanis call it the rise of militant Islam that is threatening to sweep over Punjab after acquiring an ideological sway over NWFP's tribal and many other settled areas; moreover, they have supporters and safe havens in Karachi that also happens to be the largest Pushtoon town in the world. Taliban and others of the ilk have given guerrilla style battles to Pakistani Army and given it several humiliating setbacks. Militant Islam is a radical threat to Pakistan today as a state. The famous Lal Masjid affair brought this consciousness to most Pakistanis that this is a threat, serious and very near.

It was followed by a rare kind of political agitation by the lawyers of the country who rose up as a result of General Musharraf's arrogant self-confidence, forgetting that the people of Pakistan have never reconciled themselves with military rule, even though they have essentially been under military rule from early 1950s to the present – spanning a period of over fifty-eight years. They do not know what to do about the situation because not all their experiences with the army have been negative. For instance, in the early 1950s, the army stepped in to suppress communal riots against Ahmedis or Qadianis, and have done humanitarian work during floods. But the eleven years of Ayub Khan's rule cured the people of their fascination for the Pakistan Army as a national institution, as evidenced by two notable movements against Ayub Khan in 1964 and in 1968–69. The temper of the people and their beliefs have always been democratic. To this day the people of Pakistan are not reconciled with dictatorship and they have shown this by repeated political movements against despotism that had all but succeeded with Ayub conceding all the demands of the agitators in 1969. But the army intervened yet again and Ayub was overthrown by his favourite subordinate, General Yahya Khan. Then in 1977, an intense agitation took place against poll rigging by the perceived civilian despot, Zulfikar Ali Bhutto. This too partly succeeded; in that he accepted the main demand of the agitating parties, united in Pakistan National Alliance, that is re-election. But he lost too much time conceding it, and before the agreement could be signed, the army chief moved in, took over and later hanged the ex-PM. The next agitation was in 1983 against General Zia that was bloodily suppressed by him after ousting Bhutto. It could be suppressed because it took place mainly in one province, Sindh. A protest against the government in 2007 that gloriously, if partially, succeeded, was the lawyers' agitation at General Musharraf's expense. The lawyers succeeded in forcing the reinstatement of Chief Justice Iftikhar Muhammad Chaudhry twice – who was dismissed by the president. Later the lawyers and others, superficially for the restoration of the judges, launched another agitation against Musharraf's presidentship if he did not restore them and retire from the national scene. This continued well into 2008. He was forced to resign in August 2008.

In the meantime, various political ills have afflicted Pakistan's polity. To enumerate a few will be instructive. The 1971 experience has conclusively proven that Islam alone does not provide a strong enough cementing factor to hold ethnically separate provinces together. The Muslim League party, the creator of Pakistan, had been dramatically rejected in East Pakistan as early as 1954. After that, the Muslim League has been a handmaiden of all dictators, all of whom either became presidents of the Muslim League or made use of its support for their rule. General Zia's distinction was that he favoured the support of more extreme religious parties, particularly the Jamaat-e-Islami. What is thus needed to hold Pakistan together is not common religion, but a well functioning democracy, based on strict federal principles. If that could be provided, there will be chances that various ethnic identities in the provinces will be able to accommodate one another, and help the country evolve into a functioning democracy with a reconciled and largely satisfied people.

Pakistan is today divided along ethnic fault-lines. Bengali nationalism had resulted in the carving out of a new country, Bangladesh, in place of East Pakistan in 1971. There is the Sindhi nationalism, with Sindh remaining restive and alienated under all civilian and military regimes. Baloch nationalism was strong even in 1947, as it is today, and it is now engaged in a military struggle against the Pakistan Army – unequal though the fight is. Nobody believes that the Baloch nationalists will be able to defeat the Pakistan Army, but that has not stopped them from carrying on a guerrilla war in Balochistan. Also in Balochistan, another movement is all too cognizable: the Taliban.

The Taliban has two facets: one is Islamic extremism of the al-Qaeda kind, although they differ in degrees of extremism and some religious particulars. The second significance of the Taliban movement is that it also represents a Pushtoon nationalism of a non-secular kind. The Taliban thus combines the appeals of Pushtoon nationalism and the religious fervour of an extreme Islamic faith. They, and their ilk, are out to conquer the world for Islam, and that will give them power. The Taliban is also dominant today in many tribal areas of NWFP and their influence is spreading in the rest of the province, and even beyond. Taliban-like movements are also flourishing in Punjab – where the Pushtoon element is absent, that is, religious nationalism is lacking. In Punjab, purely Islamic extremist (ipso facto sectarian) movements are gathering strength. It is to be noted here that these had been working in close mesh with the army in the past, which means that the Musharraf regime was actually hoist with its own petard. But the outside world has nothing serious to fear from the Islamic extremist parties in Punjab, because they find their enemy inside their own community.

But rural Sindh has a special orientation: Z.A. Bhutto's mystique still works, helping the PPP garner votes. However, the hearts and minds of the aware ethnic Sindhis favour Sindhi nationalists, even though the votes go to the PPP. On the other hand, among urban Sindhis, a new ethnic identity has arisen: it comprises mostly the 1947 migrants from India's northern provinces, whose sons and daughters now flaunt a nationalism of their own, calling themselves mohajirs. They politically dominate in Sindh's cities and ethnic Sindhis, mostly from rural or smaller towns or even cities, are educationally backward but have begun to be angry over losing competition for class III and IV jobs. Feelings of ethnic Sindhi nationalism began growing ugly while Urdu-speaking mohajirs from northern Indian states – the main centres of what Jawaharlal Nehru called Indo–Persian Civilization, that originated mainly in Delhi and Lucknow courts – exhibited a cultural pride that grated on Sindhi sensibilities.

The growth of the ideas of Sindhi nationalism was facilitated by the rivalry of two ethnic nationalisms in which by dominating the larger cities of Sindh, mohajirs have given ample cause to the Sindhis to be jealous of the raw power of mohajirs. The latter is now expressed through a tightly organized party called Muttaheda Qaumi Movement which often uses strong-arm tactics and does not fail to capture urban seats from Sindhs in all elected bodies. Sindhis regard them as inimical to their interests. The word mohajir has a religious undertone also: Prophet of Islam had made a hijrat (migration) from Mecca to Medina. Those who came to Medina with the Prophet were called mohajirs and were respected. Sindhis resent the descendants of refugees from India after 1947 for two mains reasons: first, they came in such large numbers and they settled only in cities and towns of Sindh, disturbing the demography. (All Sindhis especially in cities and towns face the threat of becoming a minority.) Second, and above all else, there is a competition for jobs between old ethnic Sindhis and mohajirs, causing ill will.

The social and economic conditions of Pakistan show a confusing picture. On the one hand, the country is supposed to have made much economic progress in recent years, with the government touting a 'Shining Pakistan' mantra of prosperity everywhere. For example, the roads are full of new cars, causing chaos and traffic jams in all cities. Some eight million cell phones are in use. And yet large pockets of impoverishment persist, even if as the government contends, poverty has diminished by 10 or more per cent between 2000 and 2004. The number of authentically poor Pakistanis is controversial. The government says that only 24 per cent, or less, of the population is poor in Pakistan. Many non-officials and World Bank officials think that up to 40 to 43 per cent might have incomes of less than a dollar a day (a global standard that indicates extreme poverty), while another 20 to 30 per cent, slightly higher in the income scale, would still be in the zone of those who find it difficult to make the two ends meet. The inflation rate has surged; it is officially said to be around 9 to 11 per cent, but inflation rate of foodstuffs is still 25 per cent or higher. The economic management policies conform to what the World Trade Organization, International Monetary Fund, World Bank and American Treasury recommend; the so-called 'reforms'. Regardless of what these 'reforms' may ultimately achieve, so far they have produced sharp disparities of income and development, both in terms of regions, and vertically, in terms of classes.

Thus far, Pakistan's history has more or less described a roller-coaster course. As far as foreign relations go, it has been full of ups-and-downs. The country's foreign policy vicissitudes have led to many troublesome consequences: there have been wars and periods of high tension, punctuated by periods of relative calm. In Pakistan–America relations, periods of ample American aid resulting in perceived economic prosperity have alternated with American anger and sanctions on Pakistan. With India, it has had a long and chequered history of unhappy relations during the last sixty-two years – there have been three full-scale wars, a semi-war in 1999 and several skirmishes. The first war took place in 1947–48 that did not end in a victory for Pakistan; but at least a small part of the Jammu and Kashmir state, Azad Kashmir, is still with it. Pakistan clearly lost two wars: the 1965 war may have technically been a draw, but it was a political defeat, showing once and for all that it will never be able to wrest Kashmir from India by force. The 1971 war was a decisive and comprehensive military and political defeat, resulting in the dismemberment of Pakistan. There were other periods that need to be summarized in order to take note of changes in Pakistan–America, in Pakistan–India and in Pakistan–Afghan relations.

Let us take the Pakistan-India relationship first. The relationship has been shaped largely by one major territorial dispute over Kashmir. Pakistan wanted it as part of the nation, citing the argument that Kashmir should be incorporated because it had a Muslim majority, but India has occupied it ever since 1947-48. In brief, the picture looks like this:

(i) Pakistan fought a war in 1947–48 specifically over Kashmir and acquired some areas of the old Jammu and Kashmir state, but had to leave the main prize, the Kashmir Valley, in Indian control.

(ii) It fought another war, specifically for Kashmir in 1965, and it could not win in any meaningful sense. Politically, Pakistan finally lost Kashmir to India.

(iii) In 1971 it fought a disastrous war, though not specifically for Kashmir, but India had Kashmir in mind. The main issue was East Pakistan; India was victorious and Pakistan lost East Pakistan and through the Shimla Agreement gained in Kashmir what it thought was necessary from the Indian point of view.

(iv) There was a lost semi-war in 1999, and a notable skirmish took place in 1964.

(v) There were serious war scares in 1951, in 1986–87, 1999 and, above all, in 2002.

(vi) The threat of a possible war remains, hanging like a Damocles' sword over Pakistan and India, because the Kashmir issue remains unresolved one way or another, although some claim that progress towards finding a compromise solution was made.

(vii) There have been new issues like their respective nuclear deterrents, that prevent Indo-Pakistan friendship.

(viii) Pakistan had to repeatedly threaten use of nuclear weapon on two separate occasions: in 1986 and in 2002.

Apart from the wars that have taken place and the threat of more hostilities, there were phases of negotiations between India and Pakistan. The first one lasted many years and ended in 1954-55 when Pakistan signed pacts with the West in the cold war, and India said that the theoretical agreement that had been arrived at in the UN over Kashmir (a plebiscite to decide its accession), was no longer valid. Indian position after 1955 is that Kashmir acceded to India in 1947, and it has become an integral part of India. This position has lasted to the present day, unless a new agreement is arrived at or Pakistan gives up the demand.

There was a peace agreement in 1966 that lasted for a brief period, during which new political forces emerged in Pakistan that condemned both President Ayub Khan and the peace agreement he signed in Tashkent. The episode resulted in the emergence of the leadership of Z.A. Bhutto, who had promised to fight a thousand years war with India over Kashmir.

The next peace agreement was signed in 1972, after the war in 1971. This is known as the Shimla Agreement of July 1972, signed by the Indian Prime Minister Indira Gandhi and President Z.A. Bhutto (as he was then designated). It stabilized the de facto peace between India and Pakistan that lasted all of eighteen years, during which no war took place and only one war scare occurred during the Indian military exercise called Brasstacks in Rajasthan in 1986. The exercise had caused a great deal of tension and Pakistan feared an Indian invasion. Although nothing happened, Pakistan did use the threat of nuking India late in 1986. Then, there was a major Indian initiative for peace in 1999 when Indian Prime Minister A.B. Vajpayee rode a bus to Lahore and signed a declaration with Pakistan after visiting Minar-e-Pakistan and declared that India recognized Pakistan's existence as a fact of life. But the half-war of 1999 took place over the Kargil heights a few months later and the Indians went back into their political shell of having no truck with Pakistan. Musharraf visited Agra to start negotiations in 2001 but the effort failed, and by 2002, taking advantage of a particular terrorist attack on the Indian Parliament, the Indians brought most of their deployable Army on to the frontier in an invasion mode. The whole world thought this was a serious Indian intent to fight a final war with Pakistan. It was only after Pakistani President General Musharraf gave credible guarantees to India that Pakistan would not let Islamic militants use Pakistan territory to mount attacks on Indian Kashmir that the Indian Army began to move back to its peace time stations after October in the same year. Here a fact must be added. Pakistan actually became a nuclear power sometime between 1984 and 1986. It started a proxy war in Kashmir after 1989 by sending mujahideen (Islamic warriors) to create mayhem in Kashmir. The Indians resorted to killing them, and in the process thousands of Kashmiris, some say 70,000 to 80,000, were killed by Indian troops. There were other examples of oppression and suppression in Kashmir by India.

This raises serious questions regarding India–Pakistan relations. In brief, the relations are hostage to a mindset, more prominent in Pakistan and less visible in the case of India, of basic antagonism. It has been inherited from colonial India, where Hindu and Muslim communalism arose in the nineteenth century. The Muslim communalists eventually demanded the partition of India in 1940 and got it in 1947. The mindset that contributed to the demand for Partition was a long time in the making. What Pakistan inherited from that long period was a hostile and suspicious attitude towards Hindus that grew during the colonial period, mainly after 1857; and that inherited hostility has been the leitmotif of Pakistan foreign policy from the very beginning. In competition with the Indians, Pakistan too wanted a leadership role, wherever it could get it. It began flirting with the idea of leading the Islamic world, earning derision instead from the Arab countries, such as Egyptian King Farouq's joke that Islam was invented on 14 August 1947 (when Pakistan had emerged). Nothing came of that ambition, though a certain pan-Islamic sentiment has always pervaded the Pakistani Muslim mind. Its origins lie in medieval Indian history, in which Muslim kings ruled over vast areas of India, but Muslims remained a minority – Muslims were like small islands in a sea of Hindus.

But there was no communalism during that long pre-British period of history. It was the British who started competitive communalism in India by giving jobs and representation to elected bodies on communal basis. It was a momentous change for the simple reason that the earlier Muslim rulers had made no distinctions among their subjects occasioning a communal scramble for rights or privileges. Hindus and Muslims used to be equal subjects, with equal obligations except for the fact that the Muslim rulers, like other medieval rulers, liked to be both feared and loved by all. Newly converted Hindus insisted on being seen as Muslims and one of the reasons for their conversion was that they had heard that Islam believed in equality and they would be treated differently. But they too remained subjects who did not deserve any particular favours. The favours of the Muslim rulers were reserved for Hindu rajas as well as Muslim elites who came from other countries to fight for them, with very few concessions for their newly converted religious compatriots. The Muslim elites comprised the Syeds from Arabia, accomplished people from Persia and tribal leaders from Central Asia who were honoured and given lands. Over a long period, the Muslim kings and emperors behaved like any other kings. They wanted to expand the area of their empires, and above all, wanted to be loved. They welcomed the support of people who would give it actively, while especially favouring Hindu notables, rajas and maharajas.

A lot of commonalities had come into being between the Muslims and the Hindus. The Muslim numbers continued to grow slowly and steadily, although they remained a small minority in the vast areas that now comprise three states: India, Pakistan and Bangladesh. The commonalities were ethnic, cultural and linguistic – Hindus and Muslims have shared common languages in all regions and a new syncretic language emerged in the northern areas. Based on the language of Hindus in these areas – the local Prakritik languages of northern India – this syncretic language came to be known as both Urdu and Hindi. They were virtually the same language in terms of syntax and shared a common grammar – verbs, pronouns, prepositions and many nouns and adjectives being exactly the same. Foreign Muslim soldiers and immigrants came speaking Turkish, Persian or Arabic, and used a lot of words from these languages even when they learned and used the local language. This daily intercourse produced both Urdu – totally local in its structure – and Hindi, with plenty of foreign words along with many more Sanskritic and Prakritik words. Originally local languages were written in the Devanagri or Sanskrit script while those who used more Persian and Arabic words used the Arabic script, developing the common language of Urdu.

The British, in the later 1800s, recognized Hindi as a separate language, although Urdu continued to be favoured by all upper classes, particularly Muslims, and eventually it was treated as a separate language from Hindi. Thus promoted, Urdu generally became identified with Muslim communalism, because Hindu communalists feverishly promoted Hindi as being especially dear to Hindus for their political purposes. Eventually, Muslims became distinctly antagonistic against Hindi and Hindus, and this language controversy contributed to the growth of Hindu and Muslim communalism, which ultimately resulted in the partition of India in 1947 (the Muslims had demanded partition only in 1940). As far as language was concerned, Muslims' earlier argument was that since Urdu was the language evolved by both Muslims and Hindus, it should be the national language of India. This was the demand made by Maulvi Abdul Haq in 1935 in his correspondence with Mahatma Gandhi, though this idea was fiercely opposed by the Hindus, making the gulf between Hindus and Muslims wider. This heightened Hindu–Muslim hostility is what Pakistani foreign policy inherited and the hostility grew into active antagonism aggravated by the Kashmir dispute.

Since both India and Pakistan are nuclear powers, atomic bombs constitute an important factor in creating mistrust between India and Pakistan. So long as Pakistan's nuclear weapons, sitting on tested missiles, pose the threat of destroying several cities in India in a mere four to seven minutes, which Indian would trust the goodwill or benevolence of Pakistani generals? And vice versa, how can Pakistani authorities trust Indians to never use their far bigger nuclear deterrent against the seven or eight urban–industrial centres that Pakistan has? The presence of two rival nuclear powers, so close to each other, is likely to make distrust a permanent feature. Curiously, few regard these weapons as a problem. Whether or not nukes deter and prevent war, they certainly pre-empt the possibility of friendship between India and Pakistan – despite earlier (contrary) assertions of 'bomb' lovers in both countries.

The only solution lies in working for reconciliation and friendly cooperation between India and Pakistan. This requires an effort from the grassroots to high levels to resolve the problem created by nukes – such as has been more or less achieved by France and Germany by their people-to-people reconciliation. Pakistani elites have to let unadulterated democracy prevail in all of Pakistan and also work with India, China, Afghanistan and European Union to give Afghanistan all the aid for education and social uplift of women. Then a well-conceived plan of reconciliation between the peoples of India and Pakistan should follow, aiming at friendly cooperation to resolve symptomatic disputes.

As of now, Pakistan's policies towards India and Afghanistan are unsustainable and are a prescription for running into serious trouble.

RELATIONS WITH INDIA

Everyone knows the Hindu–Muslim problem of the British Indian Empire only ended in 1947 (if it can be called an ending). It actually continues, in large measure, as two separate and mutually inimical states of India and Pakistan; the problem also survives in Bangladesh that separated itself from Pakistan. The Partition of the subcontinent was accompanied by an horrendous amount of bloodshed and world's largest ethnic cleansing. Its scars have been carried by succeeding generations also. After the Partition, the Hindu–Muslim relations worsened instead of improving, both inside each divided country and in the shape of antagonistic foreign policies of the two countries. Despite these states' different narratives about what happened and why, a few eclectic conclusions can be drawn. Both states, especially Pakistan, found it impossible to resist becoming a national security state. As a result Pakistan devoted most of its resources to building up its fighting forces. Over the years it received considerable foreign aid for various purposes, most of which were actually spent on building up the armed forces.

Pakistan, in fact, neglected its economic and social development with the result that allocations for social services, even sixty-two years later, are a fraction of what is spent on armed forces and other items. One consequence was that Pakistan very quickly joined the West in its titanic struggle with the Soviets-led bloc of nations and entered into at least three security pacts: one, bilateral mutual security pact with the US; second SEATO (Southeast Asia Treaty Organization); and third Baghdad Pact that was later renamed CENTO (Central Treaty Organization). This meant in practice that Pakistan was ready to be used as cat's paw by the United States of America. Pakistan's motivation in joining the West was to obtain American military aid so as to build up its armed forces that can, when needed, be used against India, the permanent security threat. Although the Americans always said their aided equipment was to be used only against the Communist enemies but that did not restrain Pakistan from using it against India repeatedly.

Apart from the ugly legacy of the ill-will that India and Pakistan have inherited, the dispute over the princely state of Jammu and Kashmir became symbolic of their unending confrontation. It also became symbolic of the two states' continuing to act mainly with communal motivation. If Pakistan wanted Kashmir because most Kashmiris are Muslims, India refused to agree to the proposition because Pakistan was a communal state while India was secular and plural. Looked at objectively, Indian motivation can be dubbed as a continuation of pre-independence Hindus' – and some Muslims' – determined opposition to the persistent demands of Muslims because of their dislike of Muslim demands. The Muslims, for their part, disliked the Hindus for being Hindus and being too many, too rich, too educated and too developed. Each side reciprocated the other's sentiment. Thus the courses of action adopted by the two states, in perspective, should be called communally motivated. The Indian narrative paints Pakistan, of course, as irredeemably communal. India, by virtue of the composition of its demography and its record of opposing all Muslim demands, can be perceived as being more concerned with the sensibilities of Hindus. For practical purposes, Indian policies, seen in the earlier context of Hindu and Muslim rivalry, can scarcely escape the appellation of being communal in practice.

There is no doubt that Jawaharlal Nehru was a genuinely secular leader and the fact that 160 to 170 million Muslims continue to live peacefully today in India is largely because of him. Remember his agony during the butchery of 1946–47. Otherwise, Hindu communal hatred should have driven them out or something worse might have happened. The subjective anti-communalism of the Congress, much maligned by Muslim communalists as hollow and for show only, the fact remains that even that has helped Muslims survive in India and for India continuing to stick to secular and democratic ideals, despite failures. While its failures cannot be ignored, it is also to be remembered that it continues to call itself a secular democratic republic that gives equal rights to all its citizens, irrespective of caste, colour and creed, though communal hatreds are also alive and well in India. A little bit of peep into the past should tell us that around 30 per cent of the urban Indian vote since the beginning has always gone to Hindu Mahasabha, Jan Sangh or Bharatiya Janata Party (BJP). These are Hindutva parties and can largely be called anti-Muslims.

Taking an objective overview of India–Pakistan relationship, their conduct does give the impression of a struggle between a Muslim Pakistan and an India that is largely Hindu, particularly over the Kashmir issue. Unless this could be plausibly said of India, why else would Muslims have insisted on dividing the Indian subcontinent between India where richer Hindus predominate and a Muslim Pakistan that was to be so much poorer. And why should India continue to insist on a largely Muslim Kashmir remaining a part of India – at any cost – to sustain its political narrative that is so useful in giving democratic India an honoured place in comity of nations.

Pakistan did eventually wake up to facts of life: it will not be able to wrest Kashmir from India by force. The consciousness of this goes back to at least 1971. The Shimla Agreement of 1972 was a result of that. One has no opinion on the subject that there was also a secret clause in the Shimla Agreement that recognized the Line of Control to be the final international boundary. Although I am inclined towards it as a result of many other secondary signs that would presuppose some such thing in the background. I wrote on the subject soon after in Karachi's weekly *Outlook* (edited by I.H. Burney); I still stand by it. This is not the place to enlarge on the theme of a possible secret clause in Shimla Agreement or another specific one between them, though the Indians by now should have thrown this in the face of later Pakistani interlocutors. The mere fact of such a controversy exists needs being noted. The real point to note is: how did the Pakistanis see their way ahead after actually recognizing that it cannot take Kashmir by conventional force from India. The fact of the matter is that Pakistan still thought that, damn formal agreements, one way or another, it would be able to wrest Kashmir from India by force. Confusion still persists on the subject.

To be sure, the basic differential in conventional force, including the potential of the two countries, can only stay unchanged. Pakistan decided to go headlong into a nuclear programme to break out of this strait jacket. It did not remain a secret even when the first decision was made. When was that? The government announced much later that it was 1976. One has reasons to believe, supported by the claim by late Khalid Hasan, that it was 1972. The story is however well known. In short order Dr A.Q. Khan was invited to Pakistan from Holland from where he brought the blueprints of how to manufacture centrifuges that enrich uranium. Dr A.Q. Khan was primarily a metallurgist. Therefore, he was far more interested in enriching uranium to the required degree when it becomes a fit raw material for a nuclear weapon. He had a few centrifuges manufactured by traditional workers (mistries) in Karachi and then went on improving them and ultimately he seemed to have succeeded in developing good enough centrifuges. Pakistan thus acquired atomic weapons by either 1984 or 1986, as I have discussed elsewhere. It has also to be remembered that India had warned Pakistan clearly in May 1974 that India is already a nuclear power by detonating a bomb and 'you better be aware of it and behave'. That proved an incentive for the Pakistanis to go ahead faster.

The second use of the atomic weapons was to reassure Pakistani decision-makers, mostly generals, that Pakistani defences have now become unassailable. It can do anything it likes. By the time Pakistan provided its major contribution, the mujahideen, for use by Americans (who fought the Soviet armies in Afghanistan throughout the 1980s), American opposition to an Islamic Bomb was relegated to the background. By 1988, the Soviets had thrown in the towel and the last Soviet soldier left Afghanistan in February 1989 – quite unconditionally. Pakistan, by then a nuclear power, came to acquire a dominant position in Afghanistan as the US left it alone after the Soviet departure.

This subject has aroused much curiosity as to how did the Russians give up so completely and left Afghanistan without conditions. It does seem strange. Militarily, Soviet Union was able to go on withstanding the losses that it was suffering some more if it so wanted. What was the reason that would have forced them to fold up completely and leave without uttering an explanation. I will deal with the subject a little later and I regard it as a result of some possible understanding between the superpowers, the Soviets and the US, over reverting to the content of 1907 treaty between Britain and Czarist Russia. That treaty specifically ensured the neutrality of Afghanistan as a buffer state. Which is why the US did not choose to meddle in Afghanistan and it became a gift to Pakistan.

However, we are concerned with the fact that the Russians did leave and the informal mercenary army of mujahideen, between 200,000 to 300,000, was sitting on its hands with no income but with armaments in possession. They could be a threat to Pakistan's own security. Pakistani generals quickly made use of them by starting to send them to Indian Kashmir for two purposes: first, converting the Kashmiris spontaneous, secular and non-violent movement for their political rights into an Islamic jihad. Secondly, to inflict a thousand cuts on India in the full knowledge that Indians cannot round on Pakistan with their superior conventional forces because of Pakistan's nuclear weapons.

This emboldened the Pakistani generals no end. The full story of what happened in Kashmir is not the subject matter here except that Indians somehow survived whatever Pakistan could do in Kashmir by inflicting heavy casualties on Indian Army, and the mujahideen and the Kashmiris took from it. The mere fact that Pakistan could genuinely cause trouble for India in Kashmir without India being able to make a proper military response went to the heads of the Pakistani generals. They became emboldened some more.

They tightened their grip on the civilian administration further with the result that the generals were able to frustrate the Pakistani prime minister's initiative in inviting the Indian prime minister, Atal Behari Vajpayee, to Lahore in 1999 where he said positive things and was ready to make peace with Pakistan on a longer-term basis. The generals first refused to do their protocol duty of saluting the Indian prime minister and later they set to naught the whole effort of the two prime ministers by mounting aggression from the Kargil heights. The Indian response was instant and furious. Pakistanis had to retreat and the only way it could retreat was with the Indian consent. Pakistan's prime minister made it possible with the help of the American President Bill Clinton. The Indians allowed the Pakistanis to retreat through the territory under their control.

Doubtless, after the controversial chief of army staff, General Pervez Musharraf became president, himself made efforts to make peace with India, possibly under American pressure. His effort at Agra to agree on some kind of a peace agreement failed and he returned disappointed and, in part, humiliated. After that the Islamic extremist organization, probably Lashkar-e-Tayyaba, mounted an attack on the Indian Parliament that enraged the Indians further and made the Indian prime minister order the Indian Army to invade Pakistan and half a million frontline troops gathered on the frontier and everyone in the world saw that the Indians mean business. Somehow the Indian forces did not actually invade. Why, no one really knows. Perhaps, the Indians meant only to frighten. Or maybe the Americans may have been extra active diplomatically. Nevertheless, the Indians made all the war-like noises and Pakistanis replied in kind. In the first three months of the year 2002, Pakistan made thirteen threats of using the nukes, if the Indians did actually march into Pakistan.

The Indian reply came from George Fernandes, the defence minister. He said that

> ... nuclear weapons of both countries cancel each other. For the rest, it is going to be a conventional war. But if Pakistan wants to use its nuclear weapons first, as proclaims its nuclear doctrine, let it fire the nuclear weapons first and then wait for the Indian riposte. Pakistan's six or seven major urban-industrial centres would be wiped out and those cities will be back in stone age.

However, the American diplomacy's hand seems visible and sometime in the summer of 2002 General Pervez Musharraf, the chief of army staff as well as the president of the country, made a solemn broadcast in which he promised not to use Pakistan territory against India and that he would prevent mujahideen from going into Kashmir and would also dismantle the jihadi infrastructure in Azad Kashmir. This was what the Indians wanted and probably may be American guarantees for it. By

October the Indian forces were ordered to withdraw to their peacetime stations. The hiatus of several months between July and October, during which the Indians did not do anything, remains to be explained. What was happening? Wasn't there intense diplomatic activity and some paper rustling? One does not know.

Both countries have remained engaged in arms races in all the fields – conventional armaments, nuclear weapons and rocketry in order to find the vehicle to deliver the nuclear weapons on the enemy – even today. The arms races are going strong. The situation today can only be much worse. There is the old saying that you can do anything with a bayonet except to sit on it. If it is still true, then it suggests that the chapter of war has not been closed. But it better be closed. Who knows the next war may be how barbaric.

In the process, limitations on the deterrent value of nuclear weapons have been exposed. A certain amount of primary deterrence is certainly there because no one wants a war in which nuclear weapons can be used. That includes most governments. This is the primary or preliminary deterrent value of the atomic weapons. But beyond that whether they provide foolproof deterrence against any aggression is questionable. Indians, knowing fully well that Pakistan possessed quite a noticeable nuclear deterrent, chose to make as if they are invading and many outsiders thought they would and domestic politics would have pushed the BJP bigwigs actually to go to war. Apparently some amount of deterrence has gone out of the atomic weapons – at least between two rival nuclear weapon powers: Pakistan and India. This can have a worldwide implication for other nations, particularly the US and the Russians who have the most number of nuclear weapons. Maybe they will be forced to do what India and Pakistan have been forced to do and finally the reliance may still remain on conventional weapons. But this is a debate for generals and security experts.

One consequence of nuclear devices is that it creates hubris in decision-makers of the country that acquires atomic weapons. Pakistani generals were overcome with hubris and they did what they did in Kashmir for a whole decade. That the relationship between India and Pakistan hit the nadir goes without saying. But the Pakistani decision-makers remained upbeat. Later, India overcame their confusion and they are now as proud and arrogant as any. Here is a field that security experts had better explore more thoroughly.

The Indian and Pakistani experience of confrontation since 1989 needs to be studied far more by decision-makers in both countries, and maybe abroad. One need not add that Pakistan has made its economy bankrupt in the effort to keep up with the Indian Joneses. Its political life is splintered. The society is radically divided. Its social indicators of education and health or women's welfare are shamefully low. Not that India has any better record. But the fact is that Pakistanis by their own actions have inflicted underdevelopment, poverty and misery on Pakistani citizens. Nuclear weapons have not prevented Pakistan from being defeated in the diplomatic field several times, including Agra and since. Today it is persistently supplicating resumption of negotiations with India that the Indians arrogantly refuse. They have set certain redlines and would want Pakistan to respect them. Pakistanis say they do. But the Indians are not satisfied by Pakistani actions.

How this will end up one does not know. Probably another talkathon impends. But given the differing minimum satisfaction required by either side, the prospect is not rosy, despite the many concessions made by Pakistanis and their internal situation being what it is. Among other reasons, there is the mischief the atomic weapons do. But as of now the situation is untenable for Pakistan and yet its minimum requirements may not be acceptable to India.

PAKISTAN–AMERICAN RELATIONS

Pakistan–America relations have frequently described highs and lows. Although, they remain members of two pacts: one multilateral, CENTO (that used to be called Baghdad Pact), and, of course, the bilateral security treaty with America. Its highest point was from early 1970s when Zulfikar Ali Bhutto took over until General Zia-ul-Haq perished in 1988. It was the period of highest acceptance of Americans by the Pakistani political class and the media. But Pakistanis, mostly right-wingers, blame the

Americans of having left an awful lot of mess in Afghanistan for them to clean. This is not really a fact as far as I am concerned. To my knowledge, the Pakistanis in high places were mighty happy when the Americans left Afghanistan entirely to Pakistan. Pakistan became an imperial power that acquired the suzerainty-like authority over Afghanistan through the Taliban regime that they set up in 1996. I am not concerned at this point with the good or bad of the Caliphate that Mullah Muhammad Umar presided over. The fact to be noticed was that Pakistan acquired a dominant position in Afghanistan – incidentally to the detriment of Indian ambitions and influence. They were mighty happy in Pakistan Foreign Office.

But after 2001, when American targets in New York and Washington were attacked, a rift grew in Pakistan–America relations. Pakistanis in general can be said to have been unhappy over the American invasion of Afghanistan. The question asked was, what are the Americans doing in Afghanistan for almost nine years and even talk of staying for another decade or so. (One American general has said that America may have to be in Afghanistan for the next ten years.) Such a long sojourn calls for clear explanation. The Pakistanis have expressed their unhappiness loud and clear in the media and through the statements of political leaders. But the government, first of General Musharraf and later of PPP-led coalition, has stayed a committed ally of America. The time when Americans were preparing to invade Afghanistan and was calling it a 'war against terror' was not the first time. True, Pakistan was press ganged into it – it had to join. The regime in the country received one telephone call from an assistant secretary of state to the effect that 'you are for us or against us'. General Musharraf could not afford to be against the US. It made its choice. Within no time Pakistan had agreed to be a part of invaders of Afghanistan that was being ruled by their own protégés, the Taliban. America made it Pakistan's while. In these eight years it has transferred, on the books, $11 billion. It includes, of course, defraying of the costs incurred by Pakistan military for America and its forces. There were other unavowed transfers. After all Pakistan is the chief route through which America supplies its troops. The supply-line begins at Karachi port and goes on to Torkham,

Jalalabad and Kabul. A second route is also there; it is particularly useful for supplying the troops in the southwest and southeast of Afghanistan through Karachi along the Mekran coast, Quetta, Pishin, Chaman to Spin Boldak. Pakistan's role is essential to America. It could not have invaded Afghanistan without Pakistan's assistance, especially for the supply routes. Most of American logistics passes through Pakistan.

The consequent war inside Pakistan with Taliban, al-Qaeda et al, is shocking in so far as the right-wing and religious parties are concerned. They were the same people who had first recruited, trained and sent the mujahideen for the American sponsored jihad in Afghanistan in the 1980s. It had enriched everyone concerned. But the Taliban's takeover of Afghanistan represented the second jihad for Pakistan which also must have enriched a lot of people. All religious parties are flush with money. Generals, as a whole, is the most well-to-do community in Pakistan, other than, of course, the top few industrialists and bankers. But Pakistani military found it difficult to rat on their own protégés and so soon. But they had to because of their agreement with the US. So therefore, it is only in theory that the army can be said to have been behind the move. But in practice, only partially so.

The Americans quickly noticed that there is half-heartedness on Pakistani side. The American mantra in all bilateral talks became 'do more' until about late 2007. Americans were not satisfied with the intensity with which Pakistan fought the Taliban. The Americans first complained that Pakistanis are good at catching or killing foreign mujahideen of the 1980s vintage or some others and even Afghan mujahideen are not their darlings. They arrest them; they hand over them to CIA for whatever it does with them. But they do not act the same with those Taliban that were Pakistan's own creation – who are thought to be preservable in order to be used in future. The Americans became gradually very angry. Then they began insisting on specific actions inside Pakistan.

In 2004 a convoy of 284 armed Pakistani soldiers along with their weapons and equipment, accompanied by five officers in 18 trucks, were waylaid by a few score of Taliban who 'abducted' the lot and kept in their custody for weeks in FATA. After a while the Taliban released them, with Rs 500 for each soldier as some kind of *baksheesh*, though quite a few soldiers had had their throats slit for the simple reason they were Shias. For Taliban regard Shias as worse than non-Muslims; they need to be killed in the prescribed manner: slitting of their throat.

The American distrust of Pak military has, of course, lessened lately but does not seem to have gone away completely. Various factors have entered to complicate matters. There is the Indian factor after 2005. Indians and Americans are now operating as a team in Afghanistan, particularly in the field of intelligence while Pakistanis note the number of consulates India has opened in Afghanistan and say jokingly that their foreign office boys are overburdened with work, issuing visas to Afghans from all over Afghanistan who are anxious to go to India via what was Soviet Union to New Delhi! However, American assessment of Pakistan's actions even up to 2005 was adverse. It became more so later. Pakistan was 'not doing enough'. But after the PPP-led coalition government took over, and the Pakistan Army's highest commander changed, the Americans are relaxed and happier. Pakistan is fiercely engaged in warfare against the Taliban and tribesmen in FATA. Up to three million IDPs (internally displaced persons) have already been counted. The number of deaths is high. Both army and Taliban have lost heavily.

To revert to the US attitude, a notable issue is the Americans have been firing rockets from unmanned drone aircrafts. These are guided electronically and are said to be very accurate; all they need is accurate intelligence about which house to aim at – a fine example of technology and trained manpower on the ground – they do their work. On the ground in Pakistan are not only the drones kept in a special secret base, probably not very far from Islamabad. With them there must be a certain number of people who service and maintain them. No aircraft can go on flying without servicing and maintenance. Then they have to be provided with precise intelligence of which house to target at in a village. That requires a whole network of spies arranged by CIA. All these personnel have also to be defended and saved from Taliban. For the safety of both kinds of personnel, there are Special American Forces stationed somewhere close by.

The drone attacks have taken a fairly big toll of human lives inside FATA areas. But each time Americans claim there was a high value target that was taken out; it is immediately followed by a chorus in Pakistanis from FATA and elsewhere that most of the deaths are of innocent men, women and children. If they blow up a house, the household people have also to disappear with the house whether or not there was a high value enemy of the US. A lot of bad blood has been created by the drones.

Earlier there was a ridiculous situation: after a drone attack the Americans said little other than that a high value target has been hit. But the Pakistanis always complained of high level of collateral damage: innocent men, women and children who had nothing to do with the war or at least the high value targets. Pakistan government used formally to call the American ambassador and handed over a protest note. Americans always kept quiet. At some stage, they got fed up and leaked the news to their own serious newspapers and electronic media that drones are stationed in Pakistan as are its Special Forces and the CIA – for setting up an intelligence network with Pakistan's consent – and without whom drones are of no use. The Americans were tired of receiving bogus protest notes for which they must have already agreed. The agreement did, of course, provide Pakistan a fig leaf for denying reality. Instead they misled their own people. But somehow the Pakistan government thought it feasible to do such shameless chicanery in this age and day.

The fact is now all know that drones are stationed somewhere in Pakistan as are the Special Forces to safeguard drones, maintenance personnel and the CIA and its network. The earlier claims that Pakistan has not permitted America to station any troops has proved to be false. Even the PPP-led government has accumulated enough material against itself to be used as and when the opposition chooses. The fact is that the drones sit on Pakistan territory with the Pakistan government's permission, as do the other personnel.

At one stage, there were red faces in Islamabad, of course. The PPP government did finally admit through its defence minister that 'We have permitted a drone to land (in Pakistan)' – just that and no more. What a joke! What the drones do after landing is not mentioned. Is there only one drone in Pakistan? There is no doubt that the Right-wing religious parties were out in the field shouting for withdrawing from the war and saying it is not our war; it is America's war and we have no business fighting it. The main conservative party, PML (N), is against drone attacks and generally takes a nationalist line. But it has adopted no clear stance. In fact, it supports the war as Pakistan's own but not the drones. It is against drone attacks. Who supports the drone attacks is not clear. Those who claim the war to be Pakistan's own should have the moral courage to accept the presence of drones in Pakistan and its operations. In the recent phase, in 2009, American objections to Pakistani behaviour have become fewer. They apparently appreciate Pakistan's military offensive against Taliban in FATA and Malakand division.

It is certainly a war. It is taking place. It is taking a heavy toll of human lives on both sides. And yet what is the fight about and why is not being clarified. There are no clear answers to what does the Pakistan government want other than to establish its own writ in all Pakistan areas. Why did it lose its writ? How did it lose it? Was it sleeping? Why did it not nip the trouble in the bud? What is the future? What precisely are the objectives is not clear, except one: to please the Americans. No doubt the Americans are promising far more money; $ 750 million for FATA's economic development. Then $ 1.5 billion aid is being promised to stabilize Pakistan's economy. Military aid will continue as before. There are other smaller aid proposals. But if this is the price and the war is being delivered for American satisfaction, what is there in it for ordinary Pakistanis? Is this an adequate technique for defanging Taliban and winning over the hearts and minds of the tribal people? Are artillery shells and bombs from aircrafts and helicopters the proper means of winning hearts and minds of a people?

There is much uneasiness. Americans, many claim, are still not happy with Pakistan. Their suspicions are that Pakistan wants to have a high profile role in Afghanistan after the war and that it intends running a rivalry with Indians; the ISI and RAW had squared off for a contest long ago. There appears to be no major change on any side: America, Pakistan, India or Afghanistan. Where will it lead is anybody's guess.

RELATIONS WITH CHINA

Pakistan was among the very first powers that recognized China in 1949. At the time, it was seen as something bold and unusual to recognize a big new communist power so easily. There was no hint or mention of what the West had done after the 1917 revolution in Russia. Among other reasons there was the potential Chinese weight. This weight was seen as being a decisive influence over a large chunk of Asia. The huge population of China and the recognition that the Allied Powers had already accorded to China by including it among the big five (influential) powers of the world that required special privileges in the new UNO.

China, for its part, took the anti-communist zeal of the West in its stride and made no noticeable moves except in Tibet and regarding Taiwan as a rebellious province. It accepted Western anti-communist pacts as a fact of life and did not make any counter-moves. The Chinese had warmly welcomed British and Pakistan's recognition and showed great friendliness. China's decision to encourage and befriend Pakistan ever since requires not merely notice but some explanation: it was so strangely one-sided. China has given a lot to Pakistan while Pakistan cannot be seen to have done any major service to China, other than one: it was to act as a go between America and China when the Chinese decided that it was time to make up with the West.

That had to do with the ups and downs in the Sino–Soviet relations. There was a split in the Sino–Soviet relations in the mid 1950s when Nikita Khrushchev refused to give China technology for nuclear weapons. It was in fact a complete break between the two, though the world woke up to it later. People were surprised when there was an open war between China and Russia for the demarcation of their borders in Central Asia. That the Chinese moves against the Soviets were so completely inexplicable that they still require research on the motives by both communist powers.

Some boldness can still be noted in the Chinese decision to go all out in the support of Pakistan after having made a break with Nehru's India in 1958–59. China removed all stops. It gave whatever it could because it was itself a developing country on its frequent admissions. It gave Pakistan all its war industries; it was a true transfer of technology. In the 1965 war between Pakistan and India, China supported Pakistan to the hilt, though it did not fully come to it. The war did not last long enough for China to enter it nor was Pakistan in a mood to fight India in the manner the Chinese may have envisaged. Its military and other technological aid to Pakistan included many projects and, above all, two working nuclear reactors in Chashma, the Gwadar port and far more in prospects.

The Soviets wanted China to play a big role in Asia to spread communism that China did not want to do. It remained content with a restrained help to sharpen local contradictions wherever possible and treading a careful course in international matters. It did recruit many supporters in the third world. But the position of Pakistan remains probably unique. The fact is that China has done a great deal in political support, in industrial-cum-military field and in other matters. But few can find any return of these favours by Pakistan: nothing substantial is on record that Pakistan did for China. The Chinese support and aid has been totally one-sided without requiring Pakistan to do anything in return. It was and still is a feudal country; there has been not even the mention of the word reform. Why? This is China's unusual international behaviour. The possible explanations are two: one, that China is motivated by longer-term strategic considerations and does what is to be done irrespective of what the recipient says or does. In this case, it wants a balance of power between India and Pakistan with the desire to have India checkmated by Pakistan to whatever extent possible with its help.

The second is Pakistan's seniority in recognizing China in Asia and possibly the role it expects Pakistan to play in various eventualities, although this too is a part of the strategic considerations. Some have found a kind of mutual attraction in the chemistry of the Chinese and Pakistani leaders since way back in 1954 Afro–Asian conference in Indonesia. Prime Minister Muhammad Ali Bogra got on very well with the legendry Chou en Lai who had given an unusual amount of time and attention to Ali. Then later it is said that a six-hour long one-on-one meeting between PM Hussein Shaheed Suhrawardy and Mao himself in Beijing in 1956 had created a relationship that facilitated the harder international business. The one favour that Pakistan is supposed to have done to China is to arrange a secret meeting between Henry Kissinger with the Chinese leaders in Beijing in 1971. These are all the claim that Pakistanis have made.

Pakistan has been allied with the West since 1953. Earlier still it was Pakistan that was wooing the Americans. One has dealt with this subject elsewhere: the US made friends and pacts with Pakistan after Nehru's rejections of US overtures seemed irreversible. If Pakistan Foreign Office could see that wooing America would hinder its friendly exchanges with China, the history would have been different. The US probably tacitly was, or became, of one mind with China's longer term strategic view of India's ambitions.

The West has also treated China differently from the very start. The overthrow of Chiang Kai Sheik was accepted by all without reservations. Pakistanis were mentally ready to recognize China. Old American-Chinese hands had been going round saying that these Chinese are different and some far-sighted Western diplomats expected the Sino–Soviet friendship breaking down soon enough. Indeed a French ambassador in New York, when asked about any possible war in near future, said that he does not see any major war except possibly at some stage a war between the Soviets and the Chinese communists. That reading could only be based on the history of Sino–Russian relations over the centuries. The lesson drawn was that national animosities are more important than ideology. No doubt, that is what happened in history. There was a war between Russia and China at the end of 1960s. And communism could not keep them together as a fraternity. Initially the two red giants did not work together but fell apart by the middle of 1950s, despite their common dislike of the West. It is to be remembered that Dr Kissinger's visit to Beijing took place because the Chinese had recently fought the Russians and the whole world saw that the two communist powers were on two different trajectories. China was ready for rapprochement of sorts with America and it did follow.

After the 1970s, Pakistan has come even closer to China without any frown on the Western visage. China is accepted by many Pakistanis as being able to do what the Americans were ready to do in selling civilian nuclear reactors and other technology. Many confidently expect that China would extend that sort of favour to Pakistan also and it would be, if it takes place, a new development.

Needless to say that there is a strange characteristic of Chinese aid of all kinds to Pakistan: it has given industries, completed projects, some spectacular like the Karakoram Highway, a deep seaport and many other things. Here it is necessary to understand why China does that. How far and how long can strategic reading go over this question? The way the Chinese have spent and have done countless services to Pakistan without expecting any financial and other return is something unusual, as noted before. China and India may be on different wavelengths but there is no real prospect of another India–China war, though a cold war is possible.

Both sides are prepared to accommodate each other and remain at peace. It may be said that the top concern in Beijing is its split with Russia. That the Russians and the Chinese have been trying hard to make up is also true. The Shanghai Cooperation Organization's (SCO) formation shows that they have made up to a notable extent and the SCO is a Sino–Russian dominated organization. Both Russia and China are now non-communists. They have made up after their capitalistic economic reorientation. And still China's policies towards Pakistan are in no danger of a serious change. Indeed, the Chinese are continuing to do what they can for Pakistan. It is only Pakistan's inability to implement or help implement more than what it is doing.

However, it can be said that China is playing a big part in Pakistan economy despite Pakistan being in a hopelessly tight grip of America. Indeed the Americans are underwriting Pakistan's spendthrift ways without earning as much gratitude while China is making up the differential between what Pakistan should have done financially for what China is now obliged to do. In a manner of speaking, both China and America are on the same page in so far as Pakistan is concerned. The Americans are trying to modernize Pakistan Army and the Chinese are trying to make Pakistan economy stronger, if only the Pakistanis were to do their part of the job. In fact, Pakistan's relationship with China and America is based on a common rebound from India. The harsh fact is that Indians do not seem to have any desire to get involved in Pakistan at all.

AFGHANISTAN: IS THE GREAT GAME OVER?

Rivalry between the British and Russian Czarist empires in Asia, known as the Great Game, have defined the politics of succeeding superpowers for the area to this day. They have been vying with each other to occupy, or bring under their dominating influence, Central Asia. It became especially intense in the nineteenth century. Each wanted to have maximum of areas in Central Asia under its influence. It was dangerous business. Eventually, an understanding was arrived at between the British and Russian empires that set limits to each other's ambitions and agreed on the rules of the game. They signed a treaty in 1907. It identified areas of either side's influence. Either side was to have an implicit right to intervene in its designated areas – north and south of the latitude that runs through Iran's capital Tehran: in the north of it lies Russians' zone and south of it were areas where Britain was free to make significant moves. After the Second World War, the US took over British privileges with its originally reluctant consent. It concerned mostly Iran then. In so far as Afghanistan was concerned, it was kept entirely out of contention between the two empires; its neutrality was specifically recognized with the stipulation that it will remain a neutral buffer state between the areas of Russian and the British (later American) influence. That situation lasted until 1970s when things began to change.

It may be remembered that during the Second World War's Tehran summit of Allied Powers in 1942 had agreed to abide by the main provisions of 1907 treaty and Stalin accepted on behalf of the Soviet Union all the rights and obligations of the Czars. Which is why the events in the 1970s in Afghanistan created a grave crisis. What happened in early 1970s was that King Zahir Shah was overthrown by his cousin Sardar Muhammad Daud and it was commonly known that Daud was being supported by Afghanistan's recently united Communists. This was treated in cold war terms as a victory of the Soviets over the West. The West began thinking of retaliation. The place from where any attack, military or non-military, could be mounted had to be Pakistan for geographical and political reasons, mainly because of ethnic commonalities between Afghanistan and Pakistan. All Western undercover agencies quickly made Peshawar their operational headquarters for the purpose and devised a plan of action.

Who precisely proposed what is still mostly speculation. But at times it is hard to resist speculating about events that obviously look like being driven by geo-strategic considerations. The circumstances of the time help one to look in a certain direction. The Americans were smarting under heavy blows they were receiving in Vietnam and men like Dr Henry Kissinger were at the helm in the US (the National Security Advisor): for men like him the idea of taking on the Russians in Afghanistan should have been tempting. The West somehow collected adequate funds and bought Russian equipment from Egypt for the use of the new fighters that Pakistan was to procure. The very fact that the entire West could be so easily mobilized illustrates the issue's strategic significance.

Any number of Afghan people, mainly Pushtoons, were prone to come under the influence of Afghan religious parties that had been brought to Peshawar by 1976 to make it their centre of operations to inspire and lead the pro-West insurgents. The war was fought basically by (mercenary) volunteers. The authorities paid an advance to these volunteers and promised more on their return, or in case of their death or serious injury, substantial benefits were to accrue to their families. The modus operandi was that small groups of mujahideen would go into Afghanistan and inflict whatever damage they could on the infrastructure or kill Soviet soldiers.

What started the show, as indicated, was a series of dramatic events in Kabul in early 1970s. First, King Zahir Shah of Afghanistan was overthrown by his cousin Sardar Muhammad Daud. This was taken in the West as a victory of the Soviets because the Communists were seen to be the main supporters of Daud. The purpose of the war was to counter Afghan Communists' capture of power in Kabul by defeating the Soviet Army so as to destroy the PDPA government once and for all. The West began by first enticing Sardar Daud, who showed readiness to walk over to the Western camp, if the West were to recompense Afghanistan adequately. The Shah of Shahs, the King of Persia, promised him a grand sum of $ 2 billion as a loan and a token of $ 200 million was actually paid. Sardar Daud, of course, could not resist this temptation. He only asked for some time to fix up the Communists. What that meant was that he needed an interval of time to eliminate the newly united Communist parties.

The Communists found out what was afoot as a 'breaking news' soon after the words were spoken, and Sardar Daud was reported to have said in a secret conclave that he was going to do away with the Communists first and then would walk over to the West. Having learned this, the recently-formed People's Democratic Party of Afghanistan, that earlier used to be Khalq and Parcham parties, decided to pre-empt Daud. They had him killed first and the event became known as Saur Revolution of April 1974. That served as the signal for the war to begin. Pakistan played its part by organizing, training, indoctrinating and providing the fighters. The Western powers, led by the US and other leading NATO powers, played theirs: they provided adequate funds, enough equipment of Russian origin to be able to promote the fib that the equipment was snatched from the Russian troops during the fighting and thus came to be in mujahideen's hands.

However, it was Pakistani generals who organized the main show. The Russians entered the land-locked neutral Afghanistan on 26 December 1979, although actual warfare had begun earlier. The details of the warfare are not important today. Suffice it to say that by 1987, the Russians appeared to have been convinced that they cannot safeguard either the PDPA government or keep the country united. They agreed to negotiate with Pakistan and others concerned. The Geneva talks ended in a number of agreements. The Russians started withdrawing from Afghanistan unconditionally and the last Soviet soldier left Afghanistan in February 1989. The West had won hands down. The Americans were all too happy and could be heard murmuring variants of: 'We have avenged our Vietnam debacle by making Afghanistan a Vietnam of the Soviets'.

The Americans left everything to Pakistan vis-à-vis Afghanistan. Thereafter, all the fighters and remaining equipment became Pakistan's inheritance. But the Pakistanis had got much more than mere equipment and some money. They had learnt the technique of fighting an inherently stronger enemy in a manner that can be officially disowned. Pakistanis perceived their own position to be unassailable due to their nuclear deterrent that was simultaneously deterring India too – up to a point in time, circa 2002. The recently unemployed mujahideen, irregular volunteer army that they assembled, became available to serve as a ready reserve for Pakistan. The latter used them in Kashmir in the 1990s with plausible deniability from late 1980s onward where a spontaneous political agitation by Kashmiris of the Valley had slowly gathered momentum against India's rigging of the 1987 polls. It was spontaneous as well as a secular movement. Pakistan apparently collected some more money from wherever it could and used it on the mujahideen on roughly the same terms as were given to them for Afghanistan operations. They were sent into Kashmir with some Pakistani volunteers, supplied by many jihadi parties like Lashkar-i-Tayyaba, Jaish-i-Muhammad, and Lashkar-i-Jhangvi, in order to convert the ongoing agitation in Kashmir Valley into an Islamic jihad for eventual merger of Kashmir with Islamic Pakistan. The original agitation was indisputably secular in character. But Pakistan was determined to convert it into a jihad by giving it a religious purpose. It calculated that it would be beneficial to Pakistan in future. By and large, in this too the pro-West Pakistan succeeded – but only up to a point. For, a good many Kashmiris remained under the influence of National Conference and Mufti Muhammad Saeed's People's Democratic Party, that are largely secular as well as pro-India.

The point to note about Pakistani calculations was that by repeating the indoctrination that produced mujahideen for fighting in Afghanistan earlier and intensifying it for anti-Indian Kashmir insurgents was meant to result in strong religious sentiment trumping the Indian pro-parties narratives. Which is why the Kashmiri insurgents as well as non-Pushtoon volunteers became even more intolerant, more obscurantist and more revivalist. The new volunteers received the same kind of training that ISI had earlier imparted to 'Afghan' mujahideen, only more intense. However, it did not yield Pakistan a clean victory in Kashmir over India. While the Indians suffered heavy casualties and could do nothing serious in retaliation because of Pakistan's nuclear weapons, they were not defeated; the Indian Army by 2002 was raring to go at Pakistan, ignoring the latter's nukes. The later neutering of Pakistani nukes in Indian generals' minds was a huge setback to Pakistan that made General Musharraf to eventually offer a solution to the Kashmir problem that fundamentally recognizes India's sovereignty over all of Kashmir. That India did not catch hold of this tempting Pakistani offer may be attributable to hubris over its notional 'victory' in 2002. Not jumping at the Pakistani offer might prove expensive for India, for there might not be another ruler strong enough soon to sell the idea to Pakistanis, given current political trends in Pakistan and India not having any intelligent long-term Pakistan policy.

In so far as the Indians have suffered and also in so far as their image in the rest of the world has suffered, it can be counted as victory of sorts for Pakistani generals, albeit pyrrhic. And the extent to which Pakistan has been unable to wrest Kashmir from India should correspondingly be treated as Pakistan's defeat. During the year 2002 it was clear that either there would be an actual nuclear war between Pakistan and India or Pakistan will have to climb down, if not abandon the idea of demanding Kashmir. It is hard to say whether Pakistan would ever abandon the jihadist notions, though it has reduced their ferocity greatly, though not completely. Musharraf went farthest to please the US and India by virtually recognizing India's sovereignty over Kashmir, as noted. The big question is how long can Pakistan remain so tame as to go on extending recognition to Indian sovereignty over Kashmir. If a succeeding, non-democratic government reverts to earlier hard line – a realistic fear – both Pakistan and India will be back to square one, their relationship worse than before, with both having ever larger nuclear arsenals.

Whether or not Pakistan won anything in the two jihads of 1980s and 1990s, many Pakistani generals certainly became extraordinarily rich and politically powerful. This could also be counted as some kind of their personal success. Pakistan's greatest victory was an unconfirmed report, though I vouchsafe its purport; the Americans had actually promised Pakistanis that the US can have no long-term interest in Afghanistan and that they will have to leave it alone – in order to return to the hoary understandings of 1907. 'But you – meaning Pakistanis – can go ahead and do what you want to do in Afghanistan'. This pleased the Pakistani generals no end. A whole country was being given to their care. Pakistan thus became a suzerain – for a while. It is somewhere here that people should look for the origins of the idea of Afghanistan providing 'strategic depth' to Pakistan.

How successful Pakistan has been as an embryonic or mini-imperial power is obvious. Indeed it is possible to say that it was a gross failure. The Russians withdrew by February 1989 and it could cobble together an Islamic Afghan government in Peshawar only in 1992 to be taken to Kabul in an American C130 aircraft by the then Prime Minister Nawaz Sharif. The latter installed it in Kabul the same day after which he went to the Grand Mosque of Kabul to offer a thanks-giving prayer. This long period for the formation of the government and then that government's lasting only half that time that it took to form yields a lesson. The new Afghan government dissolved itself in eighteen months into any number of civil wars. The country became fragmented. Any number of mini Afghanistans came to be ruled by district commanders or warlords who owed no allegiance to any single or central authority. Afghanistan state was truly destroyed, though Pakistan remained for a while some kind of a suzerain – for historians' purposes.

Today Pakistani officials loudly complain that the Americans were not fair to leave the whole of the Afghan mess to be cleaned by them. They made no such noises at the time. Instead they appeared to be punch happy with the end result and began entertaining big imperial dreams of how Afghanistan would add to Pakistan's strategic depth. Factually Afghanistan after 1993 underwent a change: it became a space for many mini-Afghanistans ruled by many warlords. Each warlord exercised the functions of a state within his own small domain: what law and order there was, was given by him; the administration of justice was by his men; he would collect what taxes-cum-extortions could be collected. These are functions of a normal state. This basic discontinuity of Afghanistan was cut short after the civil wars ended and this happened actually twice: once after President Dr Najibullah had left the presidential palace to seek refuge in a UN compound, leaving behind gathering chaos and splintering of the state in which the seven religious parties could never succeed in re-creating even a short-lived Islamic government in Afghanistan by their own efforts and the second time was after the Islamic government had failed to hold the country together later by 1993 and the Taliban gradually came to conquer some 80 per cent of the country between 1994 and 1996.

In the situation following this second civil war, the Pakistani generals' ingenuity did the trick. They came up with a second harvest of mujahideen called the Taliban for use in Afghanistan. They had similar qualities to those of earlier mujahideens only more intense. These young students of madrassas were given similar military training, were indoctrinated even more on the same old basis of putting additional beliefs and opinions of Wahabi and Salafi schools of Saudi Arabia on basic Deobandi orthodoxy of the subcontinent. Taliban were even more obscurantist, revivalist and backward-looking; their aim was to set up an Islamic Caliphate of exactly the kind that was established by Prophet Muhammad in Medina and later his four right-guided Caliphs, ran in Medina. Taliban were introduced in Afghanistan in 1994 and by 1996 they had won over 80 per cent of Afghan territory. That is when they set up their own Caliphate in Kabul with Mullah Muhammad Umar as the Caliph of all Muslims (in theory) and ruled only in Afghanistan's Pushtoon areas.

It would be interesting to remember how did the Taliban win. There was intense propaganda about their piety before they entered any city that proclaimed: 'We are only Taliban (students); we have no political aims; see, we are carrying Qurans over our heads'. This is how they entered a city without resistance. But behind them was the muscle – a small posse of Pakistan Army guided by an ISI's Taliban minder. They did not have to fight in most places. The gullible and naïve Muslims of Afghanistan could not doubt that a student of madrassa carrying Quran on his head could be anything but what he said he was. That is how, mostly by trickery they won most parts of Afghanistan, though occasional use of force and later repression were found necessary.

The most decisive consideration is what kind of a rule the Caliphate imposed? It is hard to be quite accurate here. But the objective fact remains that much of the world recoiled from recognizing the Taliban regime, although it ruled without much opposition for five years. Only three pro-Western Muslim countries – Pakistan, Saudi Arabia and UAE – could bring themselves up to recognizing it. No other country could force itself to recognize them. Why? Because its conduct towards women was shocking to the entire civilized world. It stopped women's education for an indefinite period – until adequately equipped and learned female teachers were available; all women were thrown out of government services because of the proximity to males. All kinds of minorities, sectarian or religious, were oppressed, particularly the Hazaras, for whom the fate seemed to have ordained only slitting of their throats. And this is what Taliban have been doing in Pakistan's own tribal areas (Khurram Agency) on a fair scale wherever they have seized control. Their cultural policy was demonstrated by what they did to Bamyan Buddhas: huge historic statues carved out on the mountain sides. Against the whole world's pleas to save this great legacy, it was destroyed by engineers by using dynamite. And their punishments to all and sundry were swift and horribly harsh. Who could want to live under such a regime?

And yet there are those who love the Taliban heartily and work for them, spend on them and are even ready to die for them. Two mutually contrary facts have to be acknowledged: on the one hand, there is a larger number of volunteers from parties like Taliban, TNSM and various others like al-Qaeda and some Central Asian formations, plus the intolerant and violence-promoting parties like Lashkar-i-Tayyaba, Lashkar-i-Jhangvi and Jaish-i-Muhammad work with them. On the other hand, there are those who hate Taliban and most other Islamic bigots that love and practice violence supposedly for the greater glory of Islam, as if Islam needs this kind of violence. Anyhow, Islamic extremists get recruits all too easily. There is no conscription or coercion. But many do join them.

Funding for them is ample, mostly from the trading class. It is wrong to think that the Muslims do not give in charity the way the Christians or Hindus do. The amount of free food that is available in the city of Karachi for any hungry person is an eye-opener. There are many centres of various welfare trusts that collect charity, on the one side, and spend it on feeding the hungry, on the other. One of the centres one has seen was providing free food everyday for approximately 23,000 people twice a day. And this is not just one trust. There are many. No religious party or no religious organization is short of money, no matter how violence-prone it is. A lot of money comes from outside, meaning thereby other Muslims living in other Muslim countries, including contributions from countries like Saudi Arabia, UAE, other Arab countries and now there are Muslim charities in Western countries that are also getting into the act.

Neither money nor volunteers are a problem for them. That is one side of the picture.

The other side of the picture is that take any particular area of the subcontinent, the majority of Muslims live by a code of actual conduct that is an amalgam of Deobandi orthodoxy and Barelvi school's practices. Which is how popular culture grew over time. People go in droves to religious shrines, the occasions are actually festivals in honour of famous Sufi saints. They offer various forms of prayers amid strange shows of devotion to the particular saint there. Most Barelvis observe the sanctity of a saint or Sufi from whom their ancestors used to take instructions even on religious matters. The Deobandi school is more austere and does not believe in going to shrines or offering demonstrative prayers through music or offer presents there. But those festivals were how a large number of people were fed for days on end. A larger number of people are now becoming more clearly aware of the fact that there are four main maslaks or sub-sects among Sunnis from which they have to choose one to belong to. One is talking mainly of the majority of the subcontinent's three countries – India, Pakistan and Bangladesh – and all having chosen Hanafi fiqah. In the Hanafi maslak in South Asia these were two versions: Deobandis and Barelvis. There are three other maslaks and, additionally, there are many religious sects and religious minorities. All of them have coexisted and traditionally all have been tolerated. It is only now that questions are being raised: which is the majority and whether it will permit the other maslaks and sects or minorities to practice their particular religion freely.

This is likely to remain an unresolved question as it has come down from centuries past. The pressing question of today has an urgent practical dimension. Taliban are on the move. According to BBC, the NWFP government actually controls (in the middle of May 2009) only 38 per cent of its territory. This is an alarming figure, though not surprising. The fact of the matter is that Muslims have started becoming far too conscious to which maslak they belong to, particularly among the Sunnis. Some 70 per cent Muslims of India, Pakistan and Bangladesh are Sunnis and all of these are plural societies. Historically, there has been tolerance of all sects and maslaks to coexist peacefully and other smaller sects or religions were free to practice their religion. This is ceasing to be the case now. Intolerance of the 'other' is growing. This is a dangerous trend.

Islam is as plural as any other religion. There are over a 100 sects in Islam and even Sunnis have at least four maslaks to belong to. But in practice nobody knows how many are Deobandis or belong to other maslaks, or sects other than Barelvis. The Barelvis claim to comprise the largest majority of the subcontinent's Muslims. Deobandis controvert this claim and there is their own claim that Deobandis are the authentic Sunni Muslims and the majority belongs to it. What is clear is that Deoband has provided most mosques with their imams. The imams do not in practice interfere with people's actual faith and allegiance to whichever maslak they may belong. Sects, however, remain separate; there is no doubt about that. But there is a great admixture or overlap of the Barelvis and Deobandis in the subcontinent because both belong to the same Hanafi maslak. They used to offer prayers usually in the same mosques and did not care whether the imam was a Deobandi or a Barelvi, though there doctrinal and minor differences pertain to namaz. But these differences are minor and historically made little difference. But not any more in most places; the Barelvis' and Deobandi followers of the same maslak are now antagonists, even in FATA. In the West, many mosques are locked up because of disputes over whether it belongs to Deobandis or Barelvis. There were minor riots in Britain over the question of which group owns which mosque and some mosques were closed on court orders.

Today the question of questions in Pakistan is: whether the Taliban and other religious extremists from north-western areas will eventually inherit Pakistan? No one is sure they will be put down or will eventually triumph? Pakistan government has ordered a war to the finish. It should be permissible for all sensible people to doubt the government's claim that it can, through mainly military action, put down this religious militancy that is intolerant, violent and well-armed with modern weapons and possesses an ideology of setting up an Islamic Khilafat (Caliphate) in the country where Shariah would be the law of the land. Once you formulate the proposition thus, there is much confusion and ambivalence. The Taliban take advantage of that.

Some people have, in practice, chosen to submit to them but

most have migrated from their ancestral homes to other peaceful areas inside Pakistan to escape destruction of their property or suffer deaths. And on the day of the writing over two and half million Pushtoons are refugees from their own land. The question being pondered on a fairly large scale is: can this government in Islamabad suppress a particular interpretation of Islam? Can it successfully subdue so well-armed and trained groups as the Taliban? It may be news to many but it is a fact that a thin slice of Muslims, especially in the cities, are actually a votary for modernism and liberal values: they are primarily democrats and believe in tolerance. Their physical survival would be impossible if the Taliban or their ilk were to succeed. They are votaries of the constitutional democracy who own this country's constitution and believe in rule of law – whether or not these values are adequately respected by rulers in Pakistan.

The immediate question agitating the minds of many is: shouldn't the government in Islamabad be persuaded not to rely mainly on the military muscle as the Americans are forcing them to do on pain of penalties and are encouraging compliance by ampler aid. The solution of the problem according to most Pakistani liberals and democrats is that give the people, all the people of NWFP, including the Federally or Provincially Administered Tribal Areas, all the political, social and economic rights. Let them receive something concrete from a democratic government which it can and should provide. Once it has provided full citizenship rights and social services, particularly jobs for most young people who join the labour force every year plus the provision of education, health service and other infrastructural services, the government will then become entitled to both victory by working out a system that can win wider popular support by isolating the intolerant militants. True, it will have to face fierce opposition from Taliban who have so far been winning and from other militants, foreign fighters, local warlords, and fierce but also circumspect resistance by feudal lords comprising the political class of the country that otherwise instinctively tends to agree with the West, being traditional toadies.

There is no clear or easy solution of this conundrum. All one can say is there is a democratic alternative that the government happens to be somehow unable to adopt, largely because of

America, NATO powers and indeed Pakistan's own political class. The liberals think that military force is not an adequate answer to religious intolerance. Political education and tolerance plus social improvement in the lives of common people is the way to deal with the extremists efficiently enough – if sustained over time. Once this government begins doing the right things, it will get tremendous amount of popular support to enable it to go ahead with its programme more easily.

On the other hand, if the government insists on pursuing the line the Americans are forcing it to adopt, the future of Pakistan will be dark indeed. Its growing Talibanized areas would be much more dangerous for the rest of the subcontinent. The reason why Americans want to keep Pakistan confined to the job of constantly fighting its own Taliban can only be to keep the Taliban and other Islamic warriors embroiled inside Pakistan territory so that they do not go and make trouble for American and NATO forces in Afghanistan. Look at the problem from no matter which angle, it is a very short-term and a narrow-minded approach. This will not win them much respite either. The American aim of keeping Taliban and other extremists engaged in warfare inside Pakistan thus comes down to providing a temporary cover to the Americans for a long enough time in which they can devise and execute their exit strategy from Afghanistan. That can only mean giving expensive liabilities to Pakistan and retaining what strategic assets they might succeed in creating.

But the US is not winning the war; the chances of losing it are now greater than of winning. That makes for a horribly difficult situation for Pakistan. If the Pakistan government freely owns the war along with domestic democrats and liberals against Islamic extremism, it may gain the lasting support of the liberals and democrats (or the intelligentsia). The question is does the social order help or sustain the intelligentsia? In contrast, the feudals and other rich gentry, including the otherwise useless political class, sustains this mockery of fighting Islamic bigots in the name of a bogus Islam. But the media is now reasonably free, despite its freedom being nibbled away by the government's octopus-like 'agencies'; it remains insufficient to solidify popular support for the cause of liberalism and modernism, though if it can strengthen itself and fend off the governmental and bureaucratic mafia by relying on mainly unsold intellectuals. It can help solidify its own freedom and strengthen the intelligentsia. Looking at media today, there appears to be powerful forces behind the scenes, domestic as well as foreign, that have ensured only former Army and civilian bureaucratic commentators now shall go on dominating all the media. Whose design is it?

Problems That Will Not Go Away

(I) ISLAM

Remember that Pakistan was born amidst controversy. All nationalist Muslims, most of the Muslim section of the Indian intelligentsia, including scholars who belonged to various religious orthodoxies of Islam, were opposed to the carving of a new country for Muslims out of India. The entire Deoband school was opposed to the idea of Pakistan. So were most Shias. Also, remember that Muhammad Ali Jinnah was opposed, in the 1946 election from his Bombay constituency, by Hussain Bhai Lalji who was the president of the All India Shia Federation. But once Pakistan came into being, Islam began to sit heavily on Pakistanis; clerics who had opposed the Pakistan idea to begin with, changed tack and started controversies, ancient and new, regarding what constitutes Islam's requirements in a predominantly Muslim country. Leaders of religious parties began arguing that 'you have carved Pakistan out of India in the name of Islam, so Islamic Shariah will have to be its supreme law'. Muslim League leadership had no answer to this and it was greatly embarrassed and confused. Pakistan has wrestled with this ideological crisis, virtually from day one. Apart from the old secular opponents of the Pakistan idea who had previously found no reason to support this religious-sounding demand, quickly came to accept it as a fait accompli once it came into being and there was nothing more to be done. But the religious leadership carried their old differences with the largely secular Muslim communalists who had led the Muslim League, a paradoxical stage further. Recall again that the more interesting contest over the idea of Pakistan was not between Hindus and Muslims, but within the Muslim intelligentsia itself. The intelligentsia – religious scholars, nationalist Muslims and most Muslim leftists – felt no need for a (separate) Pakistan, though later nearly all leftists and a few religious scholars began supporting it, because it had become the demand of the Muslim masses. But most of Musliın League leaders riding on the crest of popularity among the Muslim masses had no reasoned answers to either the nationalist Muslims' objections, or those of the religious elements. After Pakistan came into being, the religious right mounted a shrill ideological offensive against the first Muslim League government in Pakistan, led by Jinnah and Liaquat Ali Khan. Their chief argument, as already noted, was (to repeat ad nauseam) that, 'since Pakistan came into being by Muslims' efforts and (supposedly) for the sake of Islam, it must then be run in accordance with the injunctions of Islam'. What are those injunctions? 'It is the learned ulema, well-versed in the religious lore and literature of Islam who will tell you what Islam demands of you'. Maulana Ataullah Shah Bukhari is known to have been the first to make this demand in Multan, said to be with political malice aforethought.

Quickly, Maulana Abul Ala Maudoodi, the founder of Jamaat-e-Islami, came up with the idea, along with Muhammad Asad (an Austrian Jew converted to Islam who later renounced Islam), propounded the idea of a uniquely Islamic state that would be run strictly in accordance with the Shariah, that is, the Quran and Sunnah (the oral traditions and examples of the Holy Prophet). This state was to be radically different from secular democracy and capitalism; it was also to basically differ from godless communism, and so on. It was to be something quite new; purely Islamic for upholding the Quran and Sunnah as the grundnorm (supreme law) that will cover all aspect of individual conduct vis-à-vis all structures of the state. The Muslim League leadership remained at a loss over how to react for some time; it had, until then, dealt in the empty rhetoric of Islam without actually meaning anything other than to garner support or votes of the Muslim community in India, by denouncing the Hindus' much-hyped malice, intolerance and economic exploitation of poorer Muslims as the basic rationale of the two-nation theory.

This confused contest continued between a Muslim League leadership that actually believed in Western-style democracy and ordinary capitalism and the Islamicists, for most of the first two years. But the Leaguers did finally come up with a via media between Western-style democracy and Islamic injunctions in the shape of an Objective Resolution in 1949 – to be made the introduction of the new state's constitution, then on the anvil. The League leadership hoped that this compromise would satisfy the ulema while the League government would be left alone to create and run a (basically) democratic structure of the state, to be run in accordance with the model of democracy it knew, that is, a Westminster-style parliamentary system, with a capitalist economy and fundamental rights for all. It did not envisage a uniquely different kind of a state with a wholly different kind of economy which was, actually, in its view, neither feasible nor desirable because no one had known until then what an Islamic state and Islamic economy were. Moreover, it was felt that this experiment might not be suitable for this age because these were things that had not been seen before. There were too many grave doubts about the whole project. But the League leadership dared not openly express its doubts, much less its opposition, for fear of being dubbed as being opposed to the dictates of the Quran and Sunnah in a Muslim state. For, on the question of what Islam implied, the ulema had more credibility, than westernized Muslims.

But the Constituent Assembly passed the Objective Resolution that the semi-secular leadership of the Muslim League government had come up with in 1949. Like most compromises it left both sides less than wholly satisfied. While the semi-secularists of the Muslim League variety conceded a lot to the mullahs, the mullahs were not entirely satisfied with those concessions but had no rational objections to offer against this measure. Although those who believed in a secular setup for Pakistan initially thought that they were not conceding too much to the mullahs, but the Objective Resolution did establish the normative principle that sovereignty belongs to Allah and not the citizens, despite the fact that it was to be exercised through the elected representatives of the people. The fact was that the people were no longer to be sovereign, and that, in the uncertain pursuit of what Islam implied, any number of illiberal concepts could be introduced at later stage, as indeed they were. It was also conceded to the mullahs that the purpose of the state would be to enable Muslims to live their lives in accordance with the tenets or demands of Islam. What that implied was neither clear to anyone nor did anyone know about any agreed set of Islamic injunctions to be 'imposed' by the state on individuals which was to be compulsorily followed by them. But it opened the door wide to the mullahs or semi-mullahs to push in any number of non-democratic concepts or practices into the body politic. While it was not a totalitarian concept, and it did not satisfy either the mullahs or those who wanted democracy's norms to be followed, it managed to wholly destroy the philosophical basis of democracy: sovereignty of the individual. The struggle between the Islamicists and Pakistan's rulers over Islam's supposed requirements in Pakistan, has continued unabated ever since, especially after Zulfikar Ali Bhutto's Pakistan Peoples Party came into power in the last days of 1971.

The 1971 events opened the breach wider still. Jamaat-e-Islami and other religious (Islamic) parties condemned the PPP as a secular party – and not merely a secular party but also a socialist one to boot – categories which are somehow thought to be inimical to Islam. Bhutto had a truly many-sided personality: he conveniently betrayed his own principles, rode rough shod over all the opposition in a futile bid to act despotically while being an elected prime minister, but he also managed to produce a Constitution that more or less satisfied the main schools of thought in the country. But this Constitution's new concessions to Islamicists were even more far-reaching and inconsistent with liberal democracy, although the structure envisaged in it was of a parliamentary democracy. But he did not live by that Constitution. Within hours of the promulgation of the Constitution, he imposed a state of Emergency in which he ruled like a dictator – and paid for it. In the end, General Zia-ul-Haq overthrew him and had him tried for murder in the Lahore High Court. Zia's victory opened the door wider still for further Islamization, as he started an intense one-sided propaganda both against secularism and democracy, for being opposed to the basic tenets of Islam. In short, Zia's political stock-in-trade was more Islamization of Pakistan. He forced the people in government service in Islamabad to offer prayers inside the premises of the Secretariat or in their own offices.

It is true that the actual conduct of all governments in Pakistan has been more or less secular, with indispensable elements of rule of law for non-political cases – but without them claiming to do so. The Objective Resolution had no drastic effect on day-to-day governance. But in terms of ideas and concepts, too much had been given to the Islamicists, although it failed to satisfy them. It simply whetted their appetite for demanding more as a measure of gaining additional influence, power and pelf. What they really desired was their own coming into the seats of power. But in the meantime, governments in Pakistan had, Islam or no Islam, no compunction in putting themselves in the service of the United States of America and participate in its titanic ideological war against atheistic communism, if required. By 1953–54 Pakistan was safely in the American camp against USSR and China. Later on in the 1970s, there was intense international intrigue among the intelligence agencies of Pakistan, Britain, America, Iran and Germany and several Arab countries over undertaking a grand operation to wrest Afghanistan from falling to the communists' or fellow travellers' hands.

The coup by Sardar Mohammad Daud against King Zahir Shah had both frightened and encouraged the West because the pro-communists had supported Daud against Zahir Shah, and it was feared that these leftists might soon inherit Afghanistan. This would undo the old agreement between Imperial Russia and Imperial Britain that Afghanistan, the buffer state between the two, which was informally adhered to by the Soviets and the US after 1945, despite the old Anglo-Russian Treaty of 1907 having been overtaken by history. Daud was sought to be weaned away from these leftists. The Shah of Iran promised railways for that land-locked country and promised a $ 2 billion loan. That did the trick. Daud was won over but he pleaded for time to suppress the communists. Meanwhile, the Leftists heard of what was afoot and they preempted the West by overthrowing Daud in the nick of time. That was the Saur Revolution of April 1978. This unhinged all Western schemes and a new and more aggressive Western policy towards Afghanistan for sub rosa action was soon evolved. Like most other such strategic policies, it contained both the carrot and the stick components. The stick part of it comprised the invitation extended to the seven recognized religious parties in Afghanistan to Peshawar, the cockpit of international intrigue in the 1970s. Most of these religious parties of Afghanistan had come to, or established their headquarters in, Peshawar by 1976. Gulbuddin Hekmatyar had certainly come and started living in Peshawar since 1975. Thus the recognized right-wing religious parties of Afghanistan, all believers in various Islamic (Sunni) maslaks, had based themselves in Pakistan to mobilize a growing number of Afghan refugees in Pakistan.

It is futile getting into the arcane questions about who schemed against whom and for what precise reason. What is true is that a military-led Pakistan was up to its neck in this international intrigue, as a result of which Afghanistan was sought to be forced to give up its traditional neutrality, and come into the comity of Western nations. Pakistan was only too happy to cooperate in a campaign of sabotage and resistance against the Soviet Army in Afghanistan (beginning 26 December 1979), to be waged from bases in Pakistan against successive pro-Soviet governments in Afghanistan. The Tarakai's and later Hafizullah Amin's government is supposed to have pleaded with the Soviets to send troops to defend the new leftist government in Kabul The Soviets obliged. But by entering into Afghan territory they had violated the remnants of the commitments of the 1907 Treaty between Russian Empire and Imperial Britain. The main terms of that old treaty were that the Russians will not cross the Amu river and come south, while Britain would not meddle in the Central Asian region. Hence the respect for the neutrality of Afghanistan, the classical buffer between the empires. That Pakistan had been sending Afghan mujahideen into Afghanistan from across the Durand Line soon after the Saur Revolution may not be a wholly different kettle of fish. At any rate, little is known about what Stalin and Roosevelt agreed to in Tehran in 1942, and whether it covered Afghanistan or not.

It is not necessary to give a blow-by-blow account of the 1980s war inspired by the West against the communist Kabul and Soviet Army, appreciatively called jihad in all Western capitals.

There is a piquant relevance of Pakistan's originally professed Islamic identity and the waging of a jihad against America's cold war enemies, the godless atheists in Afghanistan. It fitted snugly with the intense ideological propaganda of the Zia regime for home consumption, though the true motivation was basically for financial and other considerations: getting so-called aid and gaining influence in Afghanistan. All the religious parties that talk unendingly of Shariah today, and are also so anti-American, ate out of American hands only yesterday – and had their fill. That jihad lasted for almost a decade; it came to a technical end in 1987 when Geneva Accords were signed as the last Soviet soldier left Afghanistan in 1989. Detailed chronology of the Pakistani state's conduct between 1979 and 1987 is not relevant here. But what is relevant here are the dates; the jihad that is claimed to have started in December 1979, and the Peace Accords came finally into effect in 1989. When it really began is not known with any certainty, though the Afghans and the Russians contend that mujahideen raids had begun long before 26 December 1979, the date the Soviet troops entered Afghanistan, as reaction to those raids. What matters is to note how Pakistan and the West conduct their war against the Soviets. It was conducted mostly by Afghan volunteers, known as the mujahideen, though an unknown number of Pakistani Pushtoon tribesmen also took part throughout that jihad, strictly for earning some money and arms, and hopes of going to Paradise. They were bankrolled by Western powers, though an equal amount, dollar for dollar, was said to have been paid by the Arab countries, mainly Saudi Arabia, Kuwait and UAE. It would be interesting to remember that another West-inspired war between Iraq and Iran took place soon after this jihad began, and concomitantly the religious parties' – all conservative – conduct vis-à-vis the US should to be remembered when assessing their deep anti-Americanism.

However, these mujahideen were originally said to be members of the seven parties who were nicknamed as the Seven Bearded Sisters of Peshawar. But according to this writer's sporadic research, for these jihadists the lure of money was the main motivation. Each mujahid was paid a certain amount of cash for each of his jihad forays. He was given a rifle, some ammo and other equipment and some rations. He would go, fight and (or) destroy whatever installation he could, even if it was only an electricity pole. He would come back and rest and get a bonus as a part of his payments. It is estimated that during that decade something like 200,000 to 300,000 tribals, including some Pakistani volunteers had fought, each earning various sums of money. The money trail would disclose a great deal of corruption and this has societal relevance: the Islamicists' love of Islamic Shariah never came in conflict either with serving the US purposes or filching Western money to enrich themselves. That throws a blindingly clear light on the Islam being promoted by these Islamicists. In all this, the involvement of Pakistan Army's generals, particularly those in the ISI, is especially notable. Many became multimillionaires, if not billionaires. Even President General Zia-ul-Haq was believed to be in receipt of regular amounts of cash that would be left in his office by the director of CIA, who would absentmindedly bring a briefcase full of dollar bills and would equally absentmindedly forget to take it back on his frequent trips. Or so says at least one book by an American who knew these facts. None of it is irrelevant in today's Pakistan. Most Islamic religious parties are still flush with unexplained money, as are the retired Pakistani generals, both of whom do not tire of advocating an Islamic dispensation for Pakistan after having served Western purposes most of their lives, themselves. But the end product of this brood is local Taliban and other Islamic militants who are now gnawing at the vitals of Pakistan with their ideology of jihad. This version of ideology has boosted Islamic fanaticism many notches above the fanaticism of 1980s mujahideen. It is built on the safe Hanafi (Sunni) orthodoxy of the Deoband kind. On top of it, there seem to be several layers of intolerance provided by the Saudi Arabian ideologies of Wahabism and Salafiism, and the new climate of opinion throughout Middle East. It is certainly a dangerous brew now.

The outcome of that war, the jihad of the 1980s, was a clear victory for the West. The Soviets left Afghanistan unconditionally. The last pro-Soviet government of Dr Mohammad Najibullah simply collapsed and he was hanged and quartered in a particularly brutish manner. Pakistan inherited Afghanistan as a parting gift from the US. When Najibullah's government collapsed, Pakistan manufactured a government for Afghanistan, comprising the seven great mullahs, and took them on a Pakistan Air Force C-130 to Kabul. The Pakistani prime minister of the day (1992), Mian Nawaz Sharif, escorted them and went on to demonstratively offer a thanksgiving prayer in the Grand Mosque of Kabul. The jihad had yielded Pakistan (its army primarily) a geo-strategic advantage in Afghanistan; the land-locked country came into Pakistan's sphere of influence, though that bonanza did not last beyond a few years. Pakistan's original (unrealistic) dream was to acquire a strategic depth vis-à-vis India, thus. But this dream has revisited it later as the nightmare of Islamic insurgency in NWFP's tribal areas after 2001.

Other legacies of the 1980s decade of jihad for Pakistan are also notable: primarily it was the dramatic growth of the narcotics trade, based in both Afghanistan and Pakistan's own tribal areas, where heroin factories had been established by the early 1980s, reportedly with the help of American CIA. The other main gift of that decade to Pakistan is the 'Kalashnikov culture' or the rising tendency towards violence. The third legacy is the rise of militant Islam. It had begun infecting Pakistan's tribal and other Pushtoon areas. Helped greatly by the battle hardened old militants (mujahideen) who can be mobilized either by the Taliban or al-Qaeda, depending upon the terms – these mujahideen being quite partial to money. The area has seen some big-time corruption. The creation of Taliban itself was a reaction to the situation in Afghanistan, where the earlier mujahideen leaders had fallen out among themselves and would rather fight one another than rule jointly. The new mujahideen or the Taliban have, after their 2001 defeat in Afghanistan, begun the campaign for creating – within Pakistan – a more Islamic dispensation in their own areas, and form a government that would be quite like the Caliphate of Mullah Muhammad Omar in Afghanistan. The Pakistani Army had acquired the status of an Islamic rhetoric-spewing 'hegemon', but only for a few years, though it still cherishes that imperial memory of dominating Afghanistan – even if it was only riding piggyback on American aid. This new Islam is, paradoxically enough, something inherently made in the US with ample assistance of Pakistani generals, though after 9/11 it has become viscerally anti-American.

By now, a few years after the Taliban defeat in Afghanistan, this new and more extreme Islamicism has become a serious threat to Pakistan. This Islamic extremism also carries the stench of unexplained money, mostly narcotics-related though not entirely. But it overshadows all other threats to the state of Pakistan. The course of Pakistan is being undermined and subverted by the Taliban, in the name of Islam, which is now the favourite alias of the different militant outfits that are fighting against the Pakistani state for their own narrow ambitions of power. The question arises as to who is a typical Islamic militant or a Taliban? Exceptions apart, he is a local notable of one kind or another, living in the tribal areas called FATA who has enough money – often narco-related or from some mysterious source – to raise a Lashkar of even 80 to 100 men. He can conveniently style himself either as Taliban or mujahid. He becomes a quasi ruler of the area and should properly be called a warlord. He extorts taxes to run his 'Islamic' administration and dispenses a rough and ready justice, which is a mixture of Hanafi Shariah and local customs. He provides the only security the locals have. He is no scholar, well versed in Arabic or any other language, or known for knowledge of the Shariah in any depth. It is a dangerous force because he claims that his is a true Islamic state and the warlord's adoption of the Taliban appellation gives credibility to his claim. He performs all functions of a modern state, if also in an embryonic form because the Pakistan Army's power is overwhelming. These areas are Pakistan during daylight hours and become Taliban territory after dark. But of great significance is the fact that this new entity, an incipient state-to-be which the warlord runs, is basically meant to displace the Pakistani state. People of Pakistan, particularly in the NWFP and tribal areas, regard them with respect and awe, though they do not really respect or love them. They, in fact, fear them more. But since he also inspires respect for his vaunted piety and consequently not everyone can oppose or fight against him: the local population accepts his de facto rule. But this Islam, despite the respect and awe it enjoys and the fear it instils, is troublesome for most Muslims. It exacts total obedience and allows no discussion. It is intolerant and cruel to boot. Still, such warlords or Taliban claim to be running true Islamic states. And no one, not even the local mullah, dare rebut him, both being well-nigh equal in Islamic scholarship.

The more interesting and complex question is to examine the relationship between what the world has known as (and understands as) Islam and this particular version of Islam. One had already described elsewhere in essentials what this particular Islam, by way of the ideology of the Taliban, is. But what normal Islam embodies is also not above controversy. Islam has over a hundred sects, each claiming to be the true Islam, all the others being in error and, in fact, apostates. The Islamic state of any kind has to confront this hard reality of there being so many (over a hundred) sects in – or versions of – Islam. How to reconcile their respective claims of each being the only true Islam, with the need to establish a unified Islamic or Muslim state in any particular area where Muslims live, because of the diversity of religious beliefs among them, is a matter of grave importance. Moreover, no one in theory accepts the others as Muslims, as well.

If it is supposed that establishing an Islamic state is an obligation on Muslims of all sects, the difficulty begins with the fact that neither the Quran nor the commonly accepted sayings of the Prophet (Ahadees), have given any precise guidance on that question. It is true that the Prophet Muhammad did establish the Medina state. Its basis was said to be a document, *Meesaq-e-Medina* that is extant. But it is not a formal constitution. It is really an agreement to form an Ummat (or people) who would be ruled by Prophet Muhammad, in which he also said that the Jews of the area were a part of the same Ummat with the Muslims. The whole tenor of the document is one of tolerance and benign intentions. True, it is not difficult for any Islamic ruler to be benign and kind, because these are the qualities repeatedly extolled in the Quran and the Traditions of the Prophet. But the question recurs: what are the precise demands of Islam on Muslims? In so far as direct injunctions are concerned, they are to offer five prayers a day, fast in the holy month of Ramzan, give one-fortieth of one's income as zakat (or charity), go on Haj (at least once) and participate in a jihad (when necessary). So long as any ruler permits his subjects to perform these basic observances of the faith (Arkan-e-Deen), he becomes an acceptable (Islamic) ruler no matter how he may have come to power or who he is. In all Islamic sects, all rulers have to be obeyed absolutely and there is no concept of formal legal rights of the individual. For the rest, where tolerance is concerned, the Quran lays down unequivocally that there is no coercion in matters of faith.

In any version of Islam, the position of sectarian or religious minorities remains an unresolved conundrum. Originally, in Islam, there is no concept of how to actually treat a citizen, let alone protect the rights of a minority – whether of a different religion or another sect of Islam. No doubt, many would say that Islam would treat the minorities with tolerance, good sense, moderation and prudence. But the fact remains that there is no authentic body of codified law in Islam, much less a constitution or rights of the individual vis-à-vis the state, or even the Ummat. Similarly, the minorities, whether sectarian or religious, have to actually struggle to get what rights they can from the state, Caliphate or Emirate, or whatever any ruling authority is called. While there is so much emphasis on the norm that there is no coercion in matters of belief, the actions of Muslims through history have provided non-Muslims with a potent weapon: they see that Muslims have been more intolerant in action through much of their history, in inter se conflicts: in mistreating the sectarian minorities or religious minorities.

That cosmology of Islam is not so intolerant or exclusive is shown by the fact that Almighty is not the God of Musalmans alone; he is God of all of mankind, irrespective of race, colour, faith, language or sex. He says that He is kind. But the faithful, in their enthusiasm, have given Him a hundred generic names that assign Him the most superlative qualities to be found among men. But He does not hate or condemn people of other faiths. He has also said that man qua man – and not just faithful Muslims – is His viceroy on earth. All men are equal, and so forth.

It is thus possible to argue, in a general sort of way, for secularism to be fully in consonance with the spirit of Islam. To begin with, the relationship between the God and man in Islam is direct. There is no intermediary: caste, clergy of an organized Church(es) or family. There was no codified law when Islam came, national or international, though various sects have subsequently compiled a whole body of sayings, teachings and actions of the Prophet for themselves, each somewhat different for each sect, on matters of how the faithful of a particular sect are to behave. There are no injunctions of how to organize yourself politically or economically in any sect or version. Since Islam talks so much about equality and fraternity and accepts all men as equal, qua vice-regents of God on earth, without any intermediary class, caste or organization, their sovereignty should be in no doubt. If so, they will have to decide it for themselves as to what dispensation is good for them. Islam also lays down that there is no preference in His eyes, for Muslims over non-Muslims, as such.

If so, the foundation of a secular dispensation in a Muslim majority society exists. God or Prophet has not given anyone any authority over other human beings, apart than favouring a few non-democratic doctrines on which paradoxically most sects agree: 'obey the ruler, no matter how he has come to power'. The only social dictum that Islam has laid down, and all sects agree on it – and which is being widely misused by the Taliban and other Islamic extremists – is: 'promote virtue and discourage evil'. The Taliban read into it, the power to decimate a sectarian minority or kill non-Muslims, or to disregard the clear-cut Quranic injunctions of there being no coercion in matters of faith, or that 'killing of a single human being is equal to killing all the humanity'. Or even that the word Islam itself means peace, in Arabic. Islam lays great emphasis on equality, justice and kindness and welfare (ehsan). If these were to be taken as guidelines, a secular, democratic dispensation becomes the dictate of Islam. What the Muslims have actually done on this question is that they have engaged in unending contention among those who follow traditional Islam of various sects, and those, the new twenty-first century exclusivist Islam of the Taliban Caliphate wallahs. Traditional Islam accepted as legitimate even the British colonial rule because it permitted Muslims to offer prayers, keep fasts, give Zakat and go on Haj. As for jihad, the traditional Islamists have hedged it with conditions that have made it infeasible or irrelevant. The Taliban does not accept the concepts that underpin modern democracy, to have free run in a Muslim majority country. Indeed, these Taliban-like enthusiasts of Islamic Caliphate simply assume that Islam compels Muslims to live in a particular kind of state, of, by and for Muslims, whereas there is no clear injunction or recommendation in the Quran or the sayings of the Prophet regarding minorities or sects. They forget that Muslims live as small or big minorities in myriad countries where non-Muslims are majorities. Should these Muslim minorities live in perpetual conflict with the majorities? If so, what happens to those clear-cut texts about equality and fraternity of all mankind? There is a real ideological polarization here. It is thus possible to assert, without prejudice to any particular Islamic sect – except the Taliban or al-Qaeda ideologues – that an open, free, tolerant and law-governed democratic dispensation is a wholly Islamic endeavour, and without it no predominantly Muslim society is likely to live in peace, freedom or make progress.

A case in point is the Bahais in Iran after 1979, and of the Shias in Afghanistan during Taliban rule, or the current discrimination that Ahmedis, Shias, Hindus and Christians have to contend with in Pakistan at the hands of intolerant religious groups. Indeed an intolerant Caliphate by Taliban-like extremists in any Muslim majority country will be a prescription of unending oppression and suppression of all minorities: it can scarcely extend full civil rights to minorities and may actually seek to eliminate them. It cannot make equitable material progress. Such a concept is foreign to Islam.

ISLAM'S POLITICAL IMPACT TODAY

It takes two main forms. The first is that of a fair number of religious parties with their offshoots or factions. They not only represent different sects or sub-sects of Islam but also factions often led by sub-sect leaders, for example Jamiate Ulmai Islam (JUI), which has two main factions today. There is the JUI of Maulana Fazlur Rehman and the JUI of Maulana Samiul Haq. Both had a notable role to play in producing the Taliban in the 1990s and had links with the 1980s mujahideen. There is more than one Shia party and, of course, there is the Jamiate Ulmai Pakistan. The latter represents the Barelvi maslak of the (same) Hanafi school of the Sunni sect. Then there is the rich and effective party that has led the campaign for the Islamic state, the Jamaat-e-Islami (JI), now led by Senator Qazi Hussain

Ahmed. It is the most well organized political party in Pakistan, India and Bangladesh, each has apparently enough funding. Pakistan's JI also had a role in the 1980s jihad wherein its main support was for Engineer Hikmatyar's faction. Its role later declined in Afghanistan, though it did not disappear. These parties are basically sectarian parties, emphasizing the distinctions of their particular sect, sub-sect or sub-sub-sect. Their general characteristics can be summed up as: they are interested in the world of Islam or defending the Muslims against non-Muslims even in Pakistan. From where comes the threat to Muslims in Pakistan is hard to see. But these parties do exist to defend the interests of the Muslims and, in theory, to work for an Islamic dispensation in Pakistan. What that dispensation is, or should be, is a subject that occasions many and varied opinions. But as a slogan, Islamic dispensation, is shared by all of them, though what they mean in practice by Islam is their particular kind of sectarian or sub-sectarian Islam. They show they are interested in the world of Islam and most of them affect to be pan-Islamic enthusiasts. All issues that concern Muslims anywhere in the world are supposedly their issues. The only difficulty is that they have no precise and united opinion on how the country should be run politically: whether it should be a democracy or it is to be a dictatorship, is a matter on which they are quite pragmatic. They have hunted with Zia-ul-Haq's dictatorship, as a part of his government, they have also been running with democratic hares (parties struggling for democracy), during spells of struggle for democracy. Whether they are truly for democracy or for dictatorship cannot be determined either by reference to their past conduct or their clear-cut political enunciation. No one has any economic programme or any social or political reform programme. But they do fiercely insist that Zia-ul-Haq's Hudood (Islamic) Ordinances, being truly Islamic, must be retained no matter what the Muslim women of all stripes in Pakistan demand. And yet in the normal course of events, during nominally democratic phases, these parties' total share of vote varies between 5 to 9 per cent nationally.

But they enjoy an advantage. They claim to be the ulema who can authoritatively explain what Islam means or what Islam demands, although there is nothing that can be cited as their definite stance, in book form; one such luminary actually told me that his various fatwas should be consulted with, for this purpose. In short, they are politically ambiguous and have been in practice pragmatic in the corrupted sense of being opportunists. What would be their future role is hard to say. They are political parties and their primary objective is to get into or seize, power. They do not hesitate in accepting junior partnership with either democrats or dictators (if only he wants to use them). It would be safe to say that their future role is likely to be what it has been in the past.

But this new school of Islam, the militant Islam, is out to form an Islamic Caliphate on the model of what Mullah Muhammad Omar had done in Afghanistan. They call themselves the Taliban, similar to the way described here. Their Islam is strict, extremely austere and completely intolerant. Their main slogan is to fight sin, which begins as innocuously as by listening to music or watching a dance or a film; even television is an evil, as is girls' education in the vicinity of males. What they say about FM radios is not wholly known, because they do not attack the various warring FM radios in the NWFP and its tribal areas that spew intolerant Islamic edicts all the time and serve as the mouthpiece of an established, or perhaps, an emerging warlord of an area, who begins to perform the functions of a state in an inchoate form. The difficulty is that such warlords are emerging in altogether too many small places in the tribal areas as well as in some settled areas where it remains sub rosa, though these warlords, all calling themselves Taliban, continue to coerce others to extort money by way of arbitrary taxes and they fight sin even in the settled districts of the NWFP. There is a considerable degree of sympathy for the Taliban in Punjab and in Karachi City. Karachi happens to be the largest Pushtoon town in the world, larger than the Pushtoon populations in Peshawar, Kabul or anywhere else. The Taliban is making forays in Punjab and have been active in Karachi. The point to note is that mounting a large suicide bombing attack, no matter what the target, requires elaborate logistics, money, men and a local support base where they seek and find refuge, before, if not after the attack. Such long logistics chains exist in Lahore, Peshawar, Rawalpindi and many other places, in and outside tribal areas and the rest of the Frontier.

What their role would be in future depends greatly on what the nature of the Pakistani governments will be in the immediate future, and how would they tackle the question of Islamic militancy which is clearly becoming an extension of the war on terror in Afghanistan. But what happens in Pakistan will have a far-reaching effect on the rest of South Asia.

(II) ETHNICITIES'S DEMANDS

Pakistan was a part of historical India, the British Indian Empire to be precise, and was created by an Act of the British Parliament: the Indian Independence Act of 1947. But once it came into being, it faced four main problems, which remain to this day: (i) its ethnic diversity, (ii) economic underdevelopment and poverty, (iii) Islam, (iv) relations with India on a state-to-state level, almost a continuation of its earlier problems of Muslims with the majority Hindus. The fact is that there was no region of India where Muslims and Hindus have not lived as neighbours for a thousand years. They share many commonalities based on race, language, literature, folklore, common historical memories, music, martial arts, dances, paintings, architecture, economic problems (poverty mainly) and cultural and social mores including marriage and after-death rites, practical morality as well as attitudes towards women. An important commonality was caste; old Indian castes and tribal affinities survived the conversion of many Hindus to Islam (or Christianity or Buddhism). In short, the old folk cultures neither died, nor did Islam or Christianity change them.

The problem of ethnic diversity is acute in Pakistan. The reasons lie in history: Mohammad Ali Jinnah, the politician who had successfully campaigned for the Partition of India, had propounded the theory of Hindus and Muslims being two separate nations, with little in common. He came to be revered in Pakistan and was demonized in India. But denying the commonalities of race, language, culture (both folk, and what may be called high or court culture), not to mention economic problems, was, and is, tantamount to asserting that a thousand years of living together, cheek by jowl, in nearly every village and town produced no commonality. Or that Islam produced no impact on India's civilization and cultures or that a common

Indo–Persian Civilization – mainly in the northern parts of India – did not come into being or does not survive. It is true that there is a big lobby in India, the Hindutva school, that implicitly accepts Jinnah's two-nation theory, while denouncing it noisily. But so long as it goes on virtually denying the emergence and flowering of Indo-Persian civilization – studiously avoiding the mention of it at all – it actually endorses Jinnah's two-nation theory. Instead, Hindutva emphasizes on the existence of an India before Islam's arrival, glorifies it and wishes the Indians to go back to that (Vedic) civilization and culture, in mind, attitude and belief, while becoming ultramodern in science and technology, so as to acquire the wherewithal of becoming a great (military) power. Looked at closely, these two schools are two sides of the same coin: two sets of politicians creating and exploiting Muslim and Hindu communal chauvinisms, who have actually succeeded in dividing the people of the subcontinent emotionally and politically on a permanent political basis.

Pakistan's greatest problem is not ethnic diversity per se. There are many states with citizens of multiple ethnicities that are at peace with themselves and are progressing politically, economically and culturally. The problem has become acute in Pakistan because one major ethnic group, which identifies itself with the Punjabi language and culture, is too numerous and has thrown up powerful elites who have dominated the government in all its upper tiers – the bureaucracy, military, professionals and also business, industry and finance. It can be said they have ruled in a way that has, in historical fact, denied political space and economic opportunities to the nascent middle classes of all the other provinces: East Bengal (until it seceded in 1971), Sindh, NWFP and Balochistan. Politics in all the non-Punjab provinces has revolved round their relations with Punjab and the Punjab-dominated Central government. All Central governments have relied on vacuous Islamic rhetoric or other quasi-Islamic categories like Muslim nationalism, Islamic brotherhood, but not Pakistani nationalism because that would also include the non-Muslims. Complaints of all non-Punjabi ethnicities pertain to the lack of economic opportunities open to them and their lopsided share in power and resources. The central authorities tend to call all this parochialism. They preach something to the effect of: 'all Muslims are brothers, so why do you complain that all positions of vantage in the country are occupied by Punjabis – or their earlier allies, and now hated underlings, the mohajirs? Aren't Punjabis Muslims?'

Islamic solidarity in actual practice has meant that Punjab dominates all walks of life; opposition to this is not recognized as an issue and those who raise it are treated as deficient Muslims. The regional nationalists tend to retort by arguing that Islam or Islamic brotherhood is irrelevant in a predominantly Muslim country. The real question is why are the Muslims of Sindh, NWFP and Balochistan not getting their due share of political and economic power? The people are vitally interested in the economic progress of their regions to produce more jobs that will eventually ensure their political empowerment. This argument has gone on, back and forth, now for sixty years, in one form or another. It was precisely this issue that caused the break up of Pakistan in 1971, an issue that is alive and defines much of the politics in the country.

The problem is far more bitter today as a result of the centre's dogged refusal, not only to recognize the issue but to take various actions to divert, hoodwink or suppress regional nationalists. Central authorities have used the Pakistani Army to suppress Baloch nationalists four times, while the Baloch nationalists are in a perpetual revolt. The way Akbar Bugti was eliminated in August 2006 may have made Balochistan's revolt an endemic feature of Pakistan politics, and will remain so, until something substantial that resolves this whole issue, occurs. Sindh has been in a ferment soon after Pakistan's politics was perceived to be dominated by the Punjabi bureaucracy and the army, which was soon within the first few years after Independence in 1947. Sindh has also experienced suppression, and the NWFP feels wronged at the hands of those who voice the Islamic rhetoric. But the Frontier provinces, and to a large extent, Balochistan, have lately suffered a serious dilution of their nationalists' influence, due to what the centre did in another context: by encouraging and supporting Islamic extremism in both provinces and allowing the US and Saudi Arabia to adopt the mujahideen as their own wards, arming and funding them to fight in Afghanistan against the Soviets in the 1980s.

Despite the heavy and unfortunate distraction and dilution lately, the Baloch and Pushtoon nationalisms continue to survive. They remain secular entities and continue to demand true federalism in Pakistan. Their allegiance is to their nationality – how different a nationality is from a nation depends on the circumstances. They would appear to be the same entity in psychological terms, depending upon the given political opportunities. Anyway, the demand for true and substantial provincial autonomy (a share in decision-making and ownership of resources) persists.

(III) SOCIAL AND ECONOMIC DISPARITIES

Economic underdevelopment, that is, widespread unemployment and perceived poverty, is in fact common to all parts of Pakistan. But some ad hoc development has taken place almost everywhere, far more so in Punjab. And a lot of bitterness has been created by the differing quanta of new jobs being available in different provinces, with local young men in smaller provinces being the worst sufferers (women are hardly ever taken into account because few want their women to work even now). Islamabad rulers talk a lot about having arrested the process of Pakistan becoming a failed state through defaults in repaying foreign debts. First, none of the common people were responsible for obtaining so many loans from foreign governments and banks, and for spending them on projects that did not increase Pakistan's capability to repay them. Far too much was spent on the armed forces and far too little on productive enterprises. The non-military expenditures also favoured, (a) the upper classes' conspicuous consumption; and (b) a good proportion of borrowed money ended up embezzled in one way or another by the bureaucracy, mostly through kickbacks. The living standards of retired generals and bureaucrats in Lahore, Islamabad and Karachi speak for themselves – this has strengthened all manner of resentments. Sentiment against Punjab continues to grow in Sindh, NWFP and especially in Balochistan. Second, the rise of the Taliban, sectarian terrorists and Islamic extremists in general occurs among the poor or lower middle class, a section of the society that gives intimations of class war concepts. Thirdly, any development that has taken place has been uneven, both horizontally – sharply more in Punjab and distinctly less in Balochistan and Sindh (outside Karachi) – and vertically, enriching the rich gentry and leaving too many poor.

It cannot be said that big pockets of poverty do not exist in Punjab. They very much do. But the difference with other provinces is that the social elites in Punjab are far richer and are in far greater numbers. Rich individuals do exist in Sindh, Balochistan and NWFP, but they are no match to Punjab's social elites with their five-star culture. Elsewhere in the world such social conditions would have created extreme leftist movements. But Pakistan's social and economic backwardness is being massively exploited by Islamic extremists, whose rhetoric promises a better and more just life here and wonderful affluence amidst what is obviously wild permissiveness, in the hereafter. Except for some tiny groups in a few cities, there are no active leftists. Angry talk about the lack of social justice is largely absent, except for the rhetoric of Islamic extremists. The future may thus possibly belong to Islamic extremists in Pakistan – and also perhaps Afghanistan.

But it must be noted that the policy paradigm that the Musharraf regime was implementing, is based on the current neo-classical doctrines: it lays down liberalization, privatization and de-regulation as its cornerstones, and advocates for an exports-led growth, a freely convertible floating currency and minimal role of the state in the economy. This has produced considerable prosperity for the entrepreneurial, trading and banking class, thanks to extremely weak trade unions. This prosperity of the few contrasts sharply with the growth in poverty, especially the perceived relative poverty of the middle strata of 40 to 45 per cent of the people, after leaving out of account the top 15 per cent and also the bottom 40 per cent. What makes life difficult for 70 to75 per cent of the population is the continuously high rates of inflation since 2004. This creates social unrest and exasperation, in which extremist advice is more easily accepted, thus, proving this regime to be a godsend for the Islamic extremists.

(IV) STATE OF THE ECONOMY

It is a piquant situation. After almost a decade, a lot of praise was showered on General Pervez Musharraf's economic team for its wonderful economic management by IFIs like the World Bank and IMF, including private sector rating agencies. The economic team that General Musharraf had imported from the US was led by Shaukat Aziz and his buddies from New York's banking sector. His claim to fame was that he had improved many macro-economic indicators during his first four years. Some of it was true largely because he, for the first time after a decade of chaotic economic management by the PPP and PML (N) governments, initially introduced some financial discipline, and also reined in the military's constantly increasing share of resources, but only for a while. The apogee was the year 2003-04 when he returned the wonderful growth figure of 8.4 per cent of the GDP. It was claimed that Pakistan has now joined the middle-income group countries' league, and that it has broken the begging bowl and shall no longer run to the IMF to seek help. But then after 2004 it was discovered that the human development indicators began deteriorating again. Agricultural production first became stagnant and then started declining, particularly from the supposedly bumper crop of 2004 to 2008. The rate of growth in the agricultural sector has been between 2 to 3 per cent since then, virtually cancelling any benefit because of the population growth rate, which in fact might be higher than that growth rate. The consumption by the middle class was increasing in tandem with the increase in incomes. The net result was the rise of inflation due to relative shortages of goods and services. It was discovered, though the government tried to suppress and ignore the stray voices that the figures had been fudged. It was not only the agricultural sector that was stagnating, but the industrial growth too was stagnant. Its rate lately has risen to a figure between 3 to 4 per cent, while normal expansion for keeping the prices more or less stable, is traditionally between 7 to 8 per cent. Real growth requires above 8 per cent rate of growth in the industrial sector. This has not been achieved. The high growth rates that Shaukat Aziz tom-tommed and the world applauded, was based on wonderful returns from the service sector. It was a money-spinning sector, particularly the banks, which were financing middle class's consumption of utilities and cars. In the meantime there were ideological compulsions on Shaukat Aziz and his team: there was to be an unending process of sell out of the public-sector undertakings. This was in fact an old policy that the civilian governments of the 1990s had also followed. In Pakistan most cases of privatization stank of corruption. It was freely said during the four PPP and PML (N) governments' time (1988 to 1999), that every time a public-sector undertaking was sold, it was for much less than it was worth, because of back channel corruption involved between the private buyers and the ministers concerned. Musharraf's economic team was supposed to be squeaky clean. But later on, some of its privatization operations were seen to stink to the high heavens, as the PTCL and the Pakistan Steel Mills cases showed.

Take the case of Pakistan Steel Mills Corporation. It was being sold for a pittance of Rs 21 billion. The Supreme Court of Pakistan under Justice Iftikhar Muhammad Chaudhry took notice of it and stopped it. It was later discovered by media and analysts that the government had not included the price of the land on which the mills stood. Those lands alone were worth, in the market, about Rs 40 billion. Then the steel mill had stock-in-trade ready for dispatch of some Rs 9 to 10 billion. Cash and receivables were another Rs 9 to 10 billion. There was obviously some gross corruption involved. Nobody explained who was actually buying and who was behind the whole thing. The same thing was said about the PTCL, which was a profit-making concern and which was sold at pittance without necessary transparency. The chief justice of Pakistan, who had stopped both sales, earned great respect from the people. He was otherwise also, becoming extraordinarily popular because of his persistent prodding of the government over the fate of the hundreds, and some seven thousands, of people who had 'disappeared' without leaving a trace. What was, however, generally known was that they had been picked up by intelligence agencies was refused to disclose anything about the matter and blandly told that they had nothing to say. The government pleaded before the court that it knew nothing about them and that they had not been arrested by the government. The CJP paid the price for thus annoying top civil and military officials, and it is a continuing history, as he remains non-functional though he has been curiously paid his salary until the month of May 2008. The matter is in the Parliament and the parties are squabbling over the judges who had been sacked by Musharraf on 3 November 2007. At the time of writing, the case remains a subject of political pulls and pushes. The whole country has been holding its breath over its outcome. All that can be said is that President Musharraf, still sits atop the steel structure of administration left by the colonial masters that enforces its will through the army; the structure is still under his control. The PPP government in office at the time of this writing has obfuscated over the matter, and holds that it genuinely wants to restore all the sacked judges but it has to be done through constitutional amendments that have to be passed by the Parliament – a lengthy process requiring two-thirds majority in both Houses of Parliament. The outside opponents of the government that have been on the upswing throughout 2007 and the early months of 2008 are of the view that the thing can be done in 15 seconds. All that it requires is an executive order of the prime minister through a law ministry notification. The judges were sacked illegally and unconstitutionally by an executive order, and another executive order can put them back where they were. But an aside should be added here: the trouble is that the real power still resides, somehow, with Musharraf and he is still very angry with the chief justice of Pakistan for all he had been trying to do, particularly with regard to the case of 'disappearances'. The CJP may have earned kudos from the general public for his judicial activism, but the administration as a whole feels betrayed because the judiciary in Pakistan has from the very beginning (1953 onwards) been supportive, and was, in fact, a subordinate organ of the state presided over by either the governor general or the president, and, in fewer cases by the prime minister, particularly in the 1972–77 period.

Another political fact has to be noted here: there is political mayhem because of what happened in the elections on 18 February 2008. The electoral verdict was unambiguous. Elections having been substantially free, the public had rejected the Musharraf regime in toto, and in the process, also rejected the religious parties that were governing NWFP province and which had a large share in the government of Balochistan. But the result was also split. The biggest winner was the PPP, led until 27 December 2007 by Benazir Bhutto, and after her assassination in

Rawalpindi on that date, by her husband who now claims to be co-chairman of the PPP along with his son, who is supposedly the anointed chairman of the party when he comes of age (he is only 18 and studying at Oxford, now). This has brought the traditional rivalry between the PPP and PML (N), the two major winning parties, into clear relief. The PPP is the largest party in the National Assembly and controls the province of Sindh, where it was able to form its own government, though at the Centre it required outside support which the PML (N) provided. The two parties, in fact, claim to remain mysteriously loyal to their coalition that they had signed and sealed earlier on 9 March through the Murree Declaration. But the coalition government broke down on 12 May over the judges' issue with PPP continuing to run the government alone, while PML (N) continues to provide outside support. The NWFP, for example, is controlled by a coalition of the Awami National Party (ANP) led by Asfandyar Wali and the PPP. Similarly PPP has formed a government in Balochistan in coalition with almost every sardar (or notable), and has a huge government there. In Balochistan party labels do not really matter; what matters is the tribal sardars who always return from their rotten boroughs.

It is this government which is preoccupied entirely with the judges' issue and other political matters, especially its relationship with Nawaz Sharif and Musharraf, both of whom are its sworn personal enemies. That is putting the government in a bind. PPP remains mysteriously loyal to the terms of a deal that the American administration had helped negotiate between Musharraf and Benazir in 2007. The agreement remains secret to this day, although what is known is that America is probably the guarantor of the agreement. That is the reason why PPP continues to remain soft, in action, on Musharraf, though it calls him a 'relic of the past', that he is not a constitutional president, and all the rest of the Opposition rhetoric. But in terms of hard actions, the PPP only goes so far as Musharraf will tolerate. That is the political situation in which the budget for the year 2008–09 was made.

The budget is as vacuous as it could possibly be. The PM had already announced that he would not change the economic paradigm that the previous Musharraf regime was following. The government's new budget, for instance, was already stuck with the GDP growth rate objective, which was its only achievement. It had presided over three years of continuous stagnation in agriculture and industry, though the services sector continues to perform well enough. The primary quality of the economic management that can be inferred, today, from the budget is that nothing much will change. The pre-eminent characteristic of the economic management is over-consumption, particularly by the upper crest of 10 to 15 per cent of population. The government had run a long reign of low interest rates and had encouraged increased private consumption by those who could. As the new budget for 2008–09 shows, and it is a continuation from the past, that the expenditures on defence, administrative and security expenditures and debt servicing alone eat away something like 80 per cent , or perhaps more, of the total resources. The government will continue to adhere to the policy of privatization. As in the past, the entire money from the sales comes into the kitty, and is spent. The social sectors remain neglected: education does not get even full 4 per cent of the GDP and the health sector gets even less. A lot of money comes from what is fiduciary expansion in the shape of borrowings from the banking sector or foreign loans. Despite the budget document, very few actually know what is the status of the economy; but the facts disclosed can be summed up as over-consumption. This is shown by budget deficits that is now rising up to anywhere between 8 to 9 per cent of the GDP, causing inflation rates to be in double digits. It is also exhibited by a trade deficit in which Pakistan cannot pay with exports, the cost of its imports, which are nearly double its earnings abroad. The consequent result of this is that the current account deficit is at a high percentage point of the GDP. That straightaway threatens Pakistan with falling into the debt trap. Accumulated foreign loans are now around $ 46 billion, and the debt servicing figure is going to rise very fast from one year to the next, because the earlier politically motivated rescheduling of debt servicing following 9/11 is ending. There is also the unearned income of something like a little more than $ 5 billion from expatriate Pakistanis' remittances. But these are more than cancelled out by the amount of outflows by way of the foreigners' earnings in Pakistan from their investments in the services sector.

The basic picture of Pakistan's economy is provided by the high expenditures of the government as well as the social elites, which causes all the deficits. The real cause of it is excessive expenditure by the military and the uncontrolled expansion in administrative expenses of all central and provincial governments, in the name of fighting high rates of crime and various wars in the tribal areas, not to mention insurgency in Balochistan by Baloch nationalists. The basic flaw of the economy is that 50 per cent of the economy is undocumented and can be freely called black economy. The incontrovertible fact is that Pakistan's tax-GDP ratio is the lowest in South Asia, far behind even other smaller countries, not to mention India. Also there has been, and continues to be, flight of capital from the country. That results in much smaller savings rates, domestic and others, than anywhere else in the region. Pakistan ranks along with some of the failing states in the Sub-Saharan Africa in basic economic indicators. That the inflation rate may be anywhere between 12 per cent to whatever higher figure, can be inferred from episodal and random check-ups. The official figures are already about 12 per cent, and this, many think, is much understated. Food shortages continue largely because population figures are controversial, and such shortages are now a fact of life, while hoarding and profiteering by the private sector is undeniable. In Pakistan, the fudging of the figures have been resorted to from Ayub Khan's days in the 1960s. It has been refined into a fine art by the Musharraf team. Much of it is unravelled by the consequential facts.

The situation is grave for Pakistan because it was able to withstand the downward economic pulls largely because of large dollops of aid from America and the West for its role in the US' War on (Islamic) Terror. Pakistan was a valued ally and was showered with much help, the sum total of which is not really known, though the general figure bandied about is $ 10 billion. This aid plus the amounts earned through privatization plus superfluous printing of currency notes has enabled high consumption by the state as well as the upper crust of the society. How long can this go on, is difficult to say. The latest figures issued by international NGOs that compile figures on failed states, ranks Pakistan number eight in the top ten. Pakistan's economy is its Achilles' heel.

(V) NUCLEAR WEAPONS

Pakistanis were interested in nuclear technology from 1950s onward. President Eisenhower's Atoms-for-Peace programme was making most people aware of nuclear power. Pakistanis did not get any reactor until 1970s. This was the condu-type reactor given by Canada. It came on stream in 1974. Earlier there was a certain European power that had informally wanted to convey a message to the Pakistan Foreign Office that, try as you may the Anglo-Americans will not let you have a nuclear reactor. Your only chance is to design one yourself with our help and in the process we will have trained manpower of our own. The Pakistan Foreign Office perhaps knew better than this. However, the kind of nuclear programme it was interested in was basically for military purposes.

The origins of Pakistan programme was a high-level conference in Islamabad in 1972. Its background was that India and Pakistan had already fought three wars. The last one, 1971, was a decisive one, as a result of which East Pakistan became Bangladesh. The programme was entirely military in inspiration and purpose. It wanted to take revenge and to equalize the series. The powers that be saw a short cut in early 1970s through nuclear weapons. Nuclear weapons were thought to be wonder weapons and possessing them was supposed to confer so much strength and deterrence on a power that others would not dare to attack it. Pakistan embarked on this quest and the story is fairly well-known about Dr A.Q. Khan bringing certain blueprints to manufacturing centrifuges and which led to all kinds of industrial innovations.

Considering the technological backwardness, Pakistan mastered the art of enriching uranium enough to have the compound that can serve as the raw material of the atomic weapon. By 1984, Dr A.Q. Khan was able to announce that Pakistan had mastered the technology of enriching uranium. It was a dramatic announcement made at an Indo–Pakistan seminar at Islamabad. After that the world press has been full of stories about Pakistan's Islamic Bomb, Pakistani Bomb, etc. Pakistan, as noted, wanted a military capability. Since it did not have a normal reactor (until 1974) in which plutonium could be made, it adopted the direct route to the bomb by enriching uranium to the required extent and using it as the explosive material for the bomb. By 1986, Pakistan was able to threaten India to nuke it if it proceeded with its suspected design of an invasion under cover of the Brasstacks Exercise. Nothing much happened and the crisis became a memory.

And should anyone think that Pakistan thought of a military capability of atomic nature only in 1970s one can disclose from an informal interview in the 1960s with Dr R.H. Usmani, a civil servant, who for a while served on the IAEA. He was also a science man and he had headed the Pakistan Atomic Energy Commission. I talked to him about how Pakistan would have any bomb if it did not have any nuclear reactors. Upon which he said that one way or another a reactor will come our way; negotiations are in an advance stage with various powers and once we have a nuclear reactor, the high road will be wide open to bomb-making. Whereupon I ventured, to the formidable civil servant, something to the effect that IAEA checks and supervision will prevent you from doing that. He pooh-poohed the IAEA safeguards. No matter how many secret cameras they install, we can always cheat them. They can't be sitting all the time in the reactor control room. We will burn uranium slowly at the cost of having less power than rated. There will be less power because of slow burning of fuel. That will enable us to stockpile, slowly of course, enough plutonium for a bomb and then for more bombs. He was thinking of the more usual plutonium route. He probably had no idea about enriching uranium directly. That idea was brought in the 1970s by Dr A.Q. Khan to Pakistan.

As noted, Pakistan was able to have a bomb by 1984 or 1986. Some think it was 1984 and people were being reticent in making tall claims. However, the official announcement of Pakistan's nuclear capability came in January 1990 when Shahrayar Khan, the then foreign secretary, announced in Washington that Pakistan had different parts that, when put together, would make an atomic bomb. That had deleterious effects on Pakistan–American relations. But that is another story and of no great consequence now.

The credit for training several thousand Pakistani scientists in Western universities goes to Dr Usmani. He had laid a firm foundation by training a large number of scientists and technologists.

There has been childish quarrels between Dr A.Q. Khan of Kahuta Research Laboratories, which was later named after him, and Dr Samar Mubarakmand of the PAEC. Intention from the very beginning was that of a bomb. Large-scale work proceeded both in the Kahuta Laboratory by Dr A.Q. Khan and in PAEC by others.

Ever since 1986 an arms race is going on between India and Pakistan at a frantic pace in all relevant fields: conventional, nuclear and vehicles for firing the nuclear weapons from. Both countries have taken the twin-road of using aircraft for dropping the bombs as well as special missiles for carrying those bombs to selected targets at a given distance. When the bomb did come, it brought a lot of other ideas. Originally, the nuclear bombs were thought to be the ultimate deterrence. Possession of nuclear weapons ensured a country's security almost 100 per cent.

But then come 2001 and 2002. In December 2001, some terrorists attacked the Indian Parliament and an exchange of fire took place in which intruders and a certain number of security personnel of the Parliament were killed. The Indian government thought that it was Pakistan's doing and the Prime Minister Atal Behari Vajpayee declared a decisive war would ensue. He brought all India's strike forces on to the frontiers between the two countries and India made as if it would invade. Pakistanis thought that an actual invasion is imminent. So did the rest of the world. The Indians had brought all that they could mobilize for the offensive. The Hindi-Urdu words used by Vajpayee were 'Aar ya Par', meaning truly decisive, one way or another. This war scare lasted a good ten months. But the war did not take place.

Why did it not take place? It is important to know. In earlier months of 2002, Pakistan had made as many as thirteen threats of nuking India if it did proceed with invasion. We all know that bigger Western powers intervened. There was mediation. It took a fair amount of time. India wanted caste-iron assurances that Pakistan would never again allow terrorist acts in India. Apparently the Indians had convinced themselves that the job was done by Pakistan-inspired terrorists. Eventually, President Musharraf made a broadcast that contained adequate assurances. Then it is not known for sure whether there were any external guarantees by America, Britain or both or any other power for that matter. But it does look likely that Pakistan's assurance was underwritten by some Western powers, whoever they may have been. There is still much confusion about those ten months. Among the known facts are: (a) Pakistan did make promises not to allow terrorist activity in Indian territory that is planned and conducted from Pakistan; (b) there appears to have been international mediation; (c) Pakistan made promises; (d) India did withdraw its strike troops from October 2002.

There was a peculiar event in May 1998. On 11 May and a day later, India test exploded five nuclear weapons and some of its leaders taunted Pakistan that from now on it should behave. Pakistani government could not restrain itself. It exploded six atomic weapons on May 28 and 30 at Chaghai in Balochistan. Both countries' people were punch happy on their scientific and technological achievements; sweets were distributed. After that both countries got down to an intense arms race, as noted. Indian thinking was that Pakistan will be overawed by India's five nuclear test explosions. Instead Pakistan exploded six nuclear bombs and both sides are now quiet, though some sections continue to believe that India became immensely strong after its five nuclear weapons explosions and, similarly, many Pakistanis are that Pakistan bettered India by one and it can look India in the eye. One has seen what happened in 2002.

Here the point is that official beliefs in both countries are similar: India's defences are impregnable because of its nuclear triad. Pakistan also thinks its defence is unassailable whether or not it has a nuclear triad. The fact of the matter is that these beliefs need to be seen in perspective of real experience. The year 2002 is to be remembered for that. India knowing the Pakistan capabilities made a credible threat to invade it. Both countries capabilities are credible. Pakistan saw the Indian threat credible: (a) as noted, Pakistan made thirteen threats of using nuclear weapons against India and it believed India was serious about a final war; and (b) in a purely conventional war India was thought to be sure of winning and Pakistan was sure to lose. The fact that India made a credible threat of invasion while Pakistan was known to possess at least a dozen nuclear weapons, if not more, shows that Pakistan's deterrence was, to an extent, inadequate. George Fernandes, India's the then defence minister, had taunted Pakistan: let Pakistan use its nuclear weapons first in accordance with its own doctrine. And then wait for India's riposte: Pakistan's seven or eight industrial–urban centres will be wiped out by India's second strike capability; Pakistan will have to revert to the Stone Age.

So where do we stand and what about deterrence? All said and done, India did not actually invade despite wanting to do so dearly. One presumes but does not know for sure at which high level American mediation took place. But the fact remains certain that India did mobilize for actual war, kept half a million strike troops on the borders for ten months – and finally did not invade. Some conclusions have to be drawn: (a) atomic weapons' deterrence is neither 100 per cent nor is it totally absent; there is a fairly large grey area; (b) the fact that Pakistan did not use its weapons first shows that expectation of later widespread destruction of Pakistan did deter it; the conclusion emerges that while a certain amount of deterrence inheres in all atomic weapons, it is not conclusive enough. As Fernandes said one nuclear bomb can be checkmated by another such bomb. And India will then prevail. It would seem that be conventional power, in which India is thought to be superior, is crucial. An exchange of atomic weapons will be, above all, too destructive; no sane government or general can or should take the chance of such an exchange.

The Pakistani bomb carries an additional load of worry. The whole country is facing in normal times the threat from Islamic extremism of various kinds. Al-Qaeda, Taliban (both home grown and Afghan, et al) are a big and growing threat. The rest of the world has been alarmed about the insecurity of Pakistani nukes. Islamabad, both civil and military, strenuously denied at first that Pakistani deterrent is insecure; they emphasized there are rings of steel and electronic locks. No militant can filch a bomb or two to wreak havoc in a Western city. That is perhaps true enough; no odd individual can steal a few nukes.

But then there is even a bigger threat: Pakistan, the Islamic republic, can be taken over by any of the various Islamic extremist schools, what with rampant Wahabi and Salafi ideas and local extremism growing apace.

The degree of alarm felt in the Western world is so great that in some ways Pakistan's nuclear weapons have become its greatest vulnerability. Should another year or two be like 2008 or 2009, thoughts in the West will turn to pre-emptively intervening in Pakistan. Its own friends are clearly liable to move in that direction. These weapons doubtless are a grave vulnerability.

Climactic Change

This chapter takes into consideration the period from the closing months of 2006 to the opening months of 2008, largely because many dramatic, indeed climactic, events that took place in 2007, started the previous year or had their denouement in 2008 or even in 2009. By and large, the year 2007 remains the climactic year. It opened amidst the aftershocks of the killing of the Baloch nationalist leader, Nawab Mohammad Akbar Bugti, the chief of the notable tribe of Bugtis, in 2006 that started a Baloch nationalist revolt that continues.

The period also opened amidst the shadow of other portentous events: Pakistan Army, it was clear to all, had failed to put down the Islamic militancy of the Pushtoon tribesmen in the tribal areas of the NWFP. The Army had failed to subdue them and the Pushtoon militants, Taliban or whatever else they may be, had evolved a modicum of unity of command – not necessarily one firm command but several groups working in some cohesion – which the Americans regard as the link provided by al-Qaeda among the various local Islamic militants and extremists. The Pakistani Army's inability was in full demonstration when some Islamic militants owning allegiance to Maulana Fazlullah, for instance, were able to 'abduct' 264 Pakistani soldiers with 5 officers and 19 trucks without a single shot being fired. After many months the prisoners were released with Rs 500 each, though several others were beheaded. It appeared that that beheadings were of those who belonged to the Shia sect. This sharply discloses a certain characteristic of the (Sunni) Islamic militants or Taliban operating in the tribal areas: the anti-Shia stance of such militants. The Taliban and the al-Qaeda have the same belief: of regarding all Shias as kafirs, fit only to be killed. Which is also why they are called Takfiris among the Arabs.

The net result was that the Pakistani Army's aura of invincibility vanished. The Islamic militants became bolder; they later forged unity among themselves in the name of Tahreek-e-Taliban Pakistan with the aim of establishing an Islamic Caliphate. Most people in the FATA have always been virtually independent in the sense that the army, even when it is present as now, is more or less confined to its posts and barracks in the forts. The military has asked all its personnel, even as far away as Peshawar and the rest of the Frontier province, not to mix with people or go out in uniform. Popular support for the Taliban is the reason for this fear of inviting attacks from pro-Taliban elements. This insurgency is so dramatic and intense that it seamlessly merges with Taliban's war of resistance against American (and NATO or ISAF) occupation of Afghanistan. There are many similarities between the Pakistani and Afghan Taliban: both groups comprise much of the same divided tribes of Pushtoons, and have acquired the same Takfiri beliefs that can be traced to Saudi Arabian Wahabis and Salafis, which have spread through the al-Qaeda in Iraq, Afghanistan and Pakistan.

In 2007, President Musharraf was in the last year of his presidentship, according to the tightly controlled democracy that he was running. He had to be re-elected by mid-November of the year 2007. That was also the time when elections to the National and the Provincial assemblies were due. The president was preoccupied with getting those two major elections organized and 'managed'. It was commonly understood by friends and foes alike, that the elections Musharraf would conduct in November for the National and Provincial assemblies would be expertly 'managed' by what are euphemistically called in the Pakistan press as the 'agencies'. These are the undercover intelligence services of the government and of the army. They have successfully organized systematic rigging of elections to produce broadly acceptable results (to the ruler), previously. Their strategies include selective pre-poll, polling day and post-poll techniques that the main intelligence agencies – the civilian Intelligence Bureau, the ISI and the MI (Military Intelligence) – have perfected. But this time round, they saw many more difficulties in their way. They primarily needed the marshalling of civilian political support for the president's friends, to whatever degree possible. But the trouble was that the media was becoming far too independent and critical. Musharraf had, to his credit, the fact that he had tolerated criticism of the government for a fair amount of time in order to win some credibility for his vaunted 'real' democracy. But if the results of the elections were to be predetermined as well as be credible to 'some extent', something had to be done to make the media more discreet and less strident, and still not be perceived as obedient – which would again be counterproductive. The Americans had been talking too loudly and too much about democracy and freedom; they were actually seeking to involve the people of Pakistan in their war on terror, for which reason they wanted 'unmanaged' or freer elections, so that major parties like the PPP and PML (N) could be elected to power. That upset Musharraf's schemes.

There was also another major threat on the horizon. The Supreme Court was becoming far too troublesome for the bureaucracy in general, and for the intelligence community, in particular. The court was behaving as if it had no concern or care for the boss's needs and its chief justice was heading it in the direction of becoming wholly independent of the usual influence (supremacy) of the military. Earlier, throughout Pakistan's history from 1950s onward, every military intervention against, or subversion of, the Constitution was validated by the Supreme Court. There was only one instance where it did not validate such intervention, and pronounced the proclamation of martial law by General Yahya Khan in 1969 as usurpation. But that was a comfortably safe conclusion; it pleased the government of the day (the PPP government led by Z.A. Bhutto) after Yahya Khan had been deposed. At all the other times, including the 1999 intervention by General Pervez Musharraf, the military takeovers were validated by the Supreme Court.

This man, the CJP, Justice Iftikhar Muhammad Chaudhry, was creating difficulties for the bureaucracy as he went on. In consequence of Islamic militancy in FATA and Balochistan insurgency, the Pakistani intelligence agencies had started imitating the Latin American practice of picking up troublesome activists and keeping them incommunicado in safe houses or secret detention centres. This was going on in Pakistan on a fairly large scale. The head of the Supreme Court had become a pain in the neck for the bureaucracy, by summoning senior officers to the court and grilling them about the whereabouts of the 'disappeared'. The 'agencies' responded with selective releases of a few such people to appease the CJP, while most of them were not released.

The Supreme Court had also put another spanner in the works; the matter of sale of public-sector undertakings, which was thought to be conducted in a manner that raised suspicions of corruption by the government. 'He had to be disciplined', seemed to be the advice given to President Musharraf by his close aides, who also headed the various intelligence agencies. Consequently, Justice Iftikhar Muhammad Chaudhry, the chief justice of Pakistan, was called before the president of Islamic Republic of Pakistan, who sat in full military regalia, surrounded by four other lieutenant generals, also in the military dress. Here, Justice Chaudhry was presented with a charge sheet (that had earlier been circulated in the blogosphere and had reached all the media outlets). Justice Chaudhry had one look at that scandalous sheet and he said he would prefer to be tried in an open court and that he would not resign and go quietly. This was unexpected and the president left the room while the four lieutenant generals tried to persuade or browbeat him.

What precisely happened is not known, but some facts are incontrovertible: he was detained there and then, kept in the president's Camp Office in Rawalpindi for six long hours during which a new chief justice of Pakistan was administered the oath of office – who is now a controversial figure and will have to go if and when the popular agitation for the restoration of judiciary succeeds. Justice Chaudhry was then prevented from going to his chambers; he was manhandled by the police and was 'escorted' to his residence to be locked up in his own house. All official or personal transports had been taken away from his home during those six hours. The same evening that charge sheet became a 'Reference' that was sent to the constitutional body, the Supreme Judicial Council, and some members of it were flown the same evening from other cities. The Reference was taken up for hearing, the same evening in the Supreme Court building.

What was happening was being broadcast by the TV channels live: right from when the chief justice came out of the president's place to the details of the various police manhandling were shown live and subsequently in recordings also. The reaction of the country was one of outrage. A lawyers' movement virtually started from the same day, or it could be officially dated to have started from 13 March 2007, when the 'dysfunctional' CJP made his appearance at the session of the Supreme Judicial Council. The sordid drama was telecast – in parts live – from the moment the CJP had started walking from his residence to the Apex Court building, with a large crowd around him. The police again manhandled him and deposited him into a vehicle, so that his march to the Supreme Court building does not become a public rally chanting slogans in favour of the chief justice. The outside world knows the intensity of the movement. It shook up the civil society throughout the country.

One fact, however, has not been recorded yet: it is that things have greatly changed in the heartland of Pakistan called the Punjab province. The province, as a result of economic development, has now developed a new social phenomenon: an industrial and commercial middle class that has its own ideas of wanting democracy and which insists on a full range of fundamental human rights for all, as well as a government that would obey law, and so on. Moreover, the public outrage was made visible by the media and the movement of the lawyers became so intense that it greatly influenced the entire TV-watching public, mainly the middle class throughout the country.

The year 2007 was also the year when food shortages and price hikes had begun to be unbearable for the common man. It was the steady background music of economic troubles that highlighted the failures of the Musharraf regime, with people running from pillar to post to find atta (wheat flour) to make bread. This became a strong argument against the government of the day. It created a situation which could not be contained, and the climax in this particular case came on 20 July when a full bench of the Supreme Court adjudged the Reference as untenable, and reinstated the chief justice of Pakistan to his august office. This had a tremendous impact and the whole country saw how untenable the position of President Pervez Musharraf was, and his military regime, as a result, came under public ridicule. The chief justice had behaved in a dignified way during his suspension and never spoke a word about his case or did anything outwardly political. He always confined himself to the advocacy of the rule of law, separation of powers, democratic norms, etcetera. The impact of the judicial decision on the people was very high, and the lawyers' movement went on becoming more intense, and started demanding General Musharraf's resignation. 'Go Musharraf Go', became a favourite slogan that acquired great popularity, and continues to be uttered on all likely and unlikely occasions.

Throughout the months following the 20 July restoration, everyone knew that what Musharraf would finally do will be dramatic, and will surely be a matter of great public concern. Everyone remembers that the president himself had said he would deliver the 'last punch', which he finally did on 3 November, although a preview had been seen on 29 September, when the police brutally beat up the lawyers and the others. This sort of action had not been seen before and its cruelty gave intimations of something worse coming: the 3 November actions. The president, forgetting his own controversial election on 6 October, proclaimed a state of Emergency, not by virtue of being the president but by virtue of being the chief of the army staff. This was an unheard-of thing in Pakistan; all previous states of Emergency had been proclaimed by the president, regardless of who he was. In this case, Musharraf imposed not only a state of Emergency, but also proclaimed a new Provisional Constitution Order (PCO) that amended the Constitution to give the president (that is himself) the power to amend the Constitution, as and when he needed. For good measure, he also issued gagging orders on various television channels, selectively; certain anchorpersons and television journalists were sought to be dismissed, or taken off the air. Some of it happened while some did not. There is a lot of murkiness in all this because the government did not own up that it was asking for the removal of specific journalists, though it could not be kept secret from either the public or the owners of the television channels. And the main thing that the Emergency and PCO did, and which was actually intended, was to force the High and Supreme courts judges to take a new oath of office under the new Provisional Constitution Order-amended Constitution. This resulted in sixty-two judges of the superior courts refusing to take a new oath of office under the 3 November PCO. Many of them were locked up, and all of them were sacked. Many, including the chief justice and quite a few other Supreme Court judges, as well as, some High courts judges, including some chief justices, together with the leaders of the lawyers' movement, remained under house arrest for months. This created a crisis that, by and large, still continues. Musharraf got himself freed of the scourge the emerging independent judiciary had become. He now has a pliant judiciary that duly does what the top man desires.

Another major event of the year was namely, the fairly long-running and famous Lal Masjid affair that preceded the judges' case, but for its finale. It was a revolt by two main clerics of the Lal Masjid complex, in the heart of Islamabad and which included two madrassas attached with it, one for women and the other for men. The madrassas had become a centre of Islamist activists who were terrorizing the surrounding areas, threatening music shops. The girls of the madrassa for women, had formed a vigilante group that, among other things, arrested three women for supposed immoral behaviour, although it later transpired that their real fault was that they were Shia women. These female activists had also occupied a government-owned library for children nearby. They were becoming a nuisance in the entire area, and the two main clerics were delivering fiery speeches against the regime and against America's war on terror by giving full-throated verbal support to the Taliban and al-Qaeda causes. The masjid had become a transit point for the al-Qaeda and the Taliban.

Indeed the history of the masjid itself was murky from the very beginning. It appeared that the lands for the masjid and the complex ware obtained with the intercession of the highest power in the land at the time: Field Marshal Muhammad Ayub Khan, the then president of Pakistan (the 1960s) in a dubious manner probably on ISI recommendation. Anyway, the linkage of the ISI with these clerics was said to go back a long time.

PUBLIC OUTRAGE

The effect of the foregoing two events, namely, Lal Masjid affair and the botched attempt to sack the chief justice of Pakistan was tremendous. The issue of sixty-two odd superior courts judges ousted on 3 November has kept the lawyers' movement alive and the newly formed coalition government in trouble. Public assessment of the Musharraf regime has come to be very largely, if not entirely, negative. Liberal opinion was always against military dictatorship, but that was a given. Those holding a more general public opinion, particularly those who regard themselves as sympathetic to Islamic causes, were shocked by the ruthless way in which the Musharraf regime dealt with the Islamic clerics and the students holed-up inside the Lal Masjid complex. There was scarcely anyone who actually supported Musharraf, except the narrow economic elites who have been doing wonderfully well during his regime.

The lawyers' movement has gained momentum from the ruthless way the government has continued to deal with the protestors and, pari passu, the public outrage has continued to grow. The country has in fact became divided quite unequally: there was the tiny but firm support for Musharraf coming from the social elites and business groups and some pragmatic politicians on the one hand, and overwhelming public opinion which opposed the very idea of suppressing the lawyers' movement, or non restoration of the chief justice and other judges to their offices, on the other. An apogee of sorts was reached in July when the Supreme Court threw out the government's case and reinstated the chief justice. The manner in which the court was misguided and scandalous documents were produced as evidence against the chief justice, angered the court and it said so. Anyhow the judgement was entirely against the government and the chief justice was absolved of the scandalous charges, restored to his position and the government was fined Rs 100,000 for tendering scandalous document as evidence. The effect of all this, when seen in conjunction with the media and public support for the chief justice, was that the government had greatly diminished in the eyes of the populace.

Later in the year, there were shocking shortages of food and the price of wheat flour, and consequently roti (bread) for urban workers, went up sharply. Everyone saw it as the blundering ways of Musharraf's handpicked economy managers. Indeed it was a scandal: the way the figures of growth were fudged on the basis of a fictitious bumper wheat crop, and the government allowed some exports without checking the smuggling and hoarding of wheat and flour to Afghanistan and elsewhere, showed the administration to be inept and in all probability, corrupt. Along with the prices of atta and roti, other prices were also going up. The inflation rate seemed under nobody's control. The impact of the shortages of almost everything – pulses, wheat, sugar, ghee and other essentials – have continued their upward march. The impact of high inflation on public opinion could not possibly be beneficial to the Musharraf regime. Indeed, it began to be seen as an elitist regime that was working for the rich and has left the poor defenceless.

Meanwhile, the lawyers' movement continues after the Chief Justice Iftikhar Muhammad Chaudhry's second sacking on 3 November. The movement has become wholly political with the aim of democratizing the government and purging the Constitution of what the military's domination of political life has done to it. The only option left to Musharraf was to try and suppress the movement, which he tried on 3 November. This further alienated the people from his regime. The way the police and other security forces have been beating up the demonstrating lawyers and civil activists has startled everyone because of their ferocity. It was meant to show what lay for the opponents of the regime in future. But that failed to prevent both the lawyers and the civil activists from protesting.

Musharraf needed this state of Emergency to propel his programme of getting himself elected early in October, while he was still the chief of army staff. He did not stop at this gross violation of the Constitution. He went further into an unexpected terrain: contrary to democratic norms of a parliamentary system, he chose not to be elected from an Electoral College that would be formed by the new assemblies after being elected. He chose instead to be elected by the same 2002 college that had elected him , just before its term was to expire, along with the assemblies. The 2002 elections were notoriously 'managed' by the intelligence agencies that were directly under his command. Moreover, Musharraf insisted on contesting the presidential elections while still being the army chief, violating a clear provision of Constitution that bars all government employees from standing for an elected office unless they had retired from paid service two full years before being elected. But before his controversial election, a former judge of the Supreme Court, Justice Wajeehuddin Ahmed, made himself a presidential candidate. He moved the Supreme Court complaining as an individual who was directly affected by Musharraf contesting the elections as an active government employee, which he claimed was clearly against the Constitution. The Supreme Court was seized of the matter, when the state of Emergency was declared. The judgement of the court could only have been to declare Musharraf ineligible to contest the elections, since the provision of the Constitution was clear and specific. Musharraf pre-empted the court and locked up the troublesome judges, and reconstituted the Supreme Court and the High courts with pliant judges. Such a blatant anti-democratic move only served to strengthen the sense of outrage that most people felt. The movement to oust him can only grow stronger now.

WINDS OF CHANGE

The over two-year-long agitation by lawyers was an outstanding development in Pakistan's history of agitations; it stands out for its clarity of vision and objectives. Its aims included not merely the restoration of democracy in a loose sense but wanted a proper division of powers in a parliamentary system with a fiercely independent judiciary and equally free media. This sharpened the public opinion while the earlier agitations had not produced enough awareness. The lawyers have done so.

But the social system in Pakistan, being still dominated by landed aristocracy and prevalence of feudal values has sustained military's domination of the whole political system for so long. Earlier anti-dictatorship agitations were led by sections of elite groups themselves who talked in general terms of preferring democracy to dictatorship. Those leaders had been left out of the spoils of office and wanted to get back into positions of power and authority led earlier agitations. The old system has survived all these six decades largely because in the largest province, Punjab, the heartland, was dominated by feudal-cum-military elites; political awareness among masses was conspicuous by its absence and the tradition of political protest was underdeveloped.

Most people voted as they were told by the aristocratic influentials of their area. That is changing as a result of economic development and the emergence of a middle class that owes its existence to commercial and industrial progress, though still not rapidly enough. This is a major change in Pakistan. Indeed, from a long-range viewpoint, it is a harbinger of more change. Military dictators hopefully can no longer be sure of taking Punjab for granted and to make it the base of their power.

Punjab is the most populous province of the country; total populations of all the other three provinces is less than that of Punjab which houses up to 63 per cent of the total. It is important for contributing some 70 per cent of army and bureaucracy; most of the industrialists, bankers, and successful professionals or executives of multinationals have also originated in Punjab. Thus, earlier an ordinary Punjabi could identify himself with a non-democratic regime because he could find someone with whom he could relate himself to talk to him in Punjabi. That is now changing. Punjabi middle class now has contempt for its own landed aristocracy for its spinelessness. It is against the traditional alliance of the military, mullahs, business and bigger landlords who have ruled and exploited Pakistan for so long. The revolt of the thin slice of civil society in general and these changes in Punjab in particular have been corrosive of the old order. The rise of Taliban and Islamic extremism has virtually killed the awe of the army. Also electronic media have grown and are making a big impact by imparting awareness. Pakistan's press was in the lead; it struggled to free itself and succeeded to a fair extent. All in all the media is now a powerful factor in the country, though it has still to go some way in tackling the octopus of intelligence agencies.

18 FEBRUARY ELECTIONS

The significance and background of the 18 February 2008 election has been dealt with elsewhere. Here only the major problems that became acute in 2007 are relevant for the winners of the election. It bears repetition to juxtapose the major events of 2007 with the emergent confrontation between President Musharraf, 'elected' on 6 October 2007 and wide sections of opinion in the country because of the Emergency and PCO of 3 November. Musharraf had originally ordered the general elections to be held on 8 January 2008 that later had to be postponed to 18 February. What led to the postponement was the assassination of Benazir Bhutto, the PPP chief, on 27 December 2007, which the government held was done by Islamic extremists probably linked to Baitullah Mehsud of North Waziristan. That was the version given by Musharraf government's investigators. In contrast most Opposition wallahs suspect that she may have been killed either by officially linked killers with an additional bomb attack that was probably meant to create confusion. Whatever the truth may be, it was a big upset that could not leave Musharraf regime with a reputation of maintaining law and order in an exemplary manner. His own position then was highly controversial as his eligibility to be the president was under question in the Supreme Court when he locked up many of the superior court judges thought to be 'unfriendly by being too independent'. It is also noteworthy that the elections were held under strong popular pressure and also international nudging of Musharraf to hold a fair poll. These polls were finally held on 18 February.

One of the many challenges facing the ruling party is the question about the president's position. Well into the year of US presidential election, Musharraf still enjoyed wide international support from NATO powers despite the loss of much of his prestige and much-discussed doubts about his usefulness for the West. He was until recently the chief of army staff of Pakistan Army. He had seized power in a bloodless coup d'etat in 1999, obviously violating the Constitution. He ruled for over eight years as the army chief during which he had architectured a political system he called 'Real Democracy', complete with all the institutions of a parliamentary democracy but with no real democratic content, spirit or ethos. He had organized an election in 2002 after manufacturing a political party called Pakistan Muslim League (Quaid-e-Azam group) with the help of country's intelligence agencies. The elections were expertly 'managed' by the intelligence agencies, especially by the ISI, that gave a victory to the PML (Q). Thereafter, despite the superstructure of a democracy, the reality was the dictatorship of one man: General Musharraf. The party he had founded comprised deserters of, and dissidents from, well-established major parties: PPP and PML (N). This PML (Q) won handsomely in the 2002 election. Those deserters had been both bribed and coerced through a certain new department called National Accountability Bureau (NAB). They had remained under Musharraf's thumb by NAB keeping their cases undecided. Now after defeat in 2008, most have to find some way of politically surviving. Those members of the King's party who have succeeded in getting into the new assemblies – still in large enough numbers to be the third party who in a crisis can acquire crucial role though – were initially ready to defect to whichever party needed them. Most of them may join either Pakistan Muslim League (N) or Pakistan Peoples Party, if these fell out and needed reinforcements, as indeed they have done.

Meantime, the way the Western ambassadors in Islamabad were, indeed still are, frequently meeting leaders of various political parties, chiefly Asif Ali Zardari, the co-chairman of PPP, Mian Nawaz Sharif, the leader of PML (N), Asfandyar Wali Khan of ANP and Maulana Fazlur Rehman, the chief of his own faction of Jamiat-i-Ulema-i-Pakistan, who retains footholds in Balochistan, NWFP and National Assemblies with amazing frequency tells its own story. Everyone knows the purpose: it adds up to a sad tale of humiliating micro-management by foreigners. The NATO powers were originally asking these Pakistani parties not to impeach Musharraf and should agree to participate in the war on terror under their continuing Musharraf leadership. For public consumption the fib was that they are congratulating the winners on their victory in general elections. It was not that Musharraf simply should remain. The Western purposes also included the formation of a rainbow coalition government at the centre that would include nearly every winning party so as to strengthen Musharraf's hand, no matter if he is politically hated by the populace. Such was the state of love for democracy among Western governments, their unending outpouring of democratic shibboleths notwithstanding. Their rhetoric on democracy and freedom is commonly seen as hypocritical that does not go further than requiring democratic-looking institutions, not necessarily with any democratic content or adherence to well-known norms.

An important part of the background, especially after the election, was the destruction of Musharraf's prestige and acceptance as a result of recent years' developments: the rise of

Taliban and other extremist groups in tribal areas of NWFP, insurgency in Balochistan, his crude political manoeuvrings, his hatred of popular politicians like Benazir Bhutto and Nawaz Sharif, the Lal Masjid episode and the unending affair of the chief justice of Pakistan. The winning parties are not united because of Pakistan's history, personal animosities and underlying polarizations in its political life. Thus the PPP originally projected itself as a left-of-centre party that was to herald radical change. But under Benazir's leadership the domination of feudals and conservatives of PPP has grown. The traditional conservative party with Islamic rhetoric of a shallow kind was PML that today has three main factions with some relevance: one is the PML (Q), or King's party that supported Musharraf to the last, PML (N) of Nawaz and PML (Functional), led by Pir of Pagara that also must be counted to be in Musharraf's corner. Then there are regional parties that were, once upon a time, thought to be left-inclined, though no more; they are nearly as conservative in social policy as any, though some still mouth the old rhetoric. Among them several are significant from political point of view in Balochistan, though their boycott of the 2008 elections has ensured their absence from Balochistan Assembly.

In NWFP, the Awami National Party has emerged strongly; it is still secular but it believes in Pushtoon nationalism more and is quite moderate in the American sense of the term. Another regional party of note is Musharraf-supporting Muttahida Qaumi Movement (MQM) in Sindh with its twenty-five MPs; it is quite pragmatic in the sense the Americans use the term. It aspirates the quasi-nationalism of Urdu-speaking 1947-related refugees from India and its strength lies in Karachi and other urban centres of Sindh province. There are other important Sindhi nationalist groups, though they never had any presence in Sindh or National Assembly; Sindh electorally belongs to Benazir, no matter what her politics, strictly for emotional reasons of loyalty to the Bhuttos, while in other ways the ethnic Sindhi nationalist parties are popular enough. Sindhis appear to think with the nationalists but vote for the PPP, the stark contradiction notwithstanding.

Thus, today the international intrigue is all about keeping the Western wishes supreme in Pakistan. One segment, the PML (N) that has swept much of populous Punjab province is still somewhat ambiguous, though its being moderate and pragmatic again similar to American usage is in no doubt. But Musharraf simply could not tolerate Nawaz Sharif; he was determined to keep Nawaz Sharif out in the cold even though its electoral numbers enable it to control Punjab with some help from others and is also strongly represented in the National Assembly. The game in town until the first half of 2008 was said to be to rough-hew an alliance between Musharraf, PML (Q), PPP, ANP and MQM so as to keep Nawaz out, no matter if he is the most popular leader of Punjab. How Punjab was to be tackled that houses some 63 per cent of Pakistan's population was, and up to a point still is, the subject of much speculation and intrigue. The King's party was originally knocked out after its defeat in February 2008, though the others succeeded in bringing about this somewhat less than rainbow coalition that fell through because of differences in the priorities of PPP and PML (N) in May 2008. PPP is soldiering on with the support of smaller parties and is now trying hard to recruit PML (Q)'s support both to strengthen the federal government and to rule Punjab jointly with PML (Q) isolating PML (N).

If the PPP and PML (Q) do as PPP desires, it will create a black hole large enough for the Federal government and the country to fall into it because Punjab cannot be trifled with: it is the most developed province; it is the richest; it is the most industrialized and prosperous. It is now becoming politically aware, if also too slowly. The depth of this black hole is being deepened by the growing popularity of Nawaz Sharif, confirmed by the February election and acquired great legitimacy and wide support when the lawyers movement, supported strongly by PML (N) with Nawaz Sharif towering on the grand victory of lawyers on 16 March 2009. All that can be said is that the entire PPP project is misconceived, thought up probably by foreign advisers to keep Nawaz Sharif out for fear of his supposed penchant to empathize with extremely conservative Islam and discounting his pragmatism and moderation.

This kind of thinking also ignores the political realities of Pakistani politics, particularly about the ways of dealing with Islamic extremist groups like Taliban, al-Qaeda and others; in so far as the US and other NATO or US-loving powers are concerned, what they seem to require is strong military muscle and its application, from particularly Pakistan. They are supposed to have done that in Iraq and are trying to do so in Afghanistan. They desire Pakistan should play a role they prescribe. For which purpose they desire a democratic-looking coalition government, led preferably by their new friend, President Asif Ali Zardari. By some reports it seems that Washington seems to have begun to doubt whether Zardari is up to scratch. Pakistan is correctly described by some American experts as the epicentre of Islamic extremism. It is certainly a very serious problem of and for Pakistan. But it is differently perceived in the West and also by Pakistanis. Democrats and liberals in Pakistan have to fight Islamic extremist militancy for their own dear lives; it is their very own problem. But they cannot act thoughtlessly in the way the US administration has so far proceeded.

Pakistan was brought into being under Islamic-sounding rhetoric and all its conservative governments have based their rationale on the same shallow Islamic rhetoric in their struggle to suppress democratic, social and economic demands, or those of autonomy, by regional minorities. It is true that Islamic rhetoric of all the Muslim League's various factions was hollow and had no political, social or economic content; it was mostly emotional assertion of religious identity in contrast with the other religions of India as a bargaining counter for winning specific political or economic objectives. There has been a democratic deficit in all conservative politics in Pakistan whether they were military dictators or civilian regimes that invariably and largely comprised feudal aristocracy. Tackling Islamic militancy is where all Pakistanis, secular liberals especially, would treat it differently from the way NATO powers have been doing so far; liberals will bring to bear a political and rational approach on the problem and eschew a purely militaristic approach – the surest way of prolonging civil wars – though use of military force for defensive purposes would surely be necessary. The secular liberal Pakistanis cannot afford to be soft on militancy. Only, in a predominately Muslim country like Pakistan that has been fed on hollow Islamic rhetoric for more than six decades, a purely or mainly militaristic approach would be disastrous. It will invite a militant response and politically strengthen extremists.

Besides an ambiguous rainbow-like coalition government could not have lasted long in view of the underlying problems of the country that have generated polarizations. Some of these begin in the name of Islam itself and go on to be about regional or ethnic nationalisms. Islamic militancy has now absorbed Pushtoon nationalism; Baloch nationalists are ethnic as well as regional secular nationalists; and there are other consequential polarizations. Then, there is the hardy perennial of the rich-poor divide and deficit of social justice; questions of foreign policy have also kept Pakistanis divided so far. These issues will have to be sorted out, not serially but at about the same time.

The new government, over a year old, has so far presented no real programme that could inspire confidence among the people or has shown any vision of where the country is being taken. It was initially deadlocked from within. What was a hopeful document with which it began (the Murree Declaration) soon became a subject of contention between the two largest parties over implementing it. Which is why total deadlock obtained inside the government and soon spread outside. In the declaration the PML (N) and PPP unambiguously committed themselves to restore the superior court judges through an executive order that had been deposed by President Musharraf on 3 November 2007 when he imposed the state of Emergency and his several presidential orders, including the Provisional Constitution Order. There were no conditions attached to that. One of the parties, namely, PML (N) of Nawaz Sharif, was, and remained, dead set that the judges should be restored latest by 12 May 2008. It soon became clear that the leading party of the coalition, the PPP, controlled by Asif Ali Zardari is determined that the restoration has to be conditional. PPP gradually spelled out the conditions, expressed as required modalities of how the judges can be reinstated. These modalities were totally unacceptable to the judges, lawyers, PML (N) and many other parties.

On this subject, twenty-two retired judges of Supreme and High courts, including several retired chief justices, went on record that an executive order by the government would be enough or at most, it may be reinforced by a resolution of the National Assembly in order to explain the circumstances and the need for it. The factual position was simple: Musharraf took a series of steps on 3 November 2007, all of which he publicly admitted were illegal and unconstitutional. They were declared a nullity in law the same day by a large bench of the Supreme Court. Therefore they were, and remain, wholly void of law. The undoing of those actions do not require complicated modalities. But the fact of the matter was that the PPP leadership wanted to make that conditional on the passage of a constitutional amendments package by the National Assembly and which also included new conditions on the judges being restored among other things. According to newspaper reports, the first of the PPP preferences was that somehow the chief justice of Pakistan, Justice Iftikhar Muhammad Chaudhry, should not be restored and if it is absolutely necessary to restore him, his tenure should be drastically curtailed and his powers restricted. This was totally outside and indeed contrary to the Murree Declaration signed by the two major parties as the basic programme of the coalition government.

The fact was that until then Nawaz Sharif and his PML (N), judging the mood of their constituents and of the people of the country, had become inflexible: Nawaz wanted restoration without conditions or complicated modalities. He was willing to go along with a resolution of the National Assembly and then a notification by the law ministry lifting all disabilities on the judges so that they could resume their rightful offices, unburdened by any new condition. Although this government's very first action was to release the judges who had been locked up by Musharraf but it stopped at that. It did not restore the sixty-two odd judges. This became a large, bloated issue on which the two parties stayed deadlocked, with PML (N), demanding the restoration of judges latest by 12 May 2008 while the other party, PPP, twisted and turned and wanted to attach various conditions to the restoration such as noted above. That was the crisis that made PML (N) finally withdraw from the government on 13 May 2008, though not altogether from the coalition that most thought was unlikely to last long.

Nawaz Sharif and his party remain convinced that the issue of the judges' restoration was more important than all other matters because opposition to Musharraf's famous 3 November actions was that made them win their present strengths in the Parliament.

True, the country was facing mountainous economic problems: almost run-away inflation rates led by food prices. The latter were shooting through the roof week after week. There was shortage of staple food: wheat. The country is short of electricity in a strange manner. In the eight and half years of Musharraf rule, not one megawatt of power was added to the national grid and today the whole country faces power outages of eight to ten hours a day in all parts of the country. This was the terrible background.

Other macro-economic indicators also continue looking down. The economic crises could be attributed to any of these: high-budget deficit that was touching 7 to 8 per cent of the GDP, there was an external trading account deficit in which export–import deficit was close to 50 per cent of total imports remaining uncovered with export earnings. This was naturally putting strain on the current account and its deficit went up to over $ 9 billion in 2007–08 fiscal year (nearly 8 per cent of the GDP) and looked like going further up in following years. Pakistan had a cushion of $ 5 billion worth of annual remittances from expatriate Pakistanis. But that is more than cancelled by the repatriation of profits by multinationals.

All told, economic conditions were seemingly hopeless. But nobody in the government was emphasizing these matters. They were wrangling on a matter that, all said and done, is something that should not have occasioned controversy. Restoring the sacked judges should have been a simple executive action of the new government the way many judges were released from house arrests by an executive order of the PM. And that should have been that. But unfortunately that wasn't to be. Let's be clear: what impelled the Nawaz Sharif's party to be so insistent on the restoration of judges as to forget all the various crises that afflicted the country or for PPP to dig its heels in to resist the PML (N) demands, without bothering about the priorities that have to be given to various political and economic crises that have engulfed Pakistan.

The reason why PML (N) was so insistent was its political assessment of the fact that the evils wrought by Musharraf in the preceding year, 2007, were such that unless this judges' issue is cleared first, the country cannot actually concentrate on more important issues confronting it. As a political party it stood to gain from championing a cause that had fired the imagination of the whole people, particularly in Punjab. True enough, during the February 2008 election, PML (N) performed quite well in Punjab but failed to impress people in the other provinces where regional nationalisms dominate the minds. Even so, insistence on restoration of judges was calculated to take PML (N) places in future. It stood to gain substantially in future elections because it had so positioned itself as to be seen as a great champion of popular causes, opposing all that the military dictator Musharraf and his supporters abroad were doing. No one should forget that Americans are the most unpopular foreigners in Pakistan. They took Musharraf to their bosom eight years ago and made him share their unpopularity. PML (N)'s opposing Musharraf won it the support of all who felt disgusted by the amount of American interference in the country and indeed strongly disapprove their various actions in the Middle East and rest of Asia; these are seen as a US imperialist thrust into Asia by most people.

PPP had the reputation of being a party that has been opposed to all military dictators and has made tremendous sacrifices in the past, particularly by its leaders. Its founder Zulfikar Ali Bhutto was hanged by the dictator Zia-ul-Haq in 1979. Benazir, his successor to control PPP, had also suffered much at the hands of General Zia-ul-Haq and Musharraf. Benazir Bhutto was killed by an alleged suicide bomber on 27 December 2007. She had written a letter before arriving in Pakistan that said if anything happened to her in Pakistan, the ruling establishment would be responsible and had named four officials. It has remained voters' preferred party in many parts of the country. In the February 2008 election it emerged as the largest party at the Centre as well as the largest party in the Sindh province and became a respectable number two party in Punjab Assembly while it was present in significant numbers in the NWFP, though in Balochistan the PPP is a relative stranger but still it has managed to form a government in that province.

All in all, the importance of the judges' issue has overtaken everything else. It is necessary to remember Musharraf's bullying of the chief justice of Pakistan into resigning resulted in a resounding 'no' from him. The CJP thus became a symbol of resistance to a military dictator. A new democracy movement actually began in the shape of lawyers' protests against Musharraf's autocratically suspending the chief justice and later his locking him up after manhandling by the police shocked everyone in Pakistan. Most people began saying it was time the military was sent to its barracks and it should have no further involvement in politics. The lawyers' great show of strength in June 2008 has been registered on popular mind; they have been able to retain popularity and indeed made a great show of strength in mid-March 2009.

It may be necessary to ask a question: why is the judges' issue so important for lawyers? The short and sufficient answer is that the lawyers realize that unless Musharraf's actions of 3 November, meant to frustrate their movement, are undone, Pakistan cannot make progress without full democracy that requires, among other things, an assertive and independent judiciary. It is also a primary requirement of establishing the rule of law, apart from the fact of judiciary is an important pillar of democracy. The leaders of the lawyers' movement are clear that the movement is not for the sake of the person of the chief justice or other superior court judges; it is for the larger purpose of establishing a proper democracy with distribution of powers based on respect for the rule of law and for ending the blight of military dictatorships for all times.

Ending the military dictatorship and its future editions is a necessary precondition for the permanence of the democratic dispensation. The implication of the issue is that the ultimate purpose of lawyers' movement goes beyond the end of General Musharraf's dictatorship that has taken place by political manoeuvring of Asif Zardari without the necessary insurance of reducing the political influence of the military. Which is why this PPP-led democracy has weak foundations. The task is to keep generals out. Practically, it also translates into the proposition that if Justice Chaudhry has to come back, other generals' chances would diminish because as soon as he takes over, the temper of the courts will revert to what it was after 20 July 2007 when he was first restored after his being made so called 'non-functional'.

But his restoration was easier said than done. It ran smack into the US and NATO preference for the person of General Musharraf who they thought was needed for leading the war on terror.

Indeed they had a replacement of him in reserve: it is the current army chief. The PPP co-chairman's presidency is an ad interim arrangement, a largely experimental affair. The design of the deal under which this government has been formed is an American architecture. It began with reconciling Benazir Bhutto and PPP with General Musharraf and to end their mutual hostility. The Americans did succeed in uniting them. But it looks as if Nawaz Sharif was still an outsider, though some say that the US has worked through the Saudis to make him take part in the election and in the government to be formed, which required overcoming Musharraf's own reluctance to accept his return from Saudi Arabian exile. So Nawaz is not a total outsider or who has any hard objection to cooperating with PPP for government-making or even fighting the war on terror. Some claim he is Saudis' friend and was forced on Musharraf and Zardari. However that be, he is a politician who keeps an eye on what the people want and acts accordingly. Which is why he withdrew his ministers from the Gilani government on 13 May 2008 and virtually walked out of the threadbare coalition with PPP over the key judges issue, though keeps on talking of supporting the PPP in an effort to impress the Americans that his support for the war on terror and Uncle Sam is firm. But Asif Zardari's problem was to go on repeating the mantra of reconciliation, keep the alliance with Nawaz Sharif's party but without alienating Musharraf. To repeat: The whole electoral exercise was designed to produce a more representative-looking government that would work in close mesh with, and under the leadership of, Musharraf. In other words, the intention was only to give a democratic face to Musharraf so that he could be more effective in the war on terror.

But the fact of the matter is that no military dictator can abide by democracy: respect a constitution, actually respecting a Parliament, complying with rule of law or tolerate independent judiciary. These things dissolve dictatorships. These two are in fact incompatible. The difficulty is that Pakistan is a country where people have always been treated shabbily. But they remain democratic-minded. They have never been happy under military dictatorships. They have always wanted democracy and its appurtenances. But the reverse side of this was that all military dictatorships heartily hated the people but somehow wanted to show a fig leaf of a legality. They have all tried to have a constitution that would enable their power to stay supreme while there would be a showpiece parliament or provincial assemblies and Supreme Court, High courts and various other institutions. The will of the dictator has always to prevail. This contradiction has dogged the steps of all military dictators in Pakistan. The Pakistanis have been trodden upon by so many dictators. But they have always consciously loved democracy. They have managed to deny legitimacy to all dictators; and all dictators have remained on the defensive, proclaiming that full democracy is their aim too but it can come only gradually.

One of the reasons why Pakistanis are so democratic-minded is the example of India. The Indians have run their democracy more or less successfully. They have also earned praise abroad. This makes ordinary Pakistanis wish to emulate the Indians. They are inherently freedom-lovers. They are, at bottom, anti-imperialist also. Remember that Americans have after all given a lot of money as aid to Pakistan. In a number of ways they have been helpful to Pakistanis. And yet Pakistan is one country where anti-Americanism runs deep as an undercurrent throughout the society. The people of Pakistan have run three or four major pro-democracy movements and Musharraf faced one recently. The lawyers had given time to PPP and PML (N) to restore the judges and create preconditions for the rule of law. But their patience ran out and the movement is now more bitter due to PPP's manipulation through its aligned lawyers. But they remain determined to carry on for the larger goal of democracy, though many other parties besides PML (N) have joined in. But the formal movement ended in total victory at great cost to PPP's and Zardari's prestige.

The PPP has in fact acted contrary to the commitment it had earlier made by the way it has been trying to put hurdles in the way of restoration of judges forces the conclusion on all: the deal the Americans and the British had brokered between the PPP and Musharraf seems to be not only working but overrides everything. The PPP and its chief leader, President Zardari, have let it be known that he wants not only to limit the tenure of the judges but he would also want limitations on their suo moto powers to take notice of official wrongdoings they object to. The

PPP is now seen as being tutored by the US and other NATO leaders, though no longer by Musharraf as was the case until he resigned.

Some of the PPP government's actions and its choice of men and women underscore its linkages with the US. The main adviser to the prime minister on Home Affairs is Rehman Malik, who was originally a policeman and has been in the good books of the British and also probably the Americans. Hussain Haqqani who has been in America for more than a decade and is now well integrated into the American academia and think tank community; his appointment as ambassador to the US can only be called a firm assurance to the Americans. Shah Mehmood Qureshi has been appointed foreign minister who has cooperated with the Americans by way of being active in Track II diplomacy organized by the Americans. Zardari has also appointed retired General Mehmood Ali Durrani, hitherto Pakistani ambassador in Washington and another great friend of America, as the national security adviser. The attorney general of Pakistan, a man who has been doing the legal chores for Musharraf was kept in his job by Zardari for quite some time. The rumour continues to go around that many in this government have dual nationalities just as Musharraf's earlier government had others with the same qualification. It cannot be repeated too often that the issue of issues initially was judges' restoration despite other crises. But the 2009 reinstatement was against the wishes of the Americans, NATO and other pro-Western powers. Secondly, the government had to have the ability to keep the hungry and angry population in line in the face of a raging and tearing campaign by the lawyers that was supported by much of the media, most of the civil society and many of the political parties. But this government is a slow-moving and slow-thinking phenomenon that can scarcely last long. This has become clear during the time it has been in office.

The first tactic Zardari will try to do to retain effective powers is to do what Zulfikar Ali Bhutto did in 1973. When under popular pressures he helped write the 1973 Constitution in which all powers were concentrated in prime minister's office, he effortlessly shed his office of president and got himself elected as leader of the House and automatically assumed the office of the prime minister. Zardari can try to do that. But the quality of Zulfi's leadership was different. There were no scandals associated with him. Not so in Zardari's case. Many fear that the army, then, may shed its self-abnegation and takeover. The present army chief is the one who is being kept in the loop in all high political matters. Whatever may the Constitution say, what the US has managed to revive a new Troika that is running Pakistan as distinct from the troika that General Mirza Aslam Beg had imposed that comprised the general (himself), the president and prime minister in 1988. That worked unevenly during 1988–99: while Benazir Bhutto tamely stayed junior most in high decision-making in both her stints, Nawaz Sharif revolted and reduced the two offices of the president and army chief to their proper stations for a few years in his second term of office (1997–99). Indeed he tried to go further by giving a religious colouring by converting PM's to that of Amirul Momnin. That was the real reason for army takeover in 1999 and what precipitated it was General Musharraf and his cohorts refusing to accept his dismissal the way General Jehangir Karamat had done his. Musharraf caused a coup to prevent his successor being able to takeover. This new troika is more brash: it comprises the Pentagon's representative, usually the Centcom chief when the US defense secretary himself does not take the trouble to attend the matter, President Zardari and General Ashfaque Pervez Kayani. America, the Pak president and Pak COAS are the ultimate rulers today. When and if Nawaz Sharif takes over (after he is allowed to enter the Parliament) this troika will soon be in trouble.

The PML (Q) was earlier thought to be a passing show, though it has held together until well into 2009. With that hangs a strong line of speculation: sections of powers that be seem still to be enamoured of Musharraf largely in a reaction to Zardari's PPP and Nawaz's PML (N); Musharraf, while keeping a low profile at home, has been active in cultivating America's think-tank community and the political class in India. Many suspect that some shadowy forces abroad may again be grooming him to lead Pakistan for completing what he tentatively began doing: solving Kashmir problem, burying the hatchet with India and strengthening West's geo-strategic aims in Asia. It would be odd if the US still fancies a failed man for a difficult and complex job when such a fine general is available in key office. Kayani may turn out to be next man largely because democracy has thrown up a man like Zardari, on whom his past sits heavy.

The surest forecast for the immediate future is that the PML (N) will go on strongly championing popular causes and will participate in new likely agitations. A PML (N)'s Punjab government will give strategic support to such new causes. Remember as the date of lawyers' new long march and dharna approached namely 15 March 2009, Zardari had had suppressed the PML (N) ministry and clamped governor's rule over Punjab for two months to do what Islamabad pleases both vis-à-vis lawyers agitation and see if PPP can form a government by buying over PML (Q) members. Given growing unpopularity of Zardari, the upshot could only be that the PML (N) became even more popular. The net result of dismissing the PML (N) Punjab government and rule directly by the Centre (governor's rule), the net result was that the PML (N) is becoming a martyr and its popularity mounted some more first in Punjab and later elsewhere. Governor's rule was sure to be seen as of the stooges of Zardari, army and the US. PPP will begin losing popularity more or less rapidly. Whether it can survive as a united party once it demits office is doubtful.

People see its splinters flying out before long. The splinters can be more important in Punjab. Challenges to Asif Zardari's leadership will be serious in Sindh, probably from Makhdoom Amin Fahim, who is also the head of the second biggest Pir family in Sindh and a long-time PPP loyalist. In the background would be the performance of the PPP government regarding wheat, electricity and similar issues. Daily price rises create crises. These issues will make it even less popular. The Yousuf Raza Gilani government has done very little on the economic or on any of the political questions. He will continue facing questions about negotiations with some of the Islamic militants but which are meeting resistance from the Western powers which policy has also been given up and the job of managing FATA and NWFP militants has been assigned to the new army chief. It was back to the past. Many people speculate that a new election, probably sometime in 2009 or later, to be likely maybe after a short interlude of another military initiative. And such an election can only be seen in conjunction with another martial law because the next martial law can scarcely think of ruling the country directly for any length of time. But in terms of longer term politics, Nawaz Sharif is on course to winning a crushing victory in Punjab, a respectable representation in NWFP and Sindh; his domination of the National Assembly would not be too difficult an achievement.

The big political loser in the longer term is likely to be the PPP. Next time round, PPP will have a hard time winning over even all of rural Sindh. The establishment over which Musharraf and now Zardari presided had had a hand in the emergence of the mayhem caused by Islamic extremist groups, including Taliban. These have been ISI assets and the US continues to suspect that there may still be some discreetly reduced linkages between ISI and these groups. Many retired generals who had headed the ISI remain strong supporters of such Islamic zealot groups anyhow.

But the American schemes' success was also partial in 2007 because while Musharraf did resign from the army in late 2008 and earlier held the election that was reasonably fair while also issuing an agreed ordinance called National Reconciliation Ordinance to befriend the opposition politicians of PPP against whom many corruption cases he had instituted. But he also did things the US did not like: he tried to crush the lawyers' movement in which he failed. Which is why there was big trouble about the deposed judges largely because of the earlier stance of the PPP–PML (N) government; these parties were committed to restoring the Judges to their pre-emergency (2 November 2007) status that Nawaz stuck to long after PPP adopted the Musharraf line. There was irresistible pressure on the government to restore the judges to the position they were on 2 November, that is, a day before Musharraf proclaimed an Emergency and imposed his constitutional changes off his pen qua the chief of army staff.

There is no doubt about the sad state of Pakistan's economy and a constantly deteriorating law and order situation in the country. Despite that most observers are sure that far too much of unworthy political intrigue has emanated from the President House, first under Musharraf and later under Asif Ali Zardari. Musharraf's new role was to serve the West better than others and thus if this creates disruption and worsens the law and order situation he can exercise his old extraordinary constitutional powers that still exist in the current Constitution. He will be able to sack the system and begin all over again, as has happened five times since 1958. Musharraf had, up to a point, succeeded in dividing the lawyers' movement through the standard method rulers have employed through the ages: employing agents provocateurs who would cause incidents or misunderstanding that would divide the movement and the use of money or offer of well-paid job enables a government to recruit new agents provocateurs. The British had trained India's and Pakistan's security and intelligence services to do just this kind of thing. And Pakistani security agencies have, over the years, continued to perfect these techniques.

But the fact was that Musharraf became hamstrung because the elections of 18 February 2008 last have been perceived by the world as reasonably free, though EU experts have picked some holes in the exercise. But the results are still loud and clear: they were a clear rejection of not only Musharraf but also of all he stood for. That put not only him on the spot but also made Americans worried. Although partially divided, the lawyers' movement, supported by the electronic and print media and many parties, remained alive and kicking. Political intrigues and conspiracies only gave a bad name to the PPP-led government so that, if necessary, it can be dismissed by a president acting under constitutional provision, known as its Article 58 (2) (b). It could have been reformed quickly enough if the PPP and Nawaz worked together and by not taking onboard the old Musharraf buddies who are still in the Parliament to fulfil Musharraf's dear wish of dropping the Nawaz Sharif's PML (N), who was inflexibly committed to both the ouster of Musharraf and stripping off the office of the president of the powers like 58 (2) (b) and wanted the sacked judges to be reinstated in their old jobs pronto. The mutual personal animus between Musharraf and Nawaz Sharif is like a smouldering fire that has not been put out.

A second big trouble has arisen because no political party that has won in the recent election in Pakistan believes in the method of blindly hitting out at people and places in FATA even on doubtful intelligence that one or more terrorists are hiding in a place at a given time. In a predominantly Muslim country hitting out at neighbourhoods and villages on suspicion of there being one or more terrorists is calculated to create more terrorists because of the so called collateral damage is always greater. And that resulted in the popularity of the cause espoused by the terrorists just as it had been happening in Afghanistan or Iraq. It would only promote the cause of al-Qaeda and Taliban. While the Gilani government has caved in and adopted more or less the US demands, no matter if the entire north-west of the country has become a battleground. The question recurs: would Zardari succeed in ditching Shahbaz Sharif and PML (N) from the provincial government that has been in a coalition with PPP and instead act upon the dream of Musharraf: replace PML (N) with PPP and his long-time supporters, PML (Q), in the place of PML (N), and add various earlier dissidents of PPP and MQM in place of PML (N)? And can PML (N) survive in Punjab? It has done so, so far after being restored by the court.

BENAZIR BHUTTO, PPP, ZULFI – HER ARRIVAL AND ASSASSINATION

Life-chairperson of Pakistan's largest party, Pakistan Peoples Party, was a multi-faceted personality. She had inherited the leadership of the party from her father, Zulfikar Ali Bhutto, who doubtless was a many-splendoured personality. He had formed a populist party in November 1967. It catered to the intellectual needs of all schools of thought in the country. It was primarily and deeply nationalistic, committed to wrest Kashmir from India and he had talked during 1965 War with India in terms of a 'thousand years war with India'. It was loudly anti-dictatorship and pro-democracy. It talked passionately about socialism – sometimes just socialism, packaged beautifully in admiration for Mao Zedong, with slogans like 'East is Red' and the master slogan of 'roti-kapra-aur-makan' (bread, clothes and a house) and sometimes as Islamic socialism – and at other times he located himself and the PPP in Islam. One comprehensive slogan was: 'Our politics is democratic, our economy is socialistic and our polity is Islamic'.

Zulfi, as Bhutto was affectionately called by friends, became deliriously popular and went on to win big in the first general election in Pakistan's history of twenty-five years, though his success were confined to the then West Pakistan province just three years after the party's formation. The party was actually formed around his charismatic personality and leadership, who had caught the imagination of the youth in 1968 and quickly became a legend in his own lifetime. It was not so much a party as it was cult.

Zulfikar Bhutto ruled Pakistan for seven years until 1977 rather autocratically, permitting few liberties to the people and tightly controlling the press. He made many enemies but retained a hard core of loyal supporters. Being a man of many contradictions, it was he who gave Pakistan a democratic constitution acceptable to most schools. But he also proclaimed a state of Emergency quickly and suspended the enforceability of fundamental rights and kept it so until he was overthrown by the top general he had himself chosen in 1977 over several others. But his personal vindictiveness and haughtiness turned many of his friends into enemies. General Zia-ul-Haq, the army chief, was one of them. He tried Bhutto for a dubious case of murder and had him hanged in 1979.

Bhutto himself did not trust or love his party; his style of ruling was dictatorial and depended more on the bureaucracy and army. He purged his party of socialists within a few years of coming into power. While he announced land reforms twice, limiting per person land ownership, but apparently did not intentionally enforce them strictly and big absentee landlords are as big and rich today as they had ever been. In foreign policy he began by reviving the Cento pact and worked fairly closely with the US initially. But he also alienated the Americans by some of his initiatives such as calling an Islamic Summit, later by giving a call for a Third World Summit and, above all else, started Pakistan's nuclear programme with an intended military purpose. His memory and legacy has kept the party, PPP, alive for these forty years.

The Bhutto legend was inherited by his daughter Benazir, herself a charismatic personality. She was an international sensation. The first woman prime minister of an Islamic country, a modern and moderate Muslim, educated at Berkley and Oxford – and a good orator. She kept the party united under herself as an adequate successor of the great Zulfi. She completed what the elder Bhutto really wanted: coming close to the Americans and purging PPP wholesale of the admirers of socialism and winning the trust of Pakistan's unchanging ruling establishment for the PPP as a safe conservative party. Although Benazir never won the full confidence of Pakistan's famed establishment, she forced it to allow her to form two governments in 1988 and in 1993 – largely because of her ability to win even the largely 'managed' elections and her performance in doing well enough what infuriated the establishment.

But, overall, she managed to keep the Bhutto legacy alive and almost adapted it as her own; it is now Benazir's legend and it is by invoking her 'sacrifices' that her widower husband is virtually ruling Pakistan since August 2008. It is Benazir's memory, as the authentic inheritor of the Bhutto charisma that has repeatedly given PPP office at the Centre and power in Sindh with shares in parliamentary representation in all the other three provinces. Whether, this time round, a widower can inherit a wife's charisma and hold the PPP permanently. Benazir had embodied the Bhutto and can Zardari, her widower, stay as the president and party boss for long is uncertain. It will surprise many if Asif Ali Zardari goes on surviving. On the other hand, in consonance with the widespread dynastic principle with which Pakistan, India, Bangladesh and Sri Lanka are familiar it may happen. Only time will tell whether it will work in this case. Some fissures are already being discerned in PPP. However, it may be too early to say whether PPP can stay united under Zardari and provide an effective government to Pakistan beset with grave crises in many fields.

Anyway, today's political context begins with General Pervez Musharraf's takeover in 1999. Musharraf was determined to drive out the two popular politicians who had taken turns to nominally rule Pakistan twice each, between the death of General Zia-ul-Haq (1988) and the takeover of Musharraf (1999). All these four governments, two each of Benazir and Nawaz Sharif of PML (N), were dismissed by presidents who had no constituencies of their own – largely on a nod and wink from the army chief of the day. No one knows the real reason why these five governments were dismissed half way through their tenure. Each time they were dismissed, they were called corrupt and inept. All military dictators have propagated stories of civilian politicians' corruption and maladministration, though each military administration has left behind stories of even greater corruption and nepotism. As a matter of fact corruption is a part of subcontinent's civilizational inheritance: whoever has anything to give – a favour or contract – he looks for a nephew, son of a friend. It just seems natural to them. Also, are we to believe that while all civilian politicians are corrupt and bad administrators, all military ones are incorruptible and wonderful administrators, all the stories about military's massive corruption (almost all over the subcontinent) that do not get publicized are false?

The point is, Benazir had learnt one lesson: the road to Islamabad passes through Washington. No one can get into high government office in Pakistan without the approving nod of both the US and Pakistan army chief. Power in Pakistan does not necessarily reside in the high office of the prime minister, particularly if the army chief combines his job with that of the president's, which has been frequent enough; army chief has all the power but he works in concert with the US – which often translates into CIA's overseeing. Through most of the long reign of Musharraf, Benazir and Nawaz Sharif had to live in exile (in addition to initial plethora of legal cases of corruption). Benazir made full use of this period to woo the American government into leaning on Musharraf to permit Benazir to return to Pakistan for participating in the upcoming general election that was due in November 2007. This was at a time when America was convinced that Musharraf was losing his grip on Pakistan, while war against what Bush called 'Islamo-fascism' required effective cooperation from Pakistan. The US obliged her for its own reasons but long negotiations between Benazir and Musharraf were arranged by the US and British governments and they may have perhaps become guarantors of the agreement. The agreement was finalized in July 2007 in an Abu Dhabi palace, though she returned to Karachi only on 18 October 2007.

Why did the US and UK governments take such detailed interest in the Pakistan's internal politics? It was unusual. Judging from stories in international press, they were in something of a quandary: while they found Musharraf to be generally trustworthy and sincere in the cause of fighting Islamic terror, he had unavoidable limitations. He was a military dictator. He could neither be loved nor happily accepted as a popular wartime ruler by Pakistanis. He could not win people's willing support or carry conviction with his people. He could only command the army but could not really mobilize the people. The US therefore wanted him to open up, hold free election and let election winners form a broad-based government. That would give him a democratic face to lead the people of Pakistan into the US war on Islamic extremists and militants. Despite, the naivety of this judgement, that is what made US and UK ensure Benazir's and even Nawaz Sharif's, participation in the general election that finally took place in February 2008 after being postponed from January 2008. A National Reconciliation Ordinance in 2007 by Musharraf ensured PPP leaders' and many others' ability to free themselves from a plethora of legal cases of corruption.

Musharraf delivered. The PPP and PML (N), two largest opposition parties, had to accept the Western advice of a broad-based government of nearly all parties, under Musharraf, to be unified and happily wage war on Taliban, al-Qaeda and other militants in Afghanistan and Pakistan itself. PPP too is trying to live up to its promises and commitments by talking unceasingly of 'national reconciliation' and a broad-based coalition government comprising nearly all significant parties. But there were issues flowing from Musharraf's presence in the top authoritative position in what is the surviving steel structure of the empire that British colonialists had bequeathed to Pakistan. Pakistan's establishment has lovingly preserved the spirit of that steel framework. It takes its orders from the top: from Musharraf for all domestic purposes. But for the crown of yore, one can read Washington's ukase and its ascertainable wishes. Such has been the achievement of Pakistan's ruling establishment to whom all social and economic elites owe willing allegiance.

An important and relevant aside may be appropriate here. It is, in many respects, as if there was no independence in 1947. That steel structure cornered all political power quite soon – after Mohammad Ali Jinnah's and Liaquat Ali Khan's deaths and the inner core saw nonstop squabbles in the Pakistan Muslim League party that possibly also involved some great powers (UK and the US). Assassination of Liaquat Ali Khan marked this radical change.

After that bureaucracy, civil and military, has ruled with the help and advice of the US. The formal date of this radical change was the Pakistan army chief's agreement with Pentagon in October 1953 when the US promised military aid to Pakistan. After that the informal diarchy of Pakistan army chief, as the leader of the establishment, and the US has remained unbroken to this day.

Possibly the two significant developments after Benazir Bhutto's arrival in Pakistan on 18 October 2007 were two attacks on her life. The first attack came on the same day in Karachi she arrived and the second was in Rawalpindi where she was assassinated on 27 December 2007. It showed how bad was the state of law and order in Pakistan and the growing breakdown of primary state structures that have to enforce law and maintain order were on public display. The immediate questions were: how could this fell act be done? Who did it? What if the individual who killed may have been a hired gun or a dedicated Islamic militant? The real query is about who conspired to achieve the dastardly aim of removing Benazir Bhutto from the political scene? There are also subsidiary questions: how could the killer(s) be so near her and killed her with impunity? What about the security arrangements on the site of this crime in Rawalpindi's Liaquat Bagh and the area around it? How could they be so inadequate? And why was the site of the incident cleaned up with a thick water hose within hours? Who wanted the forensic evidence to be washed away? Who gave that order? Even today, there are no answers to these queries.

The issue of who killed her and how is not as significant as who arranged it? There is much controversy that can only be noted here in passing. Most PPP loyalists believe that the federal government which was controlled by Musharraf is somehow complicit while supporters of Musharraf hotly deny the culpability of Musharraf or his close collaborators. PPP supporters point to a letter Benazir wrote to Musharraf on the basis of private information she had received before returning to Pakistan in which she gave three or four names who will be responsible if she were to suffer any attack on herself after her return. Their thrust is that Musharraf and his collaborators somehow bear responsibility for her murder. Musharraf and his partisans insist that responsibility for this crime rests on Taliban or similar

Islamic extremists, especially Baitullah Mehsud. PPP government has engaged UN to investigate this crime the way it is doing for the Lebanese politician Rafique Hariri's murder. Let's wait for UN investigators' findings. In any case, this book is not a detective novel. But one point to note is the PPP's lack of trust in Musharraf, despite the deal, is profound and it continues to hold him in some way responsible for the crime.

The friends of the president, however, argue that there had been a year-long confabulations between Benazir and Musharraf behind the scenes. Some of it became public in July when the two met in Abu Dhabi which could not be kept a secret after initial denials. Thus the year-long contacts between President Musharraf's emissaries and Benazir's aides are now in public knowledge. It is no secret that Benazir had returned as a result of a deal with Musharraf that had been brokered by American and British governments. The purpose of the deal was to strengthen Musharraf's hands in his war against (Islamic) terror. Benazir was claiming all along that she would fight the Islamic extremists better way Musharraf had done thus far. There would seem to be a broad correspondence of aims between the two, both having the same American friends. Why else would Musharraf agree to cooperate with Benazir? But Benazir's murder needs an explanation.

In the aftermath of this assassination, speculation was widespread. A respected commentator's theory can be presented as a possible, if not most likely, one, though she refuses to be named: her theory is simple. She finds both suspicions about Islamic militants and the ruling authority in Islamabad as not only likely but true. What cannot be doubted is the fact that suicide bombers cannot be hired to sacrifice their life, though things may be different especially if there were links between Islamabad and different Taliban or other extremist groups. It is only for a high anti-Western cause that any Islamic zealot will happily die. Benazir was no doubt a high-value target for such people and such people will send suicide bombers. Now, that leaves out Musharraf and the anti-Bhutto elements in the army. What of them?

As noted elsewhere also, the American military and intelligence community has long suspected a continuing link between

Pakistan's ISI and not only the Taliban proper (whoever they may be) but also many other Islamic extremist groups, six of whom were recently known to be in full cry in NWFP. These have been named in a recent news report as those operating in normal type Darra-i-Adamkhel and in other agencies (districts) to be Jaish-i-Mohammad, Lashkar-i-Tayyaba, Lashkar-i-Jhangvi, Harkatul Mujahideen, Muslim United Army International and local Taliban. All of them have cooperated with both ISI and al-Qaeda in the past; all of them are as intolerant of Muslim minority sects as of the US currently – after it occupied Afghanistan and is killing Taliban and al-Qaeda. Many of them have served ISI's major interest by carrying on a jihad in Kashmir. However, there is no certainty that these are the only extremist groups operating in Pakistan; several others, all secretive, have been heard of.

The point this commentator made was that since most Western intelligence services and their bosses go on asking Pakistan to cut this umbilical cord with such extremists organizations – most of whom have served ISI's purposes in Kashmir and elsewhere in the past. If the US agencies and NATO and British generals have believed this and accused Pakistan of collusion with some, if not all of such outfits, why should we doubt possible collusion between Pakistan's 'agencies' and Islamic terrorists; it need not be a mere canard to embarrass Musharraf. The crucial point is whether all this is a thing of the past, as Musharraf went on asserting. As she said and as is known about Pakistan Army that it was thoroughly indoctrinated with quite a militant Islam from day one after General Zia-ul-Haq took over. The ISI had been thick with CIA, MI6, Savak and Mossad since at least 1970s over Afghanistan developments and Peshawar was a cockpit of international intrigue.

Then, quickly on the heels of Soviet Army's entry into Afghanistan on 26 December 1979, she said, Afghan jihad was intensified that lasted through most of 1980s. Much the same extremist mujahideen began their operations in Kashmir under the direction of ISI circa 1989. Kashmir jihad tapered off only in 2000s, especially after the US brokered understanding between Indian premier Atal Behari Vajpayee and President Musharraf around the middle of 2002 when the Indian and Pakistani armies stood on the international frontier in a belligerent mode. India continues to accuse Pakistan of failure to dismantle the infrastructure for Kashmir jihad that had been built by ISI. This observer noted a critically important point: apart from local Pakistan Taliban, al-Qaeda and its various friends from Arab and Central Asian states, the surviving nexus between ISI (or some section of it) and some of these Islamic militants operating under various names is credible. At one stage, Musharraf himself conceded that there may be some surviving elements that have preserved their links with Islamic jihadists.

Most of these militants were splinters of the mother organization, Sipah-i-Sahaba that was set up by the Pakistan Army for General Zia's purposes in Karachi in early 1980s comprising the alumnae of Masjid-i-Binnori Madrassa, along with other ethnic organizations of Sindhis and mohajirs so as to divide the people of Sindh – the only province where anti-martial law agitation under the banner of PPP-led Movement for Restoration of Democracy (MRD) was intense in early 1980s – with a view to denying as much political space to PPP as possible. They all had ISI as their handlers and nearly all of them prospered in their own spheres of influence. Islamic militants were originally useful to the army because they were militantly anti-Shia or anti-Sunni, who could be trusted to prevent or drastically reduce people's participation in the movement against army rule by taking up a growing political space from PPP and its allies by their activities. Throughout the period of 1980s and 1990s, these militants were used in Afghanistan, Kashmir and then Afghanistan again until 1996 when ISI could celebrate after installing the Taliban regime in Kabul, while India was still being administered a thousand cuts, each insufficient as a casus belli because of Pakistan's putative atomic weapons kept the Indian Army deterred – until 2002 when Vajpayee threatened a final or 'aar-par' war with Pakistan.

Along the way Pakistan Army successfully divided the population several ways to pre-empt an anti-army popular agitation by MRD in early 1980s. Military did however permit Benazir Bhutto to return from her first exile in London in 1986 after crushing the MRD movement. After 1988 the army masterminded for over a decade a daring political game of establishing 'elected and democratic' governments, complete with all the usual institutions of a parliamentary democracy – but all under strict military control. Meanwhile ISI was busy organizing the Kashmir jihad with the help of extremist groups it had helped set up. It is not irrelevant to refer to the earlier army chief's, Zia's, modus operandi; it will show how ISI has been a necessary instrument at the disposal of all army chiefs; Musharraf did not have to use ISI in the way Zia did. But he had used it to create the ruling party of his day, PML (Q), and to enlarge its support by ensuring defectors from other parties and later still for organizing virtually three jihads simultaneously. This game went on for so many years. While Zia's game was easy because the people were kept divided and diverted by ethnic and sectarian killings, later army chiefs could always ask ISI to create conditions in which the president in the 1990s could dismiss elected prime ministers four times, two from each of the two main parties – PPP (Benazir) and PML (N) (Nawaz).

Army control was ensured through five steps: (i) amending the Constitution to give the power of life and death over the whole elected system to the president; (ii) the army chief occupying the president's office did not take place in the decade after 1988 by the next army chief, General Mirza Aslam Beg who chose to remain the king-maker behind the scenes; (iii) building up a party to oppose the largest party, PPP; (iv) ISI's help was used to 'manage' the elections to produce predetermined results; and (v) the ISI skills included also managing the media: the latter was encouraged to criticize and was fed with material for stories to paint each ruling prime minister as corrupt and inept. The truth is that, apart from their natural exuberance, these two youthful prime ministers were skilfully kept at daggers drawn and to engage in unbecoming and crude political vendetta against each other while corruption did creep in decision-making. Much of this latter role of ISI cannot be legally substantiated, but is widely believed in political and journalistic circles. The point to note is that even in 2009 nobody believes that ISI will not be able to 'manage' future elections the way it has done since 1988, if need arises and the army chief of the day so orders.

This commentator noted that Islamic zealots, PML (Q) and Musharraf had a common interest in eliminating Benazir. So why could they not cooperate in achieving the common purpose?

After all Benazir and PPP had too many enemies among Pakistani generals, as Musharraf asserts, and anyway she was a strong critic of the general and had lately united with Nawaz and his PML (N), possibly as a tactic to exert pressure on Musharraf during the year-long parleys. Wouldn't that uniting of the two be seen as a threat to military's domination of Pakistani state? Why couldn't old intelligence assets be safely used?

It is now time to think of what does the 26 December incident signified. The primary and immediate conclusion has already been drawn: the rule of law in Pakistan is not strong. The strong and resourceful can do what they like with, more or less, impunity. Going by the first presumption that the rulers of the country had something to do with the assassination or that there is some involvement of what is denoted by 'agencies', it can be said that, in so far as ISI represents the 'agencies', it is basically an anti-democratic force. It has been used to steal elections or deforming them. It controls a lot of things in the country. Indeed, if the American media are to be believed, it remains in part complicit with Taliban themselves. No doubt, authorities have repeatedly repudiated the idea that ISI is a rogue outfit. It asserts that it is a disciplined force, a part of the military establishment and works only under orders. This simply shifts the argument.

ISI's involvement with Islamic extremists is a matter of historical record; it is one of the creators of earlier mujahideen of 1980s for jihad in Afghanistan and later of Taliban in 1990s. It has had the role of masterminding the jihad in Kashmir and the two militant campaigns in Afghanistan. That it is tightly disciplined may or may not be wholly true. Most of the American media thinks that there are rogue elements within the ISI that are in league with Islamic extremists they had fostered and supported, even though subsequent orders may be to go the contrary way. At one stage General Musharraf himself admitted there are some rogue elements in ISI. The American media had no compunction in doubting the intentions of even Musharraf himself. He was seen as being under the influence of the earlier philosophy, believed in by military establishment vis-à-vis Afghanistan: that it is an area vital to Pakistan security where it should acquire a dominating influence with a view to adding strategic depth to Pakistan. This particular debate about Pakistan's interests in

Afghanistan is not relevant here but this is where Taliban may still have some uses for hard-line Pakistani military officers.

But the prospect now includes frightening things: the prospect of an eventual Taliban sway over NWFP, if it goes no further. This can invite a foreign invasion or intervention in an unavoidable civil war. Taliban victory would anyhow involve a civil war because a section of Pakistan Army is generally thought to desire a victory of Islamists and would thus side with them in order to ensure their victory. That is what a civil war is. But this may surely invite foreign intervention. Why? Simply because of the existence of nukes in Pakistan, if nothing else. As it is, Pakistan Army has lost over two thousand soldiers and paramilitary troops. The threat of the nukes falling into Islamists' hands too can involve likely expansion of international terrorists' activities and may surely involve Western military intervention which may intensify and expand local civil war.

The determined terrorists of al-Qaeda and others can get hold of radioactive materials to make dirty bombs, even if they cannot get hold of or use main Pakistani atomic weapons. Anyway, they can create god knows what mayhem and where. Long before that happens, there would be at least American, if not other, intervention to prevent it. It can also signal an eventual balkanization of Pakistan. It is hard to conceive whether PPP without Benazir would be able to create order out of this growing chaos and disintegrating processes that has begun. A blood bath of rare proportions and endless conflict may necessarily be a part and consequence of unchecked Islamic zealotry. All these are possibilities dependent on one critical development: nothing too untoward need happen if the army has no strong pro-Taliban officers and it stays united under Islamabad orders. But, as a few defections or surrenders by some officers and armed soldiers without firing a shot in South Waziristan showed there would seem to exist sympathizers of Islamic extremists in the army. Hence the relevance of these fears.

Some facts signal danger: two civil wars are going on right now: one in the Frontier that may be beginning to spread to other areas: it is between Islamic extremists wanting to establish an Islamic Caliphate and Pakistan Army at the moment. Army being army with usual blinkers, it has not much of a political strategy;

it merely fights with bigger guns. And for that reason it is at a disadvantage. Benazir had supposed that she would succeed as a captain of the team including the army and the international community. In her absence, things have not developed in a hopeful direction. There was the old promise of Nawaz Sharif's PML (N) and PPP cooperating. That cooperation was short-lived. If they could cooperate at least for a couple of years, they may have been able to stabilize the situation and put the country on the road to resolving problems probably through another election that will be fought hopefully on precise issues and not simply on democracy versus dictatorship question. This latter is too vague a proposition.

It is also important to know, and it shall be known soon enough whether PPP can survive as a united party or what kind of a leadership finally takes it over. The civil society had expected that the leaders of the lawyers' movement would reinforce the leaderships of both the two major parties. But that has not happened. The party leaderships have kept their monopoly on their parties even in PML (Q). Hitherto they have not shown much vision or large heartedness so far, though they had been talking of a united struggle for democracy and sending the army back to barracks. That has partially happened as a result of army's own volition. But it retains decisive political influence. The direction these parties take in future remains to be seen, especially for the PPP. Nobody knows how would the army actually behave, now that General Musharraf has gone. The new man in is one of those who is being praised day and night by the Americans. They appear to put a lot of confidence in him and think that he is a redoubtable professional soldier who would continue to stabilize Pakistan. What precise role they have in mind for him to entertain such hopes suggests something troubling. Their formulation about stabilizing Pakistan can raise suspicion. Nothing can be said about his moves, though hitherto all pronouncements of General Ashfaq Pervez Kayani have been correct and helpful. He says he wants to detach the army from politics and he has said all the good things so far. But that is only the beginning.

True, social reforms and proper democracy can prevent most troubles, provided economic crises are somehow resolved. That is the big white hope, if also rather iffy. There are forces in the country that are pro-secular democracy and who believe in the rule of law. After all, Pakistan has been witnessing a campaign by its legal fraternity of rare intensity that has lasted two years. It can yet be revived, though some erosion is to be seen at the edges. The threat of foreign intervention is not linked to any empire-building ambitions of any great power. No European, American, Chinese or Indian can be accused of wanting to incorporate any part, much less all, of Pakistan. The main reason for it will be the existence of nuclear weapons in Pakistan. There are assertions by the military that 'its nukes are absolutely safe; there is no chance of their falling into Islamists' hands'. True, no one believes that a Taliban agent would sneak into one of the places where the nukes are stored to steal a nuke or two. That may not really be possible. There are also sure to be technical and administrative defences. But what if Taliban do overrun significant parts of tribal areas and make headway in NWFP and Punjab or a government change in Islamabad may increase the possibility of what is strenuously being asserted abroad: foreign intervention may not be a mere possibility, but may have become a likelihood. Foreign intervention may not be by only one power. The possibilities include the Americans, Israelis, Indians and maybe a NATO power or two.

All this can be prevented, provided a simple working democracy, unadorned with any adjective, is allowed to go on, with peaceful changes of governments and rule of law prevails which would facilitate economic and social reforms and conflict situations are resolved by political reforms. There will then be no threat of foreign intervention. If Benazir had lived, this possibility would have been somewhat stronger, despite her commitments to the Americans and Musharraf to carry on war on terror more vigorously.

A New Beginning

Pakistan has had its sixth election in the last twenty years on 18 February 2008. Pakistan's record on elections is peculiar. Its first free election took place after twenty-five long years of its life. Out of seven general elections so far, six are commonly adjudged as having been 'managed' by intelligence agencies, including the fifth one, in 2002 that was expertly 'managed' by military sleuths of Musharraf. But the February 2008 election stands out as quite acceptable. There were many factors that made it a reasonably free election. How could that be? There are many reasons that need to be noted.

1) The public opinion in the country has, up to a point, come of age.

2) During the Musharraf regime there was much effort to project an image of modern and moderate Islam that ensures progress. The February 2008 polls remained fairly free in pursuit of convincing the sceptical West, the donors. Also, Musharraf regime had permitted over fifty satellite TV channels, half a dozen of which were devoted to news, comments and discussions. In step with the political movements, the news channels' comments became progressively free and usually anti-government. This was tolerated long enough. That had a huge impact on public opinion.

3) Political awareness has characterized the people belonging to middle class in Punjab. Punjab is the province where maximum economic development has taken place and a fairly well-to-do middle class has emerged. It is also educated and demands, for the first time, political space to speak and act freely and participate in political activity.

4) Certain political events have contributed to the growing political awareness in the country, particularly in Punjab and NWFP. The reason for it is that America's war on terror in Afghanistan that has now moved into NWFP and its tribal areas. This was a matter close to the hearts and minds of the people of the NWFP and most people in Pakistan, being overwhelmingly Muslim, reacted angrily to American actions in Afghanistan and Iraq and their general policy of supporting Israel against the Palestinians. Anger against American policies has been a notable factor that has created anti-American feelings in Pakistan. Americans are the most distrusted and hated country in Pakistan, despite the fact that the relations of the American government with Pakistan's Musharraf regime were of the closest kind. Americans are responsible for pumping in anything up to $ 15-20 billion into Pakistan, thanks to Musharraf's role, if secret and unaccounted funds are included in eight years. But incidents like Lal Masjid and various aggressive military operations against Taliban and other Islamic militants in NWFP's tribal areas have inflamed opinion against Musharraf regime which is seen as America's stooge, doing things on Washington's dictation.

5) The year 2007 saw three major developments: first was the Lal Masjid affair. Complicating matters no end were the original linkages between the Pakistan government and the so called Islamic terrorists in both the Frontier's tribal areas and the NWFP. Pakistan's intelligence agencies had organized a whole war against the Soviets in Afghanistan in 1980s. For a decade American and Arab money with Soviet equipment (bought from Egypt) came into Pakistan for the so called mujahideen who went and fought the Soviets in Afghanistan. The subject has been dealt with elsewhere. Suffice it to say that the 1980s jihad was followed by the same sort of forces waging another jihad in Indian-held Kashmir. This too lasted close to a decade and in part, according to Indian accusations, continues in a reduced form. In this period, Pakistan had had other adventures in Afghanistan. The period 1992 onwards saw the formation of a government in Kabul that was manufactured in Islamabad and taken to Kabul in an American C-130 and installed on a Friday. Prime Minister Nawaz Sharif went with them and duly offered a thanksgiving prayer in the Grand Mosque of Kabul. This

government collapsed in less than two years and several civil wars ensued in Afghanistan. Pakistan was involved in various ways in many of them, for it tried to ineffectually influence the course of events. Among its final efforts was the induction of a new set of Islamic militants called Taliban. They were made in Pakistan's many madrassas run mainly by Jamiate Ulmai Islam of Maulana Fazlur Rehman and also by a dissident faction of the same party run by Maulana Samiul Haq; these two factions of JUI were the main forces behind the creation of Taliban. They were introduced in 1994 in the various civil wars in Afghanistan and by 1996 they had conquered some 80 per cent of Afghanistan, leaving only the strip controlled by northern areas that is peopled by ethnic minorities (non-Pushtoon) in Afghanistan.

The day, 18 February 2008, is likely to go down in Pakistan's stormy history as yet another new beginning. A general election was held under a caretaker government comprising mostly friends of President Musharraf. Although the 18 February polls were a normal general election after the completion of five years by the assemblies 'elected' in 2002 under Musharraf's heavily-amended Constitution. But they were widely expected to be 'managed' by intelligence services of the military; contrary to earlier fears of these new elections too will also be rigged, their upshot turned out to be startling. All the parties that were supporting Musharraf got a drubbing of their life, except one: the Muttahida Qaumi Movement that continues to dominate and represent the main urban centres in the province of Sindh, including Karachi; its hold on urban Sindh remains intact. For the rest, the national election returned a split decision, with PPP being the largest in the National Assembly, the second largest being Nawaz Sharif-led PML (N); this latter incidentally won a clear majority in the Provincial Assembly of the province of Punjab, the most populous and richest. PPP, however, won seats in all the four provinces, while it received a clear majority in Sindh, the second-most populous province.

In the critically important province of NWFP, a veritable revolution took place: the six religious parties' alliance, MMA, that had hitherto ruled the NWFP, was trounced. The main victors were secular Pushtoon nationalists, represented by Awami National Party. This party is being run by the grandson of famous Frontier Gandhi, Abdul Ghaffar Khan, who had largely moulded many of the gun-toting Pushtoons into those favouring non-violence and who accepted secular Indian nationalism way back in undivided India in 1920s and later; the party was originally known as Red Shirts' movement. ANP, a secular Pushtoon nationalist party par excellence, is Red Shirts' successor, has formed a coalition government in the NWFP, with PPP as junior partner. Rejected were the orthodox religious parties, MMA, who stood for converting Pakistan into a uniquely Islamic state, with Quran and Sunnah as its supreme law – in theory quite like al-Qaeda or Taliban. ANP believes in democratic and peaceful methodology of solving all problems, including the countering of what has now become an international demon, militant Islam, which, in the shape of al-Qaeda, Taliban and many other militant groups, is keeping both Afghanistan and Pakistan's tribal areas destabilized. The US is in the eighth year of its war against what it calls 'Islamic Terror' – and Pakistan has been an official ally of the US in this war – having been dubbed the non-NATO ally of the US. Pakistan's relations with the US vis-à-vis the war on terror in Afghanistan are of crucial importance from various points of view: Pakistan's economic well-being and national security are now inextricably mixed up with America's fortunes in the war. As it happens, the American war against what Bush frequently used to call Islamic fascism is not really succeeding; it produces as many Islamic terrorists as it kills, perhaps more. There is also a regular insurgency against Pakistan state by a plethora of militant groups in NWFP's tribal areas that are now moving into other Pakistani provinces. The new government in the Frontier Province and coalition government at the Centre (Islamabad) will have to resolve many complex problems of this war because the Americans are insisting on extending their military operations from Afghanistan into Pakistan's own territory – independently of Pakistan authorities.

The Americans are believed to be demanding that Pakistan should cooperate in the manner they desire. This is in sharp contrast with most Pakistanis' opinion about how to counter Islamic militancy, which is commonly recognized by all election-winning parties as primarily Pakistan's internal problem. It needs a political and democratic approach because merely bringing to bear heavy fire power alone, or mainly, as Americans tend to think it is all that is required to win this war. The US is exerting tough military and other pressures on Pakistan but also originally desired keeping Musharraf in presidential position in Islamabad with effective powers. They think these things define America's security interests. President George Bush had been sending two emissaries, John Negroponte and Richard Boucher, both of the State Department, frequently to lobby with new electoral winners to keep Musharraf with ample powers in his president's job and preserving the alliance for war fighting with the US against militant Islam. At one time these gentlemen carried back a mixed response. The Americans received ample assurances that the new government regards all that is denoted by Islamic terrorism to be alien to the traditional beliefs and practices of Pakistani Muslims and they hold it to be a major security threat to Pakistan itself. But a discrepancy in the opinions of Pakistanis and Americans came into prominence when the strategy and means of fighting this war are discussed. Pakistanis would like to employ military force minimally while striving to make more political moves to create conditions in which the appeal of the ideas of Islamic militants or terrorists is submerged and heavily diluted in other ideas and ideals – indeed a dilution approximating to being countered. Elected Pakistanis hold there is no other way. The Americans are not impressed with this stream of thought and think it amounts to appeasement of terrorists.

For good reason, Pakistanis find America's main reliance on superior fire power to be less than wise; their counter-insurgency measures, in essentials, hark back to the strategy the British Army adopted in Malaya in later 1940s and early 1950s, as partially amended by American experiences in Vietnam and that too not wholeheartedly. Americans do not like to be told that their strategy so far in Vietnam, Iraq and Afghanistan has basically failed; or that they are in a quagmire in Middle East. But Americans are the only superpower and command the growing unwilling support of all NATO and other pro-Western countries like Australia and Japan. The pressure they can bring to bear on Pakistan, with an economy that teeters on the brink of insolvency, and a political elite that has always agreed to serve as America's bag carriers throughout most of the 1946–91 Cold War and also in its two wars in Afghanistan in recent decades.

Pakistanis in political offices are now facing a painful dilemma on this question. To agree with the Americans and act on their advice is to become America's stooges and will be, before long, forced to grant them what are the rights of extraterritoriality, reminiscent of nineteenth century China. Pakistan's public opinion is not ready for it, despite knowing that they need American aid and can scarcely go flatly against American wishes. Much depends on the statesmanship of two top politicians of PPP and PML (N): co-chairman Asif Ali Zardari and Mian Nawaz Sharif (the top leader of PML (N)). Can they rise above immediate political gains and losses to become statesmen enough for taking Pakistan out of the many deep-seated crises, including the emerging one in foreign policy vis-à-vis the US and indeed the West as a whole? Experience in Pakistan during the year 2009 shows that led by the military chief, Islamabad is now content to render its National Assembly's comprehensive resolution nugatory that laid down the proper way to fight religious extremism be ineffective and has accepted the American hook, line and sinker. All that can be said is what will be will be. But Pakistan is not like Afghanistan and Iraq. Its going haywire will entail untold consequences.

Islamabad's new government has multifarious problems awaiting solutions and has to take new initiatives on which differences exist. The economy is in a sad state with all the major deficits increasing: fiscal deficit, trade balance, current account and there are growing shortages of wheat, water, other foodstuffs, electricity, gas and in conjunction with rising inflation rates, led by rising food prices that have grown beyond 20 per cent over last year. Then, there is the second insurgency in the western province of Balochistan bordering on both Afghanistan and Iran. A purely military approach, typical of Musharraf's and Americans', can no longer do; political and democratic methods have to be applied to the problems in Balochistan, including meeting many of the clearly justified demands about the Baloch owning and benefiting from their own resources.

Then, there is the whole backlog of problems created by Musharraf in trying to sack the chief justice of Pakistan for fear that an assertive judiciary will hamper him in his political schemes of getting himself elected for another five years as the president while he was still in uniform as the chief of army staff as well as holding a general election that will return his supporters in all the six Assemblies. Both jobs were due to be done by mid-November 2007. Although an appointee of President Musharraf himself, the track record of the particular Chief Justice, Justice Iftikhar Muhammad Chaudhry, as noted elsewhere, has been one of a fiercely independent judge who gave a hard time to senior bureaucrats and was threatening to summon in court top generals running intelligence services over the question of the 'disappearance' of hundreds, maybe thousands, of political activists and other opponents, without leaving any trace for years. Everybody knew that they were picked up by military's intelligence organizations but the government functionaries have remained mum, saying that they had no knowledge of their whereabouts. The intelligence agencies did start releasing some of them in ones and twos as secretly and unavowedly as they had picked up. There may still be an unknown number of people in secret jails and safe houses. Justice Chaudhry had also stopped sale of government's public sector undertakings that stank of impropriety. In short, the rulers regarded him as a pain in the neck, especially in view of Musharraf's plan of holding two important elections in which 'positive results' were necessary for Musharraf's plan to succeed to go on ruling Pakistan till 2012 (at least).

Now, as detailed elsewhere, throughout 2007 Opposition forces continued gathering steam in the struggle against Musharraf's schemes, especially of his own elections; and the second election was for national Parliament's two houses. These two elections were sure to occasion many challenges landing in the top court. Musharraf was personally vulnerable because he was the army chief on active service, receiving a salary. This is expressly barred even in the Constitution that is much-amended by himself. Hence, Musharraf crudely tried to sack the CJP on 9 March 2007. Justice Chaudhry stood his ground and wanted to be tried in an open court, if there were any charges against him. The rest is well-known history. It gave birth to the lawyers' movement there and then that succeeded brilliantly in almost exactly two years later on 15 March. The government accepted all their demands unconditionally. It shook the foundations of Musharraf's dictatorship despite his success in 'managing' to get himself elected on 6 October 2007, by a controversial Electoral

College that was in its dying days along with the 2002 assemblies. The strength of lawyers' movement all but frustrated his schemes. Also by a quirk of destiny, the American administration came to talk profusely about democracy and genuine elections in the context of troubled Middle East. The American administration's pressure on him forced Musharraf to resign from the army on 9 December 2007 and thus he lost direct control over military's intelligence agencies (that then became the privilege of the new army chief who, for his own reasons, chose to detach the army from Musharraf and created a publicly discernible distance with him). With the psychology of resistance to military domination of the governing processes spreading widely, it caused the February election to give the verdict it did. Probably an American input in the polls being free may also be considerable.

There was also the case of Musharraf's chicken coming home to roost. For over eight long years his economic team ran Pakistan in accordance with neo-laissez faire economics. His finance minister was lionized by international financial institutions and American government; the Western press gave him long loving certificates of competence. But the net result of the regime's economic ministrations was the further growth of poverty, high inflation rates, with rich becoming obscenely rich while the poor became poorer still. The economic results of the Musharraf regime of over eight years were enough to make him the most hated man. The election results showed the pain of the common people in sharp relief. It is to be remembered that Pakistan is one of the more urbanized countries in South Asia where population is virtually half urban and half rural. The majority of the rural population is poor and not simply poor. Growing incidence of landlessness forces them to buy their own food for much of the year because the growth of large farms, worked with machines and fewer farm hands, meant a large number of people being ejected from traditional tenancies. In Pakistan agriculture has been modernized to a fair extent where rich landlords or retired military officers arrange cultivation on fairly big-sized farms by using modern machinery that require much fewer human workers. The old tenants, or share croppers thrown out of their traditional agricultural work, are trekking to the nearest towns and from there to larger ones and then on to foreign countries.

Pakistan has been exporting manpower for thirty years and yet its population growth can only be called an explosion. It can be objected that given the widespread poverty and economic misery, earlier elections should have shown the same sort of results. Why that did not happen is explained by the fact most elections were more or less rigged. Additionally, the development of the media freedom and its messages on national situation was received by common people only lately.

The forceful role of the Americans in Pakistan does not need much discussion; it is dealt in another chapter, though it becomes necessary to mention it in several contexts. Distrusted as they are in Pakistan, American interest in Pakistan, however, remains intense and they closely cooperated with Musharraf regime and now with the new elected government. That has earned the epithets for Musharraf being America's man. Now Asif Zardari has taken the mantle of being America's main bag carrier. The US interests require that Pakistan economy and politics must stay oriented to just one major objective: to wage war against Islamic terror in Afghanistan and tribal areas of Pakistan. Americans think they have given ample economic and financial aid to Pakistan. Far more than $ 11 billion officially came into Pakistan during the last eight years.

Two factors have to be juxtaposed: popular rejection of US intervention in Pakistani matters and its advocacy of the war on terror, on the one hand, and America's interest in keeping Pakistan to its old course by what can only be called diplomatic arm twisting, on the other. Doubtless, American emissaries, who visit Islamabad frequently have heard an earful and clearly could see the kind of sentiments that prevail in Pakistan after the polls. But the hard fact is that they have gone back satisfied every time. The two largest parties in the national Parliament that also control the two bigger provinces are on board so far. The ANP that nominally controls the NWFP too is a part of the new government.

Post election scenario has witnessed the consequences of collecting disparate elements into a government where there has been no tradition of coalition governments and where normal politics had remained more or less banned. There are inevitable rivalries among the parties that have historical roots. PPP and PML (N) are still rivals in both Punjab and Sindh. ANP is a rival of all PMLs, PPP and religious parties in the NWFP. PML (N) takes a stiff anti-Musharraf line and has made it a central plank of its politics. Initial assembly sessions at the Centre and in Punjab saw proceedings being drowned in slogan chanting from all sides, including the elected deputies and the visitors' galleries: 'Go Musharraf Go' slogan reverberated. Although PPP seemed committed to follow a policy of keeping Musharraf with effective powers in place so as to better conduct the US war on terror, it was forced to speak like an opposition party in the initial stages. That rhetoric became a shackle on its feet. The PPP and PML (N) are signatories to two charters known as the Charter of Democracy with Nawaz's PML in 2006 and the Murree Declaration of 2008. These commit the two parties to restore full democracy, by which PML (N) means ouster of Musharraf and restoration of all over sixty-two judges sacked by Musharraf while he reconstituted the High and Supreme courts with more pliant judges. This issue continues to haunt the two parties. So long as Musharraf stayed in the President House and had the effective powers to control the bureaucracy and had the benefit of his place in the army hierarchy, the continued participation of the PML (N) in a PPP-led government was difficult. The two worked at cross purposes while their coalition lasted. Even on the day the government was sworn in by Musharraf, the ministers belonging to PML (N) wore black arm bands as a protest against Musharraf administering the oath. Then, later Musharraf went to China on a week's visit. While PPP ministers went with him, the finance minister from PML (N) refused. Continued cooperation of PPP with PML (N) in the government lasted no more than two months.

Then, PPP is itself vulnerable to splits. Asif Zardari has inherited the leadership of PPP with an unsavoury reputation. He was known as Mr Ten Per Cent during the two regimes of his wife and has had a conviction in Switzerland, though cases against Zardari in Spain and Switzerland have been dropped under Musharraf's National Reconciliation Ordinance to get him off the hook.

In the matter of leadership, his wife treated the party as a personal property and nominated the leadership to her husband, who graciously made himself only co-chairman with her nineteen-year-old student son. It is useful to remember that the party has had a stormy history. It began in 1967 as a left-of-centre party that gradually became right-of-centre party. Later Benazir brought the party far too close to Americans so that Benazir could expect US support for ensuring her coming back into power. The party activists belong to many schools of thought; many are emotional and radically inclined. Can PPP remain united with various known factions inside it? Some may rebel against this PPP regime that is sure to conduct vigorously the war as the Americans want and doing this under the leadership of Musharraf; that would put a strain on the loyalty of many PPP workers. Then, the kind of attitude PPP has adopted already on the judges issue obviously looked lukewarm, if not hostile, to the judges' cause and tried hard to wriggle out of the commitments made under Murree Declaration. This stance could scarcely be acceptable to many PPP workers, though the PPPs young Turks have stayed quiet for over a year and half. Perhaps most people underestimated her success in changing the party's character to right-of-centre. Even so, the longer-term outlook for PPP's unity can scarcely be bright. It is however true that had President Musharraf, could be left alone in office, he could one day bring forth a 'third punch' of the kind of his second that was delivered on 3 November 2007. He had to go and Zardari took over from his one-time baiter.

In the meantime, Benazir Bhutto arrived on the scene on 18 October 2007 to an ecstatic reception. Her twenty-hour long arrival procession in Karachi was bombed by a supposed suicide bomber that all but killed her, with very high fatalities of Bhutto supporters. Her popularity zoomed both in sympathy for this attack and for her exuberant anti-dictatorship rhetoric. She looked like a saviour to the common people. Later, she was brutally murdered in Rawalpindi on 27 December 2007. That again sent a wave of sympathy for the Martyr of Democracy, as she is now referred to by her followers. This wave gave a notable victory to her party, PPP, on 18 February 2008 election. In the growing national uproar throughout the year 2007 over events in NWFP's tribal areas and the Lal Masjid affair created an adverse image of Musharraf and the maximum loss for which was suffered by both PML (Q), the King's party, and the MMA for its failure to take a clear stand on Islamic bigotry. Also there was the assertive behaviour of the Supreme Court chief justice and popular support that lawyers' movement continued to gain – the electoral campaign became chiefly focused on ending not only the Musharraf dictatorship but also military's domination of political life. Musharraf lost his nerve. It had made him do what gamblers do when on a losing vein: he raises the wager dramatically by using his powers brutally. He declared a state of Emergency on 3 November that was actually an unavowed martial law and in line with what Pakistani military dictators do, he gave a new Provisional Constitution Order in his capacity as army chief that gave the president (himself) the powers to amend the Constitution in his own discretion. He did just that. And in the process he sacked over sixty-two judges of High and Supreme courts, locked some of them up in their houses and began a fresh reign of terror. The people of the country, instead of meekly submitting to a military dictator's fiat, redoubled their protest campaign. In the event, he was forced to resign under American pressure from the army and eventually held a relatively free election on 18 February.

The emerging political reality was, however, confused and messy. He had painfully negotiated a reconciliation with Benazir Bhutto for recruiting support of the PPP for his rule in 2007 so as to vigorously prosecute the war on terror probably much against his personal wishes under American prodding and perhaps with their intermediation. The ultimate purpose originally was to strengthen Musharraf's hands by making a freshly elected PPP cooperate with him so that he will be better able to lead Pakistan in West's war on Islamic terrorism. Whether as a result of some understanding between the politicians of PPP and PML (N), or because of the new army chief's demonstration of non-cooperation with Musharraf or greater accuracy in American expectations, the election results greatly surprised Musharraf. His noted supporters were defeated. All in opposition to what Musharraf stood for won conclusively. These winning parties have quickly acquired additional supporters and have managed a nearly two-third majority at least in the lower house of Parliament and might also do so in both its houses in March 2008, necessary for constitutional amendments.

What was the new government expected to chiefly do? As noted, there is a document signed by Nawaz Sharif and Benazir

Bhutto in 2006 called Charter of Democracy (dealing with what political reforms are needed in Pakistan); another is the Murree Declaration of 9 March 2008 signed by the new boss of the PPP, Asif Ali Zardari, and Nawaz Sharif of PML (N). These two documents constituted the initial political programme of the new coalition government, if also restricted to democracy's revival. This included amending away all non-democratic amendments in the Constitution made by dictators, and probably introduce some new reforms. The two sides were expressly committed to not merely releasing the superior court judges from confinement but also to restore them to their jobs to ensure an independent judiciary. The new government's first action was the release of judges. But there it has stayed till 16 March 2009 when lawyers' movement forced the Zardari-led government to unconditionally restore them to their offices. Many political prisoners are also being released, if also tardily. This was huge political defeat for Asif Zardari and PPP and its effects will reverberate in Pakistan politics.

Two major issues, however, remain unclear: what are the ideas of the PPP-led government on the economy; the entire political leadership assembled in the new government has remained remarkably ambiguous and quiet over economic matters. There is some pro forma recognition of the economy being in straits. But hardly anyone has said what needs to be done. The two documents mentioned here deal with purely political matters. This is a curious fact that can possibly hide differences to come out later or may just be due to absence of thought and research. But by and large the most difficult issues pertain to the foreign policy question of how far can Pakistan cooperate with the US strategies and tactics in the war on terror and how far can the Americans go in accommodating the new Pakistan's ideas.

At bottom was also the none-too-small matter about the fate of two individuals: first is President Musharraf. What to do with him after his over eight years of running Pakistan in a largely blunderbuss manner, having brought Pakistan into its present sorry condition. The second personage was the chief justice of Pakistan, Justice Iftikhar Chaudhry, who was released but awaited restoration to his office for nearly two years if also intermittently. Everyone knew that the entire country supported his restoration to his top legal job, but President Musharraf and the Americans have lobbied hard with the new political victors that he be retained as the president with effective powers to lead Pakistan in the war on terror. Musharraf had made it a point of prestige that he would not let the CJP return to his job that he himself had 'illegally and unconstitutionally' given to another and more pliant judge. This was Musharraf's own admission on the BBC. Justice Chaudhry did return to his court and Musharraf had also to leave his presidential palace as a result of Zardari and Nawaz agreeing on this point who did go against original US wish.

Both matters should have come much earlier because these were in consonance with the two charters; and both PPP and PML (N) were committed to do so and yet they wasted a year doing so. But then, there were the Americans with their insistence on keeping Musharraf in the job. The complication was that both the US and Musharraf had remained adamant against the judges, especially the CJP, while the entire legal fraternity and Pakistan's civil society and media were even more adamant that Musharraf should go. While Nawaz Sharif stood solidly for both as national requirement, Zardari's case was different: PPP and Benazir – and thus Zardari too – were committed to keeping Musharraf in the presidency. But just as he has gone on remaining committed and yet not do anything – so far – to really implement the charters he remained in the good books of the US and yet he intrigued with Nawaz Sharif to send Musharraf home so as to step into the presidential palace. That is how Zardari operates. Take whatever cooperation from Nawaz but do nothing for him. Between Nawaz and Zardari there seems to be a noticeable discrepancy: while Nawaz Sharif has stayed iron hard in his determination to get all the sacked judges restored to their positions, the various leaders of the PPP tried to find ways of somehow making an exception of Justice Chaudhry. It seems the deal between Benazir Bhutto and Musharraf is still being vigorously implemented except that the PPP eased out Musharraf from his job.

Remember the real issue behind the uproar against the Musharraf regime was all about the non-acceptability of the military dictatorship. It cannot be said that Pakistan has no other problems. It has several major problems. These are long standing and in the larger historical sense make-or-break problems. The sixty-two-year history of Pakistan shows that governments dictated or tolerated by its notorious establishment have failed to tackle them; it is the nature of the problems that requires a leadership that is not beholden to the military or other elements of the establishment; these problems, in fact, cannot be tackled without the full and conscious political weight of an aware people behind a truly popular leadership. The point is that these longer-term major problems cannot really be tackled unless there is a prior development: an effective transfer of power from the famous establishment, comprising economic and social elites of the society, led by bureaucracy, civil and military, who have created the problems in the first place; they are both uninterested and incapable of solving those problems. Otherwise they would not have remained problems for as long as six decades. These have been enumerated elsewhere. Here the point to be made is: people have to free themselves first from the stranglehold of the atavistic social and economic elites that have, under military's leadership, captured power which has been exercised either by the leaders of the economic and social elites, under military's tutelage or by the military directly. The first order of business, from common people's point of view, is this basic reform: transfer of power from the elite groups with feudal mindsets to the elected Parliament, representing the people. This should have been the first important step. Has this step been taken? The answer unfortunately is no.

It cannot be overemphasized that the election campaign was hugely influenced by the lawyers' movement and the victorious parties – PPP, PML (N) and ANP – won largely because of their stand against military dictatorship and in favour of undoing Musharraf's various gaucheries of the year 2007, if not those of earlier years. If the election results have been largely coloured by such open or implied commitments of the victorious parties, the first item on the victorious parties agenda should be: a) free the detained judges; b) enable all the sacked over sixty-two judges to revert to the assertive High and Supreme courts; c) purge the Constitution of the anti-democratic amendments forced by various dictators to ensure that Constitution embodies the norms of a liberal democracy; d) and finally to bid adieu to former General Musharraf. What has not been enumerated here is a reorientation of foreign policy vis-à-vis America's war on terror, and India and Afghanistan policies: these issues should be seen from the viewpoint of an independent and sovereign country that decides to pursue a policy of peace at home and abroad: Pakistan has no business to get itself involved in the superpowers' strategic schemes and plans or to be a non-NATO ally.

True, Pakistan has a serious problem of dealing with misguided Islamic warriors and suicide bombers. But Pakistan has to look at it as its domestic problem to be solved through democratic methods and not from the viewpoint or strategy of the US or the West. Pakistan's policy on India and Afghanistan should, therefore, be revised in a manner that Pakistan gets an opportunity to solve its own problems peacefully and through democratic methodology. There has to be a withdrawal from having gone too far with the US in its Asian designs. But there is no call for working against the US, or supporting al-Qaeda and Taliban. Far from it. Pakistan is a second rank Asian country that is still underdeveloped and poverty-stricken. All its policies have to remain informed with the basic strengths and weaknesses of the state and it should adopt a role that befits its actual status.

This is not to say that other problems should not be solved or should be delayed. Only, Pakistanis have to realize that they cannot really tackle the mountainous problems of according a proper place to Islam in the body politic of a democratic country; solving the perennial problem of Centre-state relations and resolving the political confrontations between lovers of strong Centre and those who stand for near-maximum autonomy for provinces. Even if Baloch insurgency is democratically ended, there will remain the more fundamental and perennial problem of poverty and underdevelopment of two-thirds of citizens of Pakistan who remain wallowing in diseases, illiteracy, poverty and underdevelopment of all kinds. Who can say that all these problems do not occupy the first priority, though in practice some sequencing will have to be undertaken. The first one is, of course, the transfer of power from an illegitimate and undemocratic establishment to the Constitution and Parliament; at present the latter only partially represents the people. Parliament will itself take time to become fully representative of the people when a growing proportion of population becomes aware of their rights; this process will necessarily be gradual. But what cannot be left to gradualism is the basic transfer of power from non-democrats to the people and Parliament and purging of the Constitution of anti-democratic articles and their replacement with measures that are in full consonance with democratic concepts and norms. This admits of no delay and should have been done as the first item on the national agenda.

But a somewhat new factor in Pakistan politics has emerged in the shape of Nawaz Sharif having matured into a statesman. That is what he and his friends think. He has realized the establishment has made a fool of both the PPP and PML (N) leadership. While these parties quarrelled and tried to harm each other, the military-led elite groups smirked and strengthened their power by showing both leaders as immature and power hungry. Nawaz now thinks that the first task before politicians is to unite to take power from the military, which is the top elite group among the ruling elites. Hence, he has worked hard to draw PPP into cooperating with him. The PPP did go along with Nawaz and they both signed a Charter of Democracy as a general programme for both. But PPP leadership, in the meantime, had moved far more closely to the US government and had negotiated a deal with Musharraf through the good offices of American and British governments, as noted. Thus PPP has a foot in both the boats: Nawaz leadership and the US camp. Nawaz plans primarily to defang the military. This is a circumstance that would influence, if not determine, what happens in the new beginning represented by 2008 Parliament. There are many other issues that immediately crowd on to the agenda of the coalition government that was formed initially. But the coalition between PPP and PML (N) broke down in two months and a final parting of ways took place in May 2008.

SIGNIFICANT FEATURES OF 18 FEBRUARY ELECTION

Although some candidates and a few of the officials did try to influence its outcome, but the upshot of this election makes it a reasonably fair election. It is true that EU observers picked holes in the exercise, its results are such that most Pakistanis have accepted the results wholeheartedly. The popular verdict is clear.

It is an unambiguous rejection of all the policies and politicians supporting now ex-General Pervez Musharraf; all his notable ministers were defeated, quite a few forfeiting their deposits. The hitherto ruling party, PML (Q), has had its number of seats sharply reduced. All opposition parties made significant advances. Overall, the result does not give any one party an overwhelming majority. It is basically a split verdict. Two major opposition parties have emerged stronger. The biggest one is, of course, Benazir Bhutto's PPP as had been widely expected at home and abroad. Closely following the PPP was the PML of Nawaz Sharif faction; it emerged second largest party in the lower house of the Parliament, called National Assembly, and is the largest single party in the Provincial Assembly of Punjab, the key province.

Politically, the victory in the key province of NWFP, where much of the action in the war on terror is, is most significant: it has gone to secular Pushtoon nationalist party, the leadership of which is descended from the famous founder of Red Shirts, Abdul Ghaffar Khan, also known as Frontier Gandhi. It is a secular, democratic and socially middle-of-the-road party and represents secular Pushtoon nationalism. One aspect of the ANP victory is heart warming even for much of the outside world as well as the intelligentsia and civil society of Pakistan: that the previous government in the NWFP comprising six religious parties' alliance MMA, that had worked in close mesh with Musharraf dictatorship for five years was almost totally decimated. A secular party emerged victorious. Its significance needs to be pondered.

In Sindh, as could be expected, the PPP has emerged as the single largest party that commands an absolute majority in the Provincial Assembly. But Sindh politics is sharply divided on ethnic lines of its populace between so called rural Sindh and urban Sindh. In the rural Sindh, PPP is the party of popular choice; people are largely moved by the mystique of the Bhutto dynasty and vote for PPP. But in urban areas in Sindh, the mohajir vote (of the descendents of 1947-related migrants from India) has gone to a party that is hard to adequately describe, called Muttaheda Qaumi Movement (MQM). It is called ethnic, though the mohajirs came from all parts of India; it represents the rather ersatz nationalism of the mohajirs; it also shares some characteristics of India's Dalit parties representing, in fact, the lumpen proletariat among the mohajirs and does not appeal to the mohajirs of professional classes; it also shares a certain characteristic with Shiv Sena of India in so far as it wants Karachi to remain dominated by mohajirs and to keep Punjabi, Pathan, Baloch and Sindhi presence to a minimum; it dominates all major cities of Sindh, especially Karachi and Hyderabad. The party is well knit, fascistic, tailored around the personality of 'Altaf Bhai', Altaf Hussain, who now lives in London as a British citizen but keeps tight control over his disciplined party, the way the Fuehrer had done over his Nazi party in Germany.

Balochistan remains what it has always been: socially dominated by tribal sardars who sometimes double as entrepreneurs; they usually are large and unaccountable landowners; as landlords who directly rule over their tenants without any effective legislation to limit their powers. This time, although the party that has formed the government, PPP, did not originally get the majority of seats in the Provincial Assembly. But it had a fair number of seats and the rest of the MPAs, mostly tribal leaders, have joined the PPP government in the province and the Opposition comprises just one member of Parliament who has been historically at odds with the chief minister who is also a tribal sardar of his own tribe of Raisanis.

The election results need explanation. Pakistan has had five elections in the last twenty years; the recent 18 February election was sixth in just over these two decades; the election held in 1977 by Z.A. Bhutto is not being counted; its consequences had cost him his life. Pakistan's record on elections is peculiar. It had had one free election in 1970 after first twenty-five years of its life. Then after that, it has had seven general elections in which six are commonly accepted as having been 'managed' by intelligence agencies, including the previous one in 2002 that was 'managed' by military sleuths of Musharraf. But the February 2008 election stands out as quite distinct. There were many factors that made it a reasonably free election. How could that be? There are many reasons that have already been noted.

The second major incident of the year was a blunder by General Musharraf on 9 March . He called Pakistan's chief justice and presented him with a ludicrous charge sheet and demanded that he should resign. The chief justice, Justice Iftikhar Muhammad Chaudhry, read it and told Musharraf and the rest of the audience of four lieutenant generals that he refuses to resign, and would like to be tried in an open court to defend himself. He was arrested there and then, maltreated in various fashions, kept incommunicado for some days and then a case was filed in the Pakistan Judicial Council, a constitutional body for dealing with judges' matters. Later, the case was referred to a full bench of the Supreme Court of Pakistan where after another two months, his brilliant lawyers succeeded, and the CJP was reinstated in his job by that full bench of the Supreme Court. But the significant part of the story was that Justice Chaudhry's refusal to resign, in response to the phalanx of generals made him a symbol of resistance to military domination and dictatorship in Pakistan in no time. The lawyers rose like one united body throughout Pakistan in defense of the chief justice, and a movement started; first to get him reinstated and later to throw General Musharraf out of power. While the CJP was reinstated to his office on 20 July 2007, the movement has not succeeded in getting General Musharraf out – not yet. But it has deeply influenced public opinion. The lawyers leading the movement became the darlings of the people. The media, including the press, gave full support to the lawyers and the chief justice's case, which became a cause célèbre. The public became intensely anti-Musharraf and impatiently pro-change. It was this 'psychosis' that spread widely among the people. These were the real reasons why the February elections returned the verdict it did.

But another aspect of the matter is the role of the Americans in Pakistan. The US requires that Pakistan economy and politics must stay oriented to just one major objective: to wage war against Islamic terror in Afghanistan and tribal areas of Pakistan. Americans think they have ensured adequate economic and financial aid to Pakistan. Many billions of dollars have come to Pakistan during the last seven years. This economic situation could not have benefited PML (Q) or Musharraf.

The Bush administration was particularly interested in the elections that were to be held in the autumn of 2007. According to the Bush rhetoric, repeated ad nauseum, that elections should be transparent. The American aim was to have the largest party, led by charismatic Benazir Bhutto, should win a large number of seats. They had helped work out a secret deal between Benazir and Musharraf in which Musharraf was to hold a fair election and she agreed to keep him in his job with effective powers to run the War together. This is the reason why PPP is talking all the time of reconciliation. But reconciliation with whom is the question. It is with parties that have supported Musharraf and his creations: the new PML (Q) and pre-existing MQM and other odd dissident groups of PPP itself and PML (N). In the American scheme of things, taking in the Saudi advice, Nawaz Sharif and his PML (N) were not to be eliminated or kept out of the government as Musharraf had wanted. The Saudis had also persuaded Musharraf, probably on America's advice, that Nawaz Sharif is as good a moderate politician as Benazir. He should be included. That is how the formal alliance between PPP and Nawaz Sharif had been accomplished. But the popular sentiment inside the opposition parties was so intensely anti-Musharraf and his henchmen in the PML (Q) and MQM that it was politically difficult for PPP to take them along. The PPP has so much hatred for MQM that it was hard to take it on board, even with a handkerchief on the nose, though an effort has been made. This hatred issues from decades of bitter rivalry and occasional mutual killings in Karachi and Hyderabad.

One upshot of the election was that as the Americans wanted the reconciliation part was reflected in government-making. The reconciliation had succeeded brilliantly in one respect: Musharraf promulgated a National Reconciliation Ordinance under which all corruption cases against Benazir and her husband Asif Ali Zardari were dropped and there were any number of other unintended beneficiaries of that. The American interest was to ensure that (i) the opposition parties that had won should not throw Musharraf out or impeach him; (ii) they should remain committed to prosecuting the war on terror the way it had been till then; (iii) that the new government should not change the economic policies that Musharraf's men had started, despite the gruesome economic results that people now see.

The two largest parties in the national Parliament that control the two bigger provinces are on board so far – after a fashion. The PML (N) ministers resigned from the federal government on 13 May 2008 on the question of non-restoration of the judges Musharraf had sacked on 3 November 2007, as the PPP had earlier agreed to. But it remains in the coalition, still, giving support from outside; PML (N)'s provincial government in Punjab still has a complement of PPP ministers. But, on the whole, this coalition seems to have no future because the PPP is unlikely to do what the PML (Q) insists upon: unconditional restoration of the judges through an executive action, which for the PML (N) is the litmus test of its goodwill. Even the ANP that is now controlling NWFP, is a part of the new government.

CHALLENGES TO GILANI GOVERNMENT

The challenges facing the winners are many. There are three sets of crises facing the new government headed by Yousuf Raza Gilani: there is the civil society's disenchantment for not reinstating the judges for so long and not being a friend of independence of the judiciary. The second concerns the high rates of inflation and food shortages at too high prices. These include a whole range of economic difficulties facing the government. The prices of almost every commodity are rising; during the years 2008 and 2009 the food inflation rate has stayed near 20 per cent. It is claimed that at the bottom of the inflationary trend is said to be the high international prices of oil and wheat coupled with plunging values of the dollar and the rise of euro. Food and its shortages, with all other prices constantly rising and with increased user charges for electricity, gas, POL and many other services pose a severe challenge to the new government. Third, there is a whole range of fundamental problems waiting to be resolved.

First of these is the rise of Islamic extremism going under the generic name of Taliban. These are many insurgent groups, comprising many factions and groups that seek before long to displace the Pakistan state from at least the Pushtoon areas and possibly also Balochistan – unless it is effectively contained, countered or fought and somehow made unpopular rather than only militarily defeated. It's a serious challenge to the state, the appeal of which is not confined to Pushtoons in NWFP alone.

The second major crisis is also an insurgency in Balochistan. A Baloch Liberation Army and other groups are struggling to overthrow Pakistan Army's control over Balochistan. There is a whole school of thought in Balochistan that believes in Baloch nationalism and wants a lot more autonomy for the province so as to own its resources under the surface or in seas along its coast. The third major challenge is the Centre-state relations in accordance with the principle of genuine federalism based on the supremacy of what the people of a federating units want. The people of three smaller provinces, namely Sindh, NWFP and Balochistan, are dissatisfied with the kind of federation that Pakistan is in which the Central government is the only real government; the provincial governments are no more than glorified municipalities. The people of these provinces want provincial governments to be real governments. This is a subject that has remained unsettled for all these six decades and more. The country suffered the trauma of a civil war, war with India and the dismemberment of the country over just this question in 1971. But both major parties are embarrassed by the problem rather than have the nerve to tackle it, head on, if necessary. The fourth crisis is an endemic one: it's a division of society between the rich few and the many poor, some dirt poor. Hitherto, the governments have pursued a paradigm under which the emphasis has been on the growth of gross domestic product (GDP) under laissez-faire conditions. The hope was more growth will someday somehow translate into reduction in poverty and unemployment, or the so called trickle-down effect. This paradigm has been followed over most of these sixty-one years except a few. What has so far trickled down is more poverty through growing unemployment.

After the Election – Straight into Deadlock

The PPP–PML (N) coalition government came into being on 18 March 2008. It completed its hundred days around the first week of June. Pakistan's burgeoning tribe of what is called commentariate is certain of only one thing. The more this government moves around, the more it stays where it was. Few could see any worthwhile initiatives in the first few weeks, except the initial step of the Prime Minister Yousuf Raza Gilani to order the release of the superior court judges detained in their homes. For the rest, the government has been hamstrung by issues that divided its main constituents who were squabbling over what to do about the judges whom Musharraf had sacked on preceding 3 November, rather than overcoming what can be called long-standing make-or-break crises. No one talked about them.

It seems pointless to talk about the economy that is rapidly unwinding itself. It was, and is, assailed by a number of negative macro-economic indicators that point to growing deficits in external trade, in the production of agricultural goods as well as very low growth in industry. The budget deficit was touching 7 to 8 per cent of the GDP and inflation rate was well and truly into double digits, leaving 25 per cent way behind. It is led by food prices that were alarmingly rising above 30 per cent during 2008 and is about 18 to 19 per cent on week-on-week basis. The government did not seem to have any ideas on what to do about the economy. Deficit in the balance of payments on Current Account was expected to be in the 7 to 8 or more per cent of the GDP in 2008; it is expected to be slightly less in 2009. As a result the small monetary reserves were rapidly wilting, taking the rupee's value down and down. The only idea the government and the central bank, called the State Bank of Pakistan, had was to impose a 2 per cent increase in the bank rate. This is the standard response of formal economists to inflation. If only Pakistan economy had been like America's or any west European country, this might have worked. As it is, Pakistan economy is loose-limbed; half of it is wholly outside the books, with the result that increasing or decreasing the bank rate can scarcely change the basic trends in it. But first, let's look at the current political crisis that is threatening the whole democratic system and many are again talking of another possible military takeover already largely because the present government is failing to come up to the expectations of the US and NATO generals as well as of Pakistani people and the influential foreign powers, and they may, finding no other way out, again opt for the comfort of dealing with a military dictator; I too find it plausible, though difficult in view of their true desires.

THE CURRENT CRISIS

Difficulties began just after the 18 February elections. The first thing that struck everyone was the length of time it was taking to form a government. It came over a month later. What was happening? One thing was being perceived by every TV watcher and newspaper reader that Western ambassadors were calling on various political leaders frequently, ostensibly to congratulate them on their electoral victory. But soon it became clear that each leader was being accosted by various Western ambassadors to impress upon the leaders just one imperative: President Pervez Musharraf should be kept in his job and newly elected politicians should refrain from doing what the election results demanded: sending Musharraf home. They began by making it clear that American president, George W. Bush, a tight buddy of Musharraf, does not want him to leave, at least not until the end of the year or beginning of the next year: his departure now would be taken in America as a setback that the then ruling Republican Party, the Government of Pakistan cannot relish.

But the fact cannot be ignored that the whole tenor and purpose of major opposition parties' campaigning for election, and also its results, were to reject Musharraf, his government, his ruling party and everything associated with him. That led to an initial deadlock. It is possible to suspect that even the PPP, that later loyally stuck to Musharraf until August, could only have been respecting the US-brokered deal between Musharraf and Benazir Bhutto, although PPP had campaigned throughout earlier years in terms of wanting pure democracy and to demolish dictatorship and that Musharraf, the president, was an 'unconstitutional head of the state' and 'had no place in a new democratic system'.

Musharraf also had many skeletons in his cupboard: (i) his getting himself elected while he was still on active list of the army, drawing a salary, was a gross violation of the Constitution. Then, (ii) he chose to get himself re-elected as president by an Electoral College on 6 October 2007 a second time that was soon to go into the shadows along with the assemblies by mid-November when Musharraf was due to retire from the army as well as his tenure as president too was expiring by about the time. Musharraf took desperate actions on 3 November 2007. All these were unconstitutional actions and were challenged. The assertive judiciary, such as it was becoming under the leadership of the chief justice of Pakistan, Iftikhar Muhammad Chaudhry would not have condoned. It was sure to find him ineligible to stand for the presidential election being still a government servant on active duty. Then there was the constitutionality of the Emergency and the Provisional Constitution Order of 3 November 2007. If these issues were to reach the Supreme Court, it was plain that the court would find him wholly outside the four walls of law and that too on various other ordinances.

Therefore, the president pre-empted the Supreme and High courts and sacked them all, setting a new condition for the sacked judges to resume their work next morning by taking a new oath that the amended Constitution by General Musharraf promulgated on 3 November 2007 or new judges would be appointed who would abide by and take oath under the thus-amended Constitution. Musharraf's imposing of a state of Emergency was not by virtue of being the president but as the army chief of Staff – a thing that was outside the scheme of the Constitution which does admit, under some conditions, a president declaring a state of Emergency which were subject to scrutiny of the judiciary. The net result of Musharraf's 3 November action was that over sixty-two judges of the High and Supreme courts refused to take a new oath that was to show that the judge taking that oath was confirming his or her allegiance to Musharraf's 3 November amended Constitution. The president had locked up most of them in their homes along with the leaders of the lawyers' movement. The struggle between Musharraf and the civil society of Pakistan began in greater earnest after November 3 with the civil society's aim being clearly to throw Musharraf out. The election results clearly said so. But that was not to be. The convenience of American president prevailed and Musharraf continued in his Presidential Palace but only till 18 August 2008 when he had to resign to escape being impeached. The deadlock that actually followed the election paralysed the new coalition government for months on end. The PPP–PML (N) coalition with PPP at the Centre was short-lived: it ended on 13 May 2008, when Pakistan's second largest party, PML (Nawaz) walked out of the Central government – and became the main opposition party in truth, though it formally continued to say it is part of the coalition, supporting the government from outside.

These developments threw a great contradiction into sharp relief between Musharraf and the newly elected political system in which nobody was prepared to admit that Musharraf is the legitimate president. But the most reliable supporter of Musharraf for several months remained Asif Ali Zardari, the new supremo of the PPP, the largest party and later the president of Pakistan since 9 September 2008. Even he has gone on record saying frequently that he did not regard him as a de jure president; he is only a de facto president with which they are forced to carry on business of the state for the sake of social peace and to avoid serious clashes between the various institutions. But the second largest party, the PML (N) led by Mian Nawaz Sharif, refused to toe the PPP line. Nawaz Sharif was firm: Musharraf should go, preferably through an impeachment process and secondly the de jure chief justice of Pakistan, Justice Iftikhar Muhammad Chaudhry, should resume his office as quickly as possible. He remained firm on this line for all of 2007, 2008 and till 16 March 2009.

The government after May 2008 is being run and led by PPP with the help of several smaller parties. The PPP-led government remained at sixes and sevens for far too long on the issue of the top judge: PPP doggedly refused to reinstate the top judge the way the civil society and legal fraternity wanted: by an executive action, because the Supreme Court itself had declared Musharraf's 3 November actions as 'unconstitutional, illegal and void in law'. Indeed even after Musharraf was shown the door, the 'democratic' government kept saying that demands of the lawyers and civil society cannot be adhered to; Pakistan's 'permanent establishment' seemed to be arguing that all Musharraf's actions of 3 November were constitutional and legal and the Constitution stood amended the way Musharraf had wanted because the new Musharraf-created Supreme Court had validated his actions the very next day.

This judicial crisis seemed to be insoluble: the reason why Asif Ali Zardari and PPP were sticking to the coat-tails of Musharraf-created judicial system is that the American and the British governments had worked out a deal between Benazir Bhutto and Musharraf in which the president promised to promulgate a National Reconciliation Ordinance that would enable PPP leaders to go scot-free in all corruption cases in various courts inside and outside Pakistan; the state would withdraw those cases. Musharraf had in fact delivered his part of the deal; the NRO has made many PPP leaders squeaky clean and all criminal cases against them were dropped, including those of Asif Ali Zardari. This is one reason why PPP did not dare not go against Musharraf earlier or let Justice Iftikhar Muhammad Chaudhry again become the chief justice of Pakistan. Justice Chaudhry could not be trusted not to strike down the NRO just as Musharraf had feared that a number of cases against him would reach the Supreme Court in which an assertive and independent court would show him the door for his gross and admitted illegalities. Bush administration too, for its part, could not forget Justice Chaudhry's embarrassing insistence on finding out the whereabouts of all those who had 'disappeared' – many of whom are thought to be in America's many secret prisons outside the US. This was the heart of judicial crisis in Pakistan ever since the election of 18 February 2008.

Then there are relatively minor matters. There was sufficient mutual distrust and hatred between Musharraf and Nawaz

Sharif. Nawaz's first priority was to get the judges restored and the second was to have Musharraf impeached. Incidentally, this proved to be good partisan politics by Nawaz Sharif from a longer-term viewpoint. By championing the cause of the judges, he was making himself into a political colossus – mainly at the expense of PPP. He has hopes for expanding outside Punjab into other provinces also because the issue of the judges touched the heartstrings of civil society throughout Pakistan. This, however, worked to intensify the determination of Asif Ali Zardari and the PPP to prevent those brave judges who have borne the unendingly long wait in wilderness for over a year, with uncertain hope of restitution. This was a grand deadlock or crisis that prevented the coalition government from doing the right thing the right way. The whole country was, and politically still is, stuck in a quagmire of endless debate.

The PPP-led government did devise a less than honest way of 'restoring' judges and yet follow the army-led establishment's ukase of saving Musharraf from the wrath of the judges he sacked. Asif Zardari's legal aides, by unavowed methods, broke the unity of lawyers' movement and broke the resolve of many of the judges who had not taken the Musharraf 3 November oath. He thought he is one up on Nawaz Sharif; he persuaded them to accept fresh appointments with one all-important concession: their old seniority in the relevant court will remain. So Farooq Naek, the PPP law minister, was able to claim that the PPP government has redeemed its pledge of restoring the judges to pre-3 November position. The claim was false because all these re-employed judges had to take what can be called the Musharraf oath, thus accept Musharraf's 3 November actions as legitimate and constitutional. But many of the dismissed judges, including the chief justice, remained out who continued to refuse to take the Musharraf oath and be re-employed, albeit with old seniority.

Nawaz naturally remained on moral high ground when he said that the judges have not been reinstated as blameless and they are only new appointees under Musharraf's new terms. Since all the actions of 3 November by Musharraf were universally condemned by most jurists of high repute as illegal and unconstitutional, the claims by legal aides of the PPP government have not been proven and indeed it was a dishonest play on words for the unwary. PPP-led government had stabbed the lawyers' movement in the back dividing it, with the aim of making it a matter of jobs of some by judges while it should have been for the sake of the independence of judiciary and to strengthen rule of law by striking down a military dictator's autocratic orders to ensure the subservience of the superior judiciary to him. Moreover, the real chief justice of Pakistan was refusing to resign and go home or take the new oath; he held he remained the legitimate chief justice of Pakistan all along and the person Musharraf appointed as CJP was, and is, illegitimate and all that Farooq Naek, Zardari's man Friday in legal matters, has done is illegal. Nawaz's dour stance was that the original CJP is right and the government is still required to do as the real CJP says or else it would be a continuation of Musharraf regime. It was a dangerous situation with votaries of two legal systems contending over two Supreme Courts' legitimacy.

This PPP-led government never seemed to have any clear ideas of what to do and how or why. Its priorities were muddled about the economy. It has left the economy to its own inherent forces but it did try to give originally many subsidies to the users or consumers. What the impact of its first budget for 2008–09 and subsequent actions were muddled. But net upshot was to be is hard to discern initially, except increase the hardships manifold of the 70 per cent of the Pakistanis and the top 30 per cent have surely survived in their old style. However, a major issue confronting the government demand immediate attention. It has to be noted that unless the judges' issue was to be out of the way, the original coalition on which the government was based could not be revived between the PPP, the largest party and the second largest party PML (N), with other smaller parties staying in. This coalition in fact did not work well and broke down formally on 13 May 2008 when the PML (N) ministers resigned from the Central government en masse. The PPP-led government muddied the situation by refusing to reinstate the wrongfully sacked judges unconditionally and by striking down a dictator's illegal orders. It refuses to openly state it.

Stated simply, it recognized as wholly legitimate all the Musharraf actions of 3 November 2007. That is how, it held that they could only be reversed or undone by purging the Constitution of the new provisions Musharraf inserted, in the prescribed manner of amending it. PML (N), supported by most of the civil society and media, said this was rubbish. It asked the larger party, PPP, to declare that Musharraf's 'orders' were unlawful and void of legitimacy and throw them out by restoring the judges by an executive order. The issue continued to be a tough deadlock. The government, however, stayed firm on going by its own constitutional interpretation. This amounted to PPP's total endorsement of what General Musharraf said and did as fait accompli in the way the so called 'establishment' wanted.

Most of the smaller democratic parties in the opposition have always regarded army dictators as totally unlawful and illegitimate; in any case they takeover by breaking the Constitution that is the source of all legal system or is the grund norm. The parties one has in mind are PPP (for a time), PML (N), if partially, ANP and many in the All Parties Democratic Movement, mainly regional nationalist parties. All democrats regard the validations of successive dictators through amendments to the Constitution made by 'elected' National Assemblies, the elections to which were usually rigged by the ubiquitous ISI as invalid, while the latter became notorious for arranging 'positive results' for their army supremo of the day. All democrats think that as and when they can get elected, they would set up a proper, formal democracy based on truly representative National Assembly that would work under the original 1973 constitution (as it was passed). Thus the dross of all sorts of self-serving amendments to this basic law has to be removed by a genuine Parliament. All democrats were in fact pleasantly surprised by the results of 18 February election; all supporters of the dictator of the day, namely PML (Q) and various other splinters of PPP, suffered heavy setbacks. Parties opposed to Musharraf dictatorship won handsomely. How did this happen? Not that efforts to obtain 'positive results' were not reported to have been made.

European election observers have published various malpractices and faulty procedures they observed in 18 February election. Even so, the atmosphere (public opinion) created by Musharraf's foolish repression and the positive feelings created by the lawyers' movement for a free and assertive judiciary had made a tremendous impact on voters. All pressures, inducements and trickery by the ruling parties and the bureaucracy could not prevent most of the voters from voting for the Opposition candidates. This was in the traditional Pakistani conditions' context a veritable revolution.

People, therefore, hoped that these winning parties should come together to recreate proper democracy and to resolve the urgent economic problems of the people in and through the Parliament; and that was to be the forum for evolving national consensus over foreign and domestic policies. Musharraf, probably on US advice, delayed the convening of the National Assembly by over a month. Strange that no party demanded an early convening of the assembly and most allowed themselves to engage in what were in fact negotiations with Western ambassadors over no one knows what for sure. Possibly there were some conditions and policy recommendations that Western ambassadors were insisting upon because most ambassadors of great powers met most leaders several times. Most active of them were the US and British ambassadors. All this farce or tragic influence peddling was saddening to watch.

What should have happened was National Assembly should have been convened three or four days after the election results were announced. It should have been up to the winning parties to come up with a government within, say, a week or so. The assembly should have started taking substantive action with the formation of the new government because problems facing the country were huge and brooked no delay. To begin with, the winning parties showed dire poverty of ideas regarding what was needed to be done in the economy and in which broad sequence. One issue required to be tackled on day one was: the over sixty-two illegally sacked senior court judges and many of them under incarceration. The Prime Minister Yousuf Raza Gilani did show awareness of the problem by ordering the release of all the Judges under detention in his inaugural address. But he stopped at only releasing them from detention and did not order their reinstatement to the position that obtained before 3 November in all High and Supreme courts – before General Musharraf did his gross illegalities and made the big assault on superior judiciary.

The opinion of best judicial minds in Pakistan was clear: all the actions of 3 November were executive actions and could be undone by executive action by the prime minister. Musharraf's illegalities being many, including his decision to stand for the presidential election while being a government servant, his choice of the Electoral College drawn from about-to-die assemblies rather than waiting for the newly elected assemblies to form a new college that were about to be elected were actions that could not have passed the test of an independent judiciary's examination. The new elections had all but changed the country and the electoral victories of the PPP, PML (N), ANP were due mainly to the impression of the voters that the parties opposing Musharraf's cruel actions and stand for free judiciary for which the lawyers, civil society and media were campaigning for so long but the judges had to go on waiting out of their courts under duress.

The PPP-led government kept on flatly refusing to reinstate them for eighteen months. The government has used despicable tactics to divide the lawyers' movement that was against dictatorship and a subservient judiciary; they were for unalloyed democracy and rule of law. Sixty-two senior court judges had refused to take the new oath out of which quite a few have been appointed anew after taking the new Musharraf-prescribed oath. They, after nearly a year's utter uncertainty broke ranks and accepted government's terms. That led to their return to the courts. But it was re-employment; they had to take the same new oath they had at first rejected. But the law minister has made them the strange promise that they can have their old seniority and yet be a new appointee. Those judges who have succumbed to government's pressure and persuasion had seriously hurt the lawyers' movement and the cause of their brother Judges' independence. They are known as PCO judges.

The parties comprising the government share this shame of this effort to break the back of such a noble and selfless movement. People say this was mainly the result of a collusion between Musharraf and PPP's chief Asif Ali Zardari, now also president, with some input from the US interests because the White House and CIA too hated the CJP, Justice Iftikhar Muhammad Chaudhry, for his persistent probing of what has happened to all those many who 'disappeared' from Balochistan. It is commonly said and believed in the media that ISI handed them over to CIA. Not for nothing many Pakistanis feel being deceived. Anyway few parties seem to differ from the views of Musharraf on (a) economy and (b) on doing as the Americans dictate. After over a year, the government has not shown its policies in any reasonable detail or what it wants to do in the economy; there appears to be no new ideas on the big political polarization that has developed on foreign policy. For all practical purposes it seems Musharraf is still running Pakistan from his retirement retreat.

PML (N), on the other hand, did not agree with PPP position. It held that actions the general-president on 3 November, on his own admission, were unconstitutional and illegal. That a new pliant Supreme Court, headed by Justice Abdul Hameed Dogar, has validated those same illegal and unconstitutional actions was only to be expected, who was hurriedly sworn in after the de jure CJP, Justice Iftikhar Muhammad Chaudhry, was sacked but only after a seven-member bench headed by Justice Chaudhry himself had declared all those 3 November actions illegal and unconstitutional. This court was the creation of Musharraf's PCO. What else could be expected of it? The general's actions were illegal and unconstitutional on his own public admission and thus are null and void. The whole issue before Pakistanis was whether to accept a Supreme Court appointed under an illegal Emergency and PCO or to define their attitude in the legality of the Chaudhry-led SC. The latter was the legal SC that had struck down the Musharraf actions as illegal and unconstitutional on the same 3 November: the Emergency, PCO and other orders of president (and General) Musharraf for gagging the media. Thus all that the government was required to do was to issue an executive order, the way twenty-two Pakistan jurists of high repute had already recommended, saying that it was not required to amend the Constitution in order to restore the judges to their positions; they could be restored by a simple executive order because they had been removed by an executive order that was earlier found to be illegal and unconstitutional. Most of the legal fraternity has stuck to this view of the matter to this day.

The PPP government has, however, continued to accept this line of thinking. Thus the matter remained deadlocked on the issue of procedure. The PML (N) had disassociated itself with the PPP-led government way back on 13 May 2008, though both sides continue, curiously, to claim that the coalition somehow exists, while the two major parties in fact behave as ruling and opposition. The two have managed, for nearly two years, to keep up the impossible charade of maintaining this coalition in the Punjab while the PML (N) now sits in opposition in the National Assembly and differs with most policies of PPP. Well, coalition, at this writing, both exists and doesn't.

Another and immediate issue that will spill over to other contexts is the question of dealing with Islamic extremists in the NWFP's – Pakhtoonkhawa's as it wants to be renamed – tribal areas. It is a social and political tsunami. It has gone on rising and sweeping across the tribal areas and now it is no longer confined to tribal areas or even to the Pukhtoonkhawa. It is slowly spreading into Punjab and Sindh. Some of the semi-tribal areas, such as the Bara and Torkham, so close to both Peshawar and Khyber Pass, may technically be tribal areas but are part of the main artery of commerce and traffic between Pakistan and Afghanistan. These areas are infested with several extremist Islamic lashkars (armies). Most NATO forces are supplied mainly by Pakistan, though the US and NATO leaders are now negotiating a circuitous route through Russia and Central Asia; because this most suitable route through Pakistan has become vulnerable to interdiction. The main route of supply for Western troops in Afghanistan remains Pakistan. Interdictions have multiple causes: two rival extremists Sunni groups, divided along sub-sectarian line, frequently resort to fighting, thus disrupting supply vehicles.

Islamabad hasn't said much in reply to the US grumbling about interdictions in public. It has nothing to gain from the groups that do it. These groups found no difficulty in reneging on the accords or reneging in practice without owning it. The Americans' implied threat of doing what they had done in Vietnam in 1970s by heavily bombing Cambodia. Their new strategy in Pakistan is to hit out at supposedly those militants inside Pakistan who recoup and reequip themselves in sanctuaries inside Pakistan (mostly in FATA) and go out to make war inside Afghanistan against ISAF-NATO forces. The US shows it is relying on what is 'hot pursuit' doctrine. Doubtless, they have repeatedly exercised this right of 'hot pursuit'. They are using unmanned drones, flying ostensibly from Afghanistan to bomb FATA villages and have, in one case on 4 September 2008, landed troops inside Pakistan who killed many women and children, whether or not they also killed any high-value target which supposedly was their original purpose. Pakistan government and most parties oppose drones' operations. Americans have not rubbed the point in but have ambiguously said they have been permitted by Islamabad to do what they are doing while some reports said they operate in and from Pakistan. Mysteriously, except some Islamic and opposition parties continue opposing Drone operations but rest of Pakistan has fallen silent. But this has nevertheless inflamed Pakistani opinion and Pakistan Army, at one stage, itself had to warn the US that more such incursions will be resisted and fired upon. But it later piped down and now meekly tolerates what is hot pursuit. Pakistan obviously has permitted the Americans to station drones, personnel needed to operate them on its soil, as the US media have claimed and Pakistanis mostly are silent.

This issue had almost breached the cosy relationship between the US military and Pakistan Army. A crisis in the Pakistan–US relationship did arise and it took much climbing down by Pakistani side. Perhaps silence by Pakistan government is dictated by discretion. It seems the US has forced silence on Pakistan government. Gone are the days of Musharraf who, it appears, had secretly permitted their special forces to stay inside the Pakistan borders. CIA is also operating freely, obviously with Islamabad government's permission and the cases of cross border hot pursuit and bombing of Pakistan areas go on, supposedly for 'taking out high value suspects' hiding there. In most cases, it turned out that the intelligence on which the Americans sent in their drones was untrue and only innocent men, women and children were killed.

Many Pakistanis go to the length of saying this is an issue that may yet make or break Pakistan. That public opinion in Pakistan is totally against America is a well-recognized fact. This, at worst, can be taken as a conspiracy theory for which Pakistanis are famous. The government of Pakistan goes on saying that no foreign troops will be allowed inside Pakistan territory. It does not say anything about what the Americans who have been sending drones every now and then from across the border or from inside Pakistan taking out houses inside Pakistan's tribal areas. This, the public opinion insists, must end. The Americans are continuing to complain that Pakistan is hosting sanctuaries from which reinforcements for Taliban are coming into Afghanistan. Last year (2008), a 40 per cent increase in Taliban attacks has been recorded in Afghanistan; no let up has been reported since. The Americans are, claimed by many to be planning big action similar to what they had taken during the Vietnam war in Cambodia. They bombed Cambodia to their satisfaction on the assumption that the Vietcong were coming through this route into South Vietnam. Despite all the destruction in Cambodia, the Americans were still defeated in South Vietnam and had to run from there helter-skelter. The destruction in Cambodia did not help the Americans' cause at all. The same can be said about repeating it in Pakistan. In this case, consequences may be far more unexpected because of Pakistan's strategic significance.

Are the Americans likely to go to the extent of making a Cambodia of Pakistan? No one can say that with certainty. The current US politics is likely to colour military action in Afghanistan and the rest of the Middle East; the US government of Barack Hussein Obama is likely to last till 2012. Obama administration's policies are still evolving. What his policies would eventually be cannot be foreseen with any certainty. While it is possible to speculate on America's geo-strategic aims that perhaps do not change with the changes of governments. But how they are implemented is a subject on which a new government does make a noticeable difference. The problem is even bigger: Pakistan is not Cambodia of those days. It is a significant part of South Asia and has a nuclear deterrent of its own and a large army that is more than quasi-modern. It can scarcely be treated like the Cambodia of 1970s. Here a mere possibility has been noted.

Pakistan government began talking about the subject after a time. It firmly said that the ideology of Taliban, the real driving force, cannot be dealt with by mere military means. The ideas are in the mind. They cannot be killed with guns. Political methodology has to be employed, if an ideology has to be contained, diluted or countered by democracy's freedoms and economic construction. That is the way to tackle the issue in which military has to be used but only defensively when it becomes necessary. The main fight against extremist ideas has to be on the plane of ideas. It is Pakistan's own problem and Pakistanis have to resolve it. The debate, however, has subsided after the American officials used their carrot and stick methodology. While relatively high levels of aid were promised, the stick's length was also shown. It does seem that spectre of a military takeover too was broadly hinted at as General Ashfaque Pervez Kayani appears to have been won over as a result of amazing number of visits by American military's top brass. Pakistan seems to have accepted American ideas of how to resolutely conduct military operations against manifestations of Islamic zealotry, such as Taliban's. Pakistan has been fighting hard against Taliban, al-Qaeda and other extremists. It can be said the Yankees have bamboozled the Pakistani government into doing what the US wants and the way it wants. It can be said that the lure of higher levels of aid plus implied or hinted threats have made Pakistan do what the US wanted. They certainly are not repeating what they were saying soon after Obama's inauguration, backed by Pakistan National Assembly's restoration; no one mentions that resolution now.

It was obvious that either Pakistan has to fully allow the Americans to do what they think is required and let that happen everyday; or it has to firmly stop them. Pakistan goes on saying that no foreign troops would be tolerated on is territory. Fine. But what are the special forces doing in the tribal areas that the *New York Times* revealed earlier? There is a whole known network of CIA in the area. Why is it being tolerated? Doubtless, the assumption made by most Pakistanis is that they would do their own fighting inside Pakistan while the Americans and others can remain confined to Afghanistan. Being non-NATO ally too does not mean disrespect for Durand Line.

The Americans had, in theory, appeared to have accepted this thinking of Pakistanis and began talking of increasing the aid for economic construction in tribal areas and the figure bandied around was of $ 750 million. That is still in the Congress. But it is subject to changes in American thinking. The Americans like to shoot first and talk later. Perhaps that is due to the hubris of being the only superpower. But for Pakistanis it poses problems and anyhow US military operations on Pakistani soil require their assent. This is a subject that the PPP-led government has not tackled upfront, except talking tough but imprecisely. Even that has subsided. What of the continuing drone attacks on Pakistan territory and people? Are not the US special forces and CIA being tolerated on Pakistan territory? What if the Americans persist in taking much stronger action in Pakistan if they think it is necessary to win the war they are fighting?

This government is, in political terms, an American creation because Musharraf was clear in his mind that he would keep Benazir and Nawaz Sharif out of Pakistan permanently and hold and win the election in November 2007 the way he had done in 2002. It was only the Americans who insisted that 'you had better let them in, hold a relatively free election, allow democracy to flourish and that will give you a democratic face and this will strengthen your position. We will ensure they will keep you in the top job(s). Unfortunately that has not happened. Musharraf did survive for a while. But later all parties combined to throw him out and out he went on 18 August 2008. What did he or the war on terror gain from his democratic visage?

THE REALITY: THE GREAT LET DOWN

The government of Prime Minister Yousuf Raza Gilani took over in March 2008 amidst much hope of strengthening governance. What has he done since is a question being asked all around the country. There is physical movement, mostly ministers flitting around in big cities or frequently visiting other countries. But there is no apparent refashioning of policies or a coherent plan that the government is implementing. The fact is largely known that the Musharraf regime had allowed many crises of huge magnitude to accumulate. But this government is not seen as tackling any of them. It makes breezy statements to reassure that it will soon control inflation; 'we will arrest the price spirals; we are at it'. Such words are not followed by concrete action to inspire confidence in the populace. This was initially a coalition government comprising many parties. It is now primarily a PPP government that is now controlled by Asif Ali Zardari, who has been elected the president also. Other parties are now left to influence policies after PML (N) walked out of the coalition just two months after government formation. President Zardari, as many perceive, appears to be altogether too involved in personal affairs that somehow require his moving around the world: Dubai, London, New York and sometimes visiting Pakistan also. The other major party in the government, as noted, was PML (N) led by Mian Nawaz Sharif that walked out of this basically PPP-led government quite early. Quite a few smaller parties are still in it: JUI (F) led by Maulana Fazlur Rehman, Awami National Party, led by Asfandyar Wali, a secular Pushtoon nationalist party that has given a lie to many who think that Talibanization is the unavoidable fate for the North Western Frontier Province. These two largely Pushtoon parties are near total incompatibles; JUI is a religious party that was quite friendly to General Musharraf and produced mujahideen and Taliban in its madrassas successively for ISI in the past and ANP is a secular nationalist party that defeated the former and has displaced its provincial government in the NWFP. What it does show is that a majority of ordinary Pushtoons chose in 2008 to vote for a professedly secular Pushtoon nationalist party in the face of the rising tide of Taliban and other extremist groups that have enjoyed the support of religious parties. And these votes also suggest that a majority of Pushtoons are ready to vote for a primarily secular Pushtoon party en masse.

There is also another ally of PPP; it is a sub-national or ethnic secular party, aspirating the hopes and wishes of mohajirs, though necessarily confined to urban centres of Sindh, particularly Karachi and Hyderabad. But it is too tightly controlled by 'Altaf Bhai', Altaf Hussain, who lives in Britain as a British citizen but controls the party: MQM. It was one of very close friends and firm supporter of President Pervez Musharraf just as JUI (F) could always be counted upon to support the military as and when the real need arises. Even so, because of this, this Zardari-controlled government has many handicaps. One of these was that since the two biggest parties, PPP and PML (N), were pursuing divergent politics that excluded full cooperation. Thus it had a clouded future. The PPP was originally a left-of-centre party that was formed by charismatic Zulfikar Ali Bhutto, who within three years of its formation in Lahore, went on to win big in the first free general election in Pakistan's history in 1970

– the first election held a quarter of a century after the formation of Pakistan. All earlier provincial and local elections were commonly seen as having been rigged. PPP was a party that was woven around the personality of Mr Bhutto and has continued to live as a result of the Bhutto legend and by now it seems to have become a cult. The party is now firmly right-of-centre one, led mostly by landed aristocrats though talks incessantly of common people, their lives and the sacrifices made by its leaders for the poor that indeed were many. This party has no specific plan or philosophy, except to talk big about the common man and to imply that it would, some day, give 'roti, kapra aur makan' (bread, clothing and house) to all. For the fiscal year (2009–10) PPP government's budget has allocated Rs 70 billion for BISP (Bhutto Income Support Programme) for poor families that will give one thousand rupees a month to each certified poor family throughout the country. There is no specific law to govern it or to determine who exactly is poor enough to be entitled to receive Rs1,000 a month. Whether this will solve the problem of poverty and unemployment or that the operation would be equitably implemented.

But the other major party was sharply focused on the happenings of the year 2007, particularly the judges' issue. It was inflexible in the demand that the sacked judges be restored to their offices without laying down conditions so as to undo the illegal and unconstitutional acts that Musharraf committed on 3 November 2007 by his executive action. The PML (N) agreed that this restoration may be backed by a National Assembly resolution, though it is not really necessary. It bases its reasoning on the lawyers' argument about the actions of General Musharraf on 3 November 2007 being wholly unconstitutional and illegal executive actions, as declared by the Supreme Court's larger bench on 3 November, itself. The PML (N) parted company with PPP in this point of fact, though not on any other ideological matters.

There were a number of indications and statements of politicians that behind the scenes intrigues were afoot from early on in 2008. One of the intrigues was attributed to former General Musharraf, later president. He insisted the judges he sacked must remain out in the cold and should not and cannot be reinstated because his actions of 3 November were later on validated subsequently by the Supreme Court that he reconstituted on 3 November. The PPP supremo, Asif Ali Zardari, bought Musharraf's reasoning and his party's government made it a point of prestige that those judges can be restored on fulfilling two conditions: first, a constitutional amendment has to undo 3 November actions because SC's validation of these provisions made them a part of the Constitution. Secondly, these judges return to their chambers can only be after their re-employment. Zardari bought these propositions and not that of six former SC judges and any number of High Court Judges. For over a year, Zardari line was official line and PPP government stuck to that position until 15 March 2009 under Zardari's influence. Meanwhile, Zardari was seen to be in cahoots with Musharraf and the army. He paid a heavy political price for siding with Musharraf and keeping sacked judges out in the cold up to two full years. Zardari and PPP got all the blame. It is now commonly doubted whether PPP can repeat the success at the hustings it achieved in February 2008. But for now, both are in power, though actually it is 1990s troika – army chief, the president and prime minister – now make the decisions.

Zardari continued to carry out Musharraf's desires and was not ready to reinstate the judges, especially the chief justice, Justice Iftikhar Muhammad Chaudhry, which he could have restored within minutes of his decision – the way Prime Minister Gilani released all the judges by a verbal executive order even before he had taken the oath of office. People see a long-term intrigue behind PPP's refusal to restore all the Judges; the intention seems to have been to isolate and hurt Nawaz Sharif and his party while preserving his (Zardari) own image of being a sagacious politician who actually wants to take all others with him. The original idea was to drop PML (N) whose leader Nawaz Sharif was a bete noire of President Musharraf and no friend of Zardari either. Nawaz, it is believed, reciprocates as much ill will towards both Musharraf and Zardari in his heart. Musharraf's advice to PPP was to take PML (Q)'s members in the coalition in place of PML (N) that had been formed before the election to the National Assembly in 2002 and many members in the Senate – in fact a majority of the Senate – and take all the others like JUI (F) and MQM. There is also a PML (Functional) led by Pir Saheb of Pagara who is an old stalwart supporter of GHQ. JUI (F) and MQM would provide along with ANP adequate strength to the government and it would be free of the constant pressure being exerted by Nawaz Sharif that the judges be restored. Zardari was attracted to the idea.

But other factors – mainly Zardari's personal ambitions and image of one who reconciliates – postponed it until after his own election as the president and a suitable occasion. The mantra the Anglo-Americans taught him was reconciliation as a basis for a broad-based government to fight Islamic extremists. Which is why he and PPP began with wooing PML (N) to come join hands and let's throw out Musharraf first. Nawaz could not have been asked for anything better. He supported the move for impeachment and even agreed to let him go scot-free if he resigns. Musharraf resigned. Pakistanis still want to know what has changed with Musharraf's departure?

It is also said that the former general still seems to think that he has a residual support in his former constituency, the generals and Pentagon. Others demur. They say that a retired general is as good or as bad as any other civilian. Only serving generals matter; retired ones do not. Be that as it may, the old King's party, the PML (Q), had been vigorously propagating that this government has been altogether too lazy and too incompetent; it has done nothing about the inflation; it has not been able to do anything to ensure regular supply of wheat or *atta* throughout the country; there are too frequent electricity breakdowns; and *atta* becomes scarce and prices shoot up temporarily in many areas which is in addition to the steady creep up of prices as a result of private trade's hoarding and profiteering. The PML (Q) is performing the role of an opposition party but would be happy to join the crowded ruling crowd. Let no one forget that up to a point the tug of war between the two largest parties, PPP and PML (N), has sometimes stymied the government on important issues, though its self-regard and self-praise leaves it little time to do anything positive or constructive.

In the period the PPP-led government has ruled Pakistan many crises have worsened. They were long in the making but their onset have broken on the country with a gale force and each crisis was seen to have struck suddenly; the government's ability to assess and perceive a crisis in the making was singularly absent.

We can divide its difficulties into political and economic ones. Let's take the economic ones first. The background is that Pakistan has largely been run by conservative landlord-ridden parties that have alternated in government whether under the generals who take one group or other of landlords and follow a policy orientation that the Americans recommend or under civilian political leaders that are landlords. Let no body forget the basic character of Pakistan state: in economic matters it has remained the same, though landlords' own practices have evolved; most landlords of above the medium size have learnt to become gentlemen farmers, use tractors and other machines; the old share-cropping system has been giving way to what is plantation-farming. That has released large numbers of share croppers – and many subsistence farmers too – who have no or little land to work on and no jobs. Villages are now full of hordes of the unemployed poor. They trek to nearest cities and from there to larger ones and eventually try to emigrate, legally or illegally.

Pakistan is a state that consumes more than it produces. The differential comes from America and other donors, though the American and other aid also means that at the end of the day, foreign debts increase. Pakistan state has also been a rentier one. For one thing, its economy does not produce the resources to sustain a military of approximately a million strong. Islamabad's effort has been to keep it as modern as Indian Army is. The motivation for what amounts to renting out its army to the Americans was that, with their help, it can be kept modernized and well trained plus some economic development would then become possible. The Americans have done their 'duty' and have given a lot of money so far. But the rest of the economy has been run and developed in a manner that was based on America's academic advice. Initially it was advised to do everything contrary to what Jawaharlal Nehru was doing in India. Later still it has always run the economy on the basis of what the Washington consensus prescribed in all successive stages.

Pakistan was usually advised against too great a local effort to mobilize resources to attain high saving rates (which will lead to high investment rates). The best thing to do was to keep the economy as near laissez faire as possible and to depend on foreigners' excess savings in the shape of FDIs (foreign direct investments) for progress in productive capacity should be oriented to the needs of foreign markets. That has been the grand design. It has been followed more or less for sixty long years under slightly differing formulations. Later, of course, this basic paradigm has been called the deregulation, liberalization and privatization or globalization. The result is that Pakistan now imports something like $ 45 billion while its exports have not gone beyond $ 19 billion. Such a huge trade imbalance can only lead to a heavily depreciated rupee that brings all manner of instability through huge current account deficits and growth in indebtedness. All this puts pressures on the price line; inflation is built into this pattern of overconsumption. The overconsumption includes the requirements of the military that actually needs a minimum of $ 500 to 600 million every year for current overseas payments, may be considerably more on occasions when new weapon systems are introduced.

This expenditure of $ 500 million does not include the replacement of major ordnance: tanks, aircrafts, big guns, etc. That requires huge amounts that have to be especially mobilized by Pakistan's Islamic and pro-Western diplomacy. The real facts about how Pakistan's armed services have been equipped and kept pace with technology change from decade to decade is not known. But ultimately the figures of the foreign debts tell its own story. Pakistan, for instance, owed something like $ 45 to 46 billion in the year 1998 soon after it had exploded six nuclear devices. In 2009 after many reschedulings and write offs, it owes $ 50 billion to foreigners and another $ 50 billion in domestic debts. That is something like 95 per cent of the GDP. It could not service its debts in 1998 that required $ 5 billion. Earlier such difficulty to service debts was felt in the year when Pakistan fought a war with India in 1971. In both cases, IMF bailed out Pakistan and put it under its own economic regime.

The root cause of the difficulty remains Pakistan's overconsumption, enhanced by military's requirements, compared to what Pakistan could possibly earn from exports. Pakistani exports have always lagged behind imports and the direct consequence of that was the influence of America dominates every field of decision-making in Pakistan. That is still the position. Pakistan was short of wheat awhile ago; it could not pay for all its oil it imports; it cannot import all the fine food stuffs that is usually imported for its upper classes. That was the crisis. What will happen is that the Americans and the IMF and World Bank would find ways of keeping Pakistan going with enhanced American influence on decision-making.

It is obvious that economic and political facts remaining the same, it would seem to suggest that the Americans would remain the only saviour; Pakistan's politics too would therefore stay under their thumb. Pakistan had finally opted for the West in October 1953 and has remained allied to the West, particularly the Americans – mainly for the sake of maintaining to some extent its deteriorating balance of power with India; the leitmotif of its policies has stayed the uninterrupted arms race with India from virtually day one. Unless this arms race ends, there would be little change in Pakistan's circumstances.

A political crisis in the relationship between America and Pakistan has also matured. Most media commentators and politicians sense that the Americans may eventually undertake military action in some of the Pakistani areas (initially perhaps in the NWFP's tribal areas). But this is going to be a make or break development as noted awhile ago. What this would mean is that the war that the West – US and NATO powers – are fighting in Afghanistan has all but extended itself to various parts of Pakistan some day. The West has already extended the operations to many areas that violates the independence of Pushtoon tribesmen on a big scale and their reaction would only be to fight more fiercely alongside the Taliban and various other extremist groups, including al-Qaeda and others. The end of this war is not in sight. This is a major and growing threat.

All Pakistanis want that the American troops should not violate Pakistan's territorial sovereignty. True, this sovereignty has become threadbare already; it is being nibbled away a little here and a little there that Pakistan government first used to deny and protest at drone attacks. It is now clear that formal protests were a charade and sometimes Islamabad pathetically protested that America is playing with fire. It was all a hoax. Americans have gone on making drone attacks; there are now no protests. All US did was to leak the news that these drones are based on Pakistan territory along with personnel for servicing the machines, some special forces to protect drones and CIA's network under a proper secret agreement with Pakistan. There was egg on some face but that led to no change. For Americans it is business as usual. There used to be much talk of playing with fire. The fire part of it now refers to the reactions in other Pakistan areas; and it will no longer be possible to confine it to NWFP's tribal areas. Most nationalistic Pakistanis' reaction may coalesce with and strengthen Taliban-like militant groups. Taliban and such like would inevitably be perceived as playing the role of a national resistance against foreign occupation because Western objectives can no longer be achieved without American boots in bulk being on Pakistan's soil. They cannot remain confined to certain areas they have occupied in the beginning. The vicissitudes of such a war need to be visualized. It would surely be by far more serious than what the West has found in Iraq or Afghanistan. The reason is that Pakistan itself has been playing with fire in the ideological games for shortsighted goals.

Pakistan from day one, indeed earlier, has been talking of Pakistan for the Musalmans of India and the greatness of Islam was somehow involved. The invocation of Islam without necessarily meaning anything concrete can only be seen as deceptive; in reality it was only a way of gathering votes for specific political purposes; it was exploiting the communal identity of Muslims vis-à-vis the larger community of Hindus. But as soon as Pakistan was formed this shallow rhetoric about Islam became a fetter on the feet of all Pakistan governments. The Muslim League governments in the initial years had little else in their repertoire than of talking about a rather ersatz Muslim nationalism for Pakistan, a thing which is seen by most Islamists to be a contradiction in terms because Islamic identity being confined to Pakistan would violate Islam's universality.

Then, the local ulema who had initially opposed Pakistan got together and demanded that since Islam was invoked during Pakistan movement (1940–47)` and this is a predominantly Muslim state, it must therefore be ruled by Islamic Shariah serving as the basic law. This upset the Pakistan government no end because they could make no real reply to this demand. Although they did want to be a mostly secular dispensation albeit with Islamic rhetoric, it was hard to say so. Muslim League leadership came up with the clever-by-half response in the shape of Objective Resolution of March 1949. It has remained controversial because the liberals say far too much has been given away to the mullahs and mullahs have not been satisfied because they want the same fruit of power for themselves in the political game being played; they saw the Muslim League having used Islamic phraseology gained power whereas the ML actually envisaged a Western style parliamentary democracy – too non-Islamic and hypocritical. This discord has continued.

Today even the unique Islamic state wallahs need to be confronted with their own contradictions: they should explain why they ardently supported the US in 1980s and called it jihad. This cause was pursued by Pakistan with the joint efforts of the American CIA, the intelligence agencies of Britain, Germany, Iran, Saudi Arabia and even Israel to produce mujahideen for the Afghan war of 1980s strictly for Western geo-strategic interests against the Soviets in Afghanistan. Why was this termed a jihad in which President Reagan tom-tommed the mujahideen as freedom fighters? These jihadis have bequeathed to Pakistan a culture and fascination for jihad for others' interests; it has also led to the huge spread of Kalashnikovs and easy money from narcotics. The process was corrupt from beginning to end. The nexus of Western cash for the jihad was never a secret. The term jihad made the jihadis, as individual, to expect paradise if they died or some more money if they came back as Ghazis. In retrospect, this cynical exploitation of popular faith of simple Pushtoons for imperial ambitions of the US – and of some bizarre aims of Pakistani generals – has never been widely discussed, much less emphasized. Pakistan Army improved upon this ignoble heritage by producing an even more committed, ruthless and non-compromising jihadis, the Taliban of 1990s by same methods.

The Taliban performed wonders, with the help of the ISI, and conquered 80 per cent of Afghanistan within two years and set up an Islamic Caliphate under Mullah Muhammad Umar. Islamabad's rulers thought that they had become the overlords of Afghanistan. That delusion lasted no more than six years but did much more damage. Soon the Americans demanded from the Taliban Caliph Mullah Umar certain concession on behalf of the US oil company, UNOCAL, that he refused. Soon enough, the US Administration found a reason to invade Afghanistan, destroy the Caliphate and occupied the country. President George W. Bush 'persuaded' Pakistan's military dictator – who until then was taken to be the suzerain of Afghanistan – to join the US-assembled 'Coalition of the Willing' and fight their erstwhile protégés, the Taliban. Not surprisingly Pakistan military quickly fell in line and joined the US-led coalition to fight war on 'Islamo-fascism', Bush's favourite description of Taliban.

Eight years down the line, Pakistan Army is seriously engaged in fighting Taliban of various hues, mostly in FATA, many Taliban-like groups' depredations now extend to places in NWFP and Punjab; indeed they seem to be spreading their operations to all parts of the country. After their formal defeat in Afghanistan the Taliban ran away to Pakistan, the only place where they could have run to. They have regrouped and they are now fighting both in Afghanistan against the West and the war is now being fought inside Pakistan areas inevitably because they have now become the sanctuary of all militant groups. The Americans are not factually wrong. There was, or is, no other place where Taliban could take refuge. It is history's big irony. Pakistan elites are now paying for the empty Islamic rhetoric that they had used over more than a hundred years in a big way.

Insubstantial, shallow and insincere, Islamic slogan mongering has now produced a monster. This could be Pakistan's nemesis. That Americans might attack Pakistan because they want to pursue the Taliban to the bitter end and at stake are Pakistan's nuclear 'assets': the means of defence have now become a vulnerability. What a big accident of history! It may soon be also be a part of the price Pakistani and other Muslims have to pay for all they have been thoughtlessly slogan mongering about Islam for over a hundred years.

The second major crisis that needs to be tackled, and is not altogether too hard to do so, there have been persistent decades-long demands from Sindh, Balochistan and NWFP that they should be given decision-making powers regarding their own areas and that their resources should be put to use in a way that they benefit the particular province. The autonomy demand for provinces has been too old and can no longer be postponed.

When 1973 Constitution was being written, the demand was raised full throated by these provinces even in that assembly over which charismatic Zulfikar Ali Bhutto presided. But the Constitution in fact, retained a thing called Concurrent List in the Constitution over which both Centre and province can legislate. But the vital detail is that Centre's legislation would take precedence if both Centre and province legislate on a particular subject. That arrangement was to be abolished in ten years time. It is now thirty-six years and it has not been abolished. What it takes to abolish it? The problem has to be looked at from the point of view of the smaller provinces. They see that the bureaucracies, civil and military, at the Centre are in fact the same in provenance as those in the province of Punjab. It is this bureaucracy's decision-making from day-to-day that gives it power, privilege and also pelf that they do not want to give up. National Assembly comprises 63 per cent deputies from Punjab; that ensures Centre's overriding powers over provinces and their resources; the Centre spends on what it likes.

To repeat, there is a terrible amount of trust deficit among the provinces. Take any major issue like division of waters of the Indus River system: Sindh frequently complains and continues to believe that Punjab is stealing its water – far more water than is its due. Balochistan has frequently accused Sindh of not giving its share of Indus River water. Frontier is terribly opposed to Kalabagh Dam on which the Centre has been dead set on implementing it. People saw that what was intended through Kalabagh Dam and Thal Canal project was to irrigate the arid soils of Bahawalpur area, where many generals have their own lands, including perhaps General Musharraf. There are differences over the provinces' shares in the profits of WAPDA: Frontier wanted that the profits of electricity generated in its areas should come back to it. Other provinces want similar things. These issues have been on the minds of lawmakers from all the four provinces. Few politicians actually trust one another. If this is not tackled honestly through reviving and empowering the Council of Common Interests, a constitutional body and by abolishing Concurrent List, big trouble will ensue. A modicum of honesty from all politicians is, however, needed. But somehow few expect it.

Then, there are the questions of social solidarity and equality of citizens. Over 70 per cent of Pakistani people is certified poor because they earn less than two dollars a day. This is the commonly accepted World Bank criterion. The poor over the years have been made even poorer by persistent high rates of inflation over the decades. The rich-poor disparity has continued to grow. The trickle-down theory of economics prescribed that let there be GDP growth, some prosperity will trickle down to the poor. In Pakistan's case it can be said with certitude that this has been tried for virtually sixty years and the disparities of income, both vertical and horizontal – between provinces and social classes – have increased. Punjab has in fact grown more and has a larger GDP than others. It has produced a fairly well to do middle class that is industrial and commercial in origin. It is true that Punjab has preserved its land-owning gentry who are political masters in the sense that most of the members of the Punjab and national assemblies are landlords, big and some very big. Similarly the provincial assembly of Sindh comprises mostly landlords, again big and very big, except its urban deputies. In the Frontier, there is an admixture of old political workers but the complement of landlords is notable. Land reforms, much tom-tommed in Bhutto's time, have never been implemented or conceived in terms of effecting real social change. Poverty for a large majority of Punjabis is as much a fact of life as in other provinces; only some social groups are rich.

Consequently the poorer classes in the villages everywhere are, under economic pressure, losing their traditional livelihood of being share croppers. They lose land because landlords are increasing the size of their actual self-farming unit and are using modern machinery that requires fewer farm hands. There is a veritable Closure Movement, particularly in southern Punjab. The evicted trek out from the villages to cities and try to emigrate to Middle East, Europe and elsewhere. In cities 50 per cent of population lives in tiny houses with insecure roofs, usually tin, asbestos or even straw mats. Their health is poor. Malnutrition is widespread and incidents of various diseases that originate in unclean water and malnutrition are high and absence of knowledge about hygiene is also widespread. Their social and economic conditions in cities are equally bad. They have no regular job; they merely eke out a living; vending all kinds of things in the streets and their women working in the homes of middle-class people as domestic helps. Neither has the state ever provided enough schools for their children nor have they ever been persuaded to send their children to schools – that do exist. Population growth rate has scarcely ever fallen. The old medieval ideas of the number of children being the Will of God, rules. And He will, one way or another, look after the new-borns. Thus, it does not matter how many children one produces! There is supposed to be the quasi-religious sanction for refusing to plan families.

Then there is the long tradition in Pakistan of military taking over the governments. Military in point of fact acts as the strongest and most well organized political party in the country. It requires a volume of resources from the economy that it can not spare. The earliest ruling politicians, or really bureaucrats in the early 1950s, actually did what amounted to renting out the army to the Americans. The unwritten and even unspoken understanding was that let the armed forces' foreign exchange needs be met by American aid and it would be at their disposal for their geo-strategic purposes. That arrangement since 1954 has continued to this day. In 1980s America needed to shoo off the Soviets from Afghanistan; it leaned on Pakistan and it obliged. All American aid was thus retrospectively justified as being in its own interests. This relationship needs to be corrected. Right now the crisis in the relations between Pakistan and America has reached a stage where Americans are growling and might one day even invade parts of Pakistan before too many months. The subject has been discussed elsewhere at some length. But here the mere fact has to be noted that the real cost of this foreign policy has to be paid by the people now who had decided nothing. Such are the wages of past political sins by unrepresentative rulers.

US Interests and Role in Pakistan

Pakistan–American relations' history begins with the initial vague Pakistani effort to woo the US into becoming a close friend of Pakistan and invest in the new country substantially. Although it was soon after the East–West cold war had begun circa 1946 initially over Iran, the US was far more interested in winning over India than the new and unpredictable country that was much smaller and poorer than India in the initial post-independence period. It is only when the US was finally disappointed with India's policies under Jawaharlal Nehru that it fell back on Pakistan on a rebound, so to say. It made the first seminal agreement with Pakistan in the autumn of 1953. It is interesting to remember who the signatory of that agreement was. On Pakistan's side the signatures were of Pakistan Army's first Pakistani commander-in-chief, General Ayub Khan and the Pentagon was the other party. Ever since, Pakistan and US are allies, though this alliance has had many ups and downs. The basis of US–Pakistan alliance was the strategic location of Pakistan's two wings: the western one at the junction of Gulf region, the southern Asian nations of Turkey, Iran and Afghanistan and the rest of historical India. The other wing would be an important addition to whatever the US was to work out by way of unity of Southeast Asia for security. Security of both the Southeast Asia and the Middle East was very much on Americans' mind for consolidating its own security (global domination).

The US gave something like $ 3 billion in the dollars of those days up till 1970 in aid that largely went to build Pakistan's armed forces. The Americans were generous in aid by Pakistani standards. But they had put one stiff condition on its military aid. None of it was to be used against any other country, except

Communist powers. Pakistan of course did not adhere to this condition. It freely used ammunition, guns, tanks, aircrafts and other equipment in its wars or skirmishes with India. At least a year before the second India–Pakistan war of 1965, the Americans were warning Pakistan not to use their equipment against India. But Pakistan had used this equipment in the Rann of Kutch skirmish (1964) and did so more freely during the 1965 war. The Americans were angry and froze all their aid in 1964. Pakistanis were greatly upset and angry by American harshness in freezing their aid, though they should have expected it. The relationship did sour on both sides for a few years.

Looking back now, it would seem that Pakistanis had perhaps always nursed a desire to have an alternative to the US, if the relationship soured. That alternative emerged after Pakistan signed the border agreement with China in 1963 that caused consternation in the West and India. President General Muhammad Ayub Khan in the post-1965 war period flirted with the idea of becoming an Asian Charles de-Gaulle: broadly and politically with the West but acting more independently in national interests. His propagandists were tom-tomming his great role in Asia as also about the potentialities of the Sino–Pakistan friendship. It was conceived as a sort of insurance policy against America withholding its aid suddenly and otherwise dictating what to do and what not to do. Indeed during that period after 1965 war and before the Americans relented later in 1960s, the ebullience of Pakistan foreign minister Zulfikar Ali Bhutto under Ayub Khan also resulted in Pakistan trying to nudge closer to Russia. Indeed Russians gave some token military aid for a short while. That made the Indians remonstrate with the Russians and the latter froze up for a long while because the Soviets simply could not annoy India for the sake of Pakistan. But later at the end of 1960s, during Dr Henry Kissinger's tenure as the foreign minister, Pakistan acted as a bridge between the US and China. Kissinger flew to China from Pakistan secretly and the rest of the story of the Sino-American détente is well known.

But the Americans displeasure over Pakistan's friendship with China did dissipate over the next few years. For one thing, the Americans did not, at that stage, fear China so much, and indeed they wanted to encourage it, as a part of their grand geo-strategy to cause a rift between two communist giants: Russia and China and Pakistan's closeness with China came in handy to the US for building bridges with it. The Americans succeeded in widening the gulf between the Soviets and China and the net beneficiary of it was Pakistan, in the sense that American opposition to Pakistan getting closer to China or taking aid from it was considerably diluted. After the Ayub period and the 1971 war in which Pakistan was finally defeated and its eastern wing became Bangladesh, the US role in installing Zulfikar Ali Bhutto as the next ruler of Pakistan has not been much discussed after the second military dictator, General Yahya Khan, had brought disaster to Pakistan. The US enthusiastically cooperated with Bhutto and he had begun by reinvigorating the remaining multilateral pact with America, the Baghdad Pact, that later came to be known as CENTO. But Bhutto also had other sides to him: he was a consummate populist leader who exploited both the latent pan-Islamist feelings among Pakistanis as well as his own version of mild CIA-approved socialism. But above all else he was a militant Pakistani nationalist who started the secret Pakistani programme of acquiring nuclear capability. The Americans were mighty angry when they discovered that Bhutto was emphatic on going ahead with this programme. It is said that the mass movement that brought Bhutto down and the way he was disposed off had had an unprovable American input.

The US was, even in 1950s, able to exercise its influence over what happens in Pakistan. No government changed in Pakistan except with their knowledge, and perhaps concurrence. But before an anti-Bhutto protest movement started in 1977, he was closely cooperating with American CIA's sub-rosa schemes in Asia. The 1980s Islamic jihad in Afghanistan was planned during Bhutto's days by the Americans, Iranians and the Pakistanis in the 1970s. The scheme was to win over Afghanistan from its neutral perch and to bring it to the bosom of the Western nations' comity in Asia, that is, Turkey, Iran, Pakistan and Afghanistan would make a fine bloc under Iranian leadership to hold up the expected Soviet march to a warm water port. On the one side, Pakistanis were in their own rather juvenile way, planning their greatness through nuclear weapons against American wishes, which aim brought Bhutto down. On the other side, Bhutto's enthusiastic participation in Western intrigues and schemes about Afghanistan had the unrealistic aim of being able to acquire more influence in Afghanistan than Iran and India in that landlocked country. But Bhutto's nuclear project overrode all other 'services' to the West and Kissinger never forgave him for this sin. But no one else in Pakistan, including the new military dictator General Zia-ul-Haq – who later became a virtual errand boy of the CIA – had the gumption to stop the nuclear programme. Such was the state of popular sentiment.

After a while the Americans began to ignore what Pakistanis were doing. Why? Because what else they were doing was jolly good from American viewpoint. They were enthusiastically helping to plan and execute the snatching of Afghanistan from a near-communist pro-Soviet government there. Americans were overly enthusiastic about this Pakistani role. A minor debate in Pakistan has gone on as to who the real architect of the Afghan jihad of 1980s was. Some Pakistani generals claimed that it was their ideas that ultimately prevailed and the Iranians, the Americans and the British merely agreed and followed, while there are others who think that it was the CIA that masterminded the whole idea and gave Pakistan a lead role in it was due to simple geographical reasons – the ready availability of the Pakistan Army which could actually achieve it. Anyhow, the US role became far stronger inside Pakistan after the 1980s, though after the peace agreement of 1987 the Americans basically lost interest in Afghanistan and, the writer has reasons to understand, that they left it to Pakistanis' wits to control chaotic Afghanistan. General Zia was, for obscure reasons, opposed to the American wishes of abiding by the agreements and the first Pakistani prime minister under a military dictator who dared to differ with his boss, M.K. Junejo, asserted and acted like an elected and democratic prime minister (with American approval). Which is how he could defy General Zia. But after the death of President Zia, a new election took place.

Incidentally, there is no reason to discuss here how Zia died because many Pakistanis, including his own son, think that Americans were somehow involved in the plane crash in which Zia perished. Others think that it was an internal affair of the Pakistan Army. But all this is neither here nor there, except that

America's finger is anyhow seen by everyone in every major political development in Pakistan and not all of it is paranoia. But on the whole, during the period from 1987 to mid 1990s, Americans had more or less given up being too closely interested in Pakistan. While the alliance survived, the Americans again became greatly concerned about Pakistan's nuclear ambitions, even though by 1986 the matter was past the stage where it could be throttled. The Americans had been very angry with Pakistan since before 1979. But later they simply ignored it because it became a fait accompli circa 1954. Pakistan became a nuclear-capable power probably by 1986, while it had mastered the technology of uranium enrichment by February 1984 on its own admission. The Americans put Pakistan under sanctions after Pakistan officially admitted in 1990 that it had one nuclear weapon in dismantled form. These sanctions have remained throughout the period of 1990s while after the explosions in 1998 more sanctions were imposed on Pakistan. The US, despite being an ally of Pakistan, has actually remained rather distant.

There was another reason for the US displeasure with Pakistan. After 1987, a non-violent secular political agitation had started in Indian-controlled Kashmir against Indian rule that began as a result of a specific cause: the rigging of 1987 elections in the J&K state. Pakistani generals by that time had become overly confident. They had helped US win a great victory over the Soviet Union and some generals actually claimed that Pakistan had reasons to be proud of virtually destroying the Soviet Union. General Mirza Aslam Beg, the new army chief after Zia, did not take over the government on Zia's death but continued to direct all major developments in the country. The so called 'democratic' governments enjoyed all the protocol but little power.

Pakistani generals saw in that situation a great opportunity of inflicting a thousand cuts on India without it being able to retaliate in any serious way. That was done through transforming that peaceful and secular political agitation for azadi into an Islamic jihad. Beg and other generals were confident that now that Pakistan has acquired nuclear capability – by then it was widely known that Pakistan had acquired nuclear capability (by 1986) – they went ahead to make Indians squirm by supporting the Kashmiris and infiltrating their jihadis among them who would fight the infidel Indian Army and the latter would be unable to do anything big because of Pakistanis' exaggerated notions of the deterrent value of the nuclear weapons that Pakistan had begun accumulating. The Americans did not like it one little bit. The Islamic jihad in Indian controlled Kashmir could only, in their view, lead to either a possible new war, perhaps involving a nuclear exchange. They wanted to discourage Pakistan from doing so but then, with the American sanctions in place, the displeased Pakistani generals simply refused to listen. They went ahead and for almost a decade they continued to do what they possibly could do in Kashmir.

It was only much later that the Indians convinced themselves that they need not be deterred. Instead, they can look forward to deterring Pakistan. The basis of their thinking was that Pakistan will have to be deterred by a much larger nuclear power of India and this came out in the crisis of 2002. The Indian 'war minister' adumbrated a new line: nuclear weapons deter nuclear weapons; the more realistic option is always conventional war.

It has now been disclosed by the ex-President Bill Clinton that Indian thinking was that let there be a nuclear war if it becomes necessary. The Indians painted a horrific picture of nuclear exchanges. Indians would lose somewhere between 300 to 500 million; they will be incinerated by Pakistan strikes. But in reply we will wipe out all 120 million Pakistanis. They would presumably take possession of the burnt out land and declare victory.

It is for thoughtful Indians to determine whether such a victory is desirable and why should a nuclear war needs to be prevented at all costs. Losing 300 to 500 million Indians apparently came easy to whoever was the interlocutor of the American officials. There is still a tremendous amount of confusion about nuclear matters. They are truly weapons of mass destruction.

The Indians probably had initially bought the notion: 'what could they do except to go to war with Pakistan which can then become a nuclear exchange in populous South Asia'. That was a frightful idea for all South Asians. Anyway, the point is the Americans did not support Pakistanis and there was not much of American aid other than what used to be called Paris Club or Pakistan Forum, organized actually by the World Bank. Pakistanis were also playing a quasi-imperial leadership role in Afghanistan in the 1990s.

They began with exporting a government to Afghanistan in early-1992. But that government did not last more than a year and a half. It broke up and various civil wars ensued and most of the country anyhow had come to be ruled by local warlords, almost one in every district. Pakistanis failed to help maintain the Afghan government's unity or effectiveness or to impose a peace of their own which they could not do for want of an Afghan national army. But later (after 1994) some of the more enterprising Pakistani generals did bring a new batch of Afghan jihadis, this time known as the Taliban, to do the job. And they did it. The Taliban was introduced in Afghanistan in 1994 and they began conquering it mainly by trickery and succeeded by 1996 in virtually taking over most of the Afghanistan, some 80 per cent of the territory.

The Taliban set up a unitary government and ruled effectively in the name of implementing their militant Islam. They set up an Islamic Caliphate in Kabul that, it is significant to keep in mind, was acceptable to all orthodox Sunni Islam in the subcontinent because the Deoband seminary in India and Jamiate Ulmai Islam in Pakistan certified it as an authentic Islamic Caliphate. The other religious parties also did not openly demur. Pakistan had by this time acquired a para-leadership role of controlling Afghanistan. It was a mini-imperialism of Pakistan, if also piggyback on American understanding and residual aid mainly for its military, despite the US disinterest. Some Western economic aid to Pakistan had also continued. But the Americans, even during the period of their disinterest, were not unmindful of their long-term preferences and geo-strategic imperatives. Among these was bringing Pakistan and India closer into a South Asian format provided by SAARC and, of course, their own geo-economic need for controlling the sources of key raw material in all parts of the globe, particularly oil and gas.

It was in that period that the Americans had promoted, through an American oil company, UNOCAL, a proposal for an oil and or gas pipeline from Turkmenistan through Afghanistan and Pakistan to India. That would cement the linkage between Pakistan and India as well as bring the entire region under American sphere of influence. But it required long negotiations with Kabul's Taliban regime that could not be concluded; the

Taliban were more inflexible than anyone expected and demanded things that the American company was not prepared to concede. Later in 2001, Americans chiefly wanted Taliban to hand over Osama bin Laden to them – whom Kabul had given asylum – but the Taliban rejected the American demands and the negotiations collapsed. But soon after the 9/11 incidents happened in New York and Washington, the Americans seem to have suddenly activated all their geo-strategic aims and desires and invaded Afghanistan. The UNOCAL proposal had gone into some kind of a coma, without quite dying. The Americans disposed off the Taliban as the ruling regime in Afghanistan in a few weeks. But the Talibanis themselves more or less safely ran away to various hideouts in Afghanistan and Pakistan. These two countries, with many Pushtoons, especially along the Durand Line, were where they could expect safe hiding places and friendly reception.

This opened yet another chapter of Pakistan–American cooperation. Pakistan was co-opted into the US war on terror or as some say press-ganged into this war because the Americans said 'either you are with us or against us'. And 'being against' the US meant that it can send you back to the stone age by bombing the way it did in Afghanistan. Pakistan Army did not require many inducements or threats; it is always only too glad to be actively cooperating with the Americans. This war made the rule of General Pervez Musharraf stronger and richer. Time was, as recently as March 2000, when President Bill Clinton could not have insulted a Pakistani president more than the way he treated Musharraf. He stopped only for four hours in Pakistan; did not allow a handshake to be filmed (if ever there was one); and he chose to speak to people of Pakistan direct through Pakistani electronic media. What he may have discussed officially is not known.

But the succeeding American president, George W. Bush, became the 'tightest buddy' of Musharraf and he has stayed by him till the summer of 2008 – a few weeks before Musharraf's resignation. This was in spite Pakistan's election of 18 February that, to put it mildly, rejected Musharraf, his friends and all his works in a decisive manner. Musharraf, however, stayed for six months after the polls, thanks to American support. Only later, around July, the Americans indicated they will not go on supporting Musharraf indefinitely. While this war was not perhaps as profitable for the Pakistani generals as the one in 1980s in Afghanistan was. It carried the risk and discomfort of bringing the 'war against terror' into Pakistan territory along with the rise and rise of Taliban power inside FATA and has since been growing in some settled districts of NWFP and Punjab is under a looming threat.

While the War goes on and Pakistan and America continue to cooperate fairly closely, new divergences are arising with the US. The US wants to go after the Taliban, al-Qaeda and various other militant organizations, hammer and tong so as to clean up the whole area. The Pakistanis, however, demur. How far can they fight their own people on their own territory? In fact Pakistan Army did exactly what the Americans had wanted – and in a fairly big way. Historically, Pakistan Army had never entered the FATA areas after 1948. Now, thanks to the Americans, it has 120,000 troops or more deployed along the border with Afghanistan and in FATA. Militant Islamic groups have kept up an insurgency in which many groups, in addition to Taliban and al-Qaeda, are involved. This is not the place to enlarge on the issue of differences within Islamist groups. (It is necessary to note even in passing that Islamist groups, qua Islamist groups, cannot be united.)

Even in the Frontier areas in Pakistan, the Muslims are in fact quite plural in matters of faith and observances; hence, the sectarian disunity among Islamic militant groups. But on certain things they are all united: Americans are up to no good; they are fighting a war that looks uncommonly like a war against Islam; they are bringing the war right into Pakistan; and have been using unmanned aircrafts to shoot at suspected targets inside Pakistan and say that they, at first, used to say have done it from outside. Later this procedure was dropped. The Americans were not satisfied with the earlier arguments of the Pakistan Army and nor are they convinced with argument now being made by the new civilian government in Pakistan after 18 February elections. But Pakistan Army did what it was told by the Americans. The net result was that it may have killed or arrested an unknown number – may be many hundreds or thousands of militants. But it also got a bloody nose; it has won only a few battles of this war. No regular professional army can win a war against committed militants that use guerrilla tactics. Pakistan Army may have lost more than 2,500 troops, including the paramilitaries. No NATO power has lost half as many soldiers.

This is a significant fact. Pakistan Army dare not act the way the Americans do in Iraq and Afghanistan. Pakistan Army is trained to fight another professional army, in fact, India's, which is much like itself. It is clueless about how to win against ideologically-fired Islamic militants who use guerrilla tactics to good effect. There is still no example of a professional volunteer army having decisively defeated political forces that fight with guerrilla tactics. The British Army, all said and done, claimed a successful tactic in Malaya in 1940s. But it had in fact to give up most of its colonial possessions; the Dutch were defeated by the Indonesians. The French were, at the end of the day, defeated decisively both in Vietnam and in Algeria. The Americans, with the largest and the richest army in the world, has had a record of failures: in Korea, in Vietnam and they do not look like winning in Iraq or in Afghanistan anytime soon. Their successes or failures in Latin America need not be discussed because many nuances have to be taken care of. How long can America stay in Iraq and Afghanistan quagmires? No doubt, some geo-strategists and neo-con thinkers – often the same people – may want to stick it out in Afghanistan, though perhaps not in Iraq. But ordinary Americans have no stomach to go on fighting against Islamic militants for decades on end – that too without realistic hopes of achieving the ultimate strategic goals.

In so far as current US policy vis-à-vis Pakistan is concerned, the Americans have made it abundantly plain that they do not like the basic idea of the new government or of the Pakistan Army making local peace deals with Islamist groups. They think it is appeasement that is likely to encourage the Islamic fighters whether they be Taliban or al-Qaeda or any other sectarian organization, all of which have adopted the tactics of al-Qaeda and are under the influence of its ideas. The Americans thought that they have arranged for a democratic government that would remain yoked to their chariot, keeping Musharraf at its head so that Pakistan can continue its role of aiding US, CIA and special forces in attacking and eliminating high value Taliban, al-Qaeda or other targets in Pakistan and would fight with militants with a view to eliminating them. Pakistanis want the American forces to stay outside Pakistan territory but may, in some way or other, the Americans have won base(s) inside the country to attack the targets inside Pakistan. This remains a sticky point between Pakistan and America. And the American thinking is not shared by all NATO powers, including France. They are, in general principle, united in fighting the Islamist forces in Afghanistan and want to avoid the war inside Pakistan too where the militants are entrenched. Pakistan Army in fact had moved the other way by making peace deals with Islamist groups and the civilian government is, willingly, supporting the Pakistan Army moves as well.

No one really knows the details of what Musharraf and Pakistan Army had conceded to the American forces regarding operating inside Pakistan territory. It is a dark, or, at best, a grey area. It is now confirmed that there are some reports of a base for training of Pakistan's paramilitary by the US special forces and CIA experts on how to fight the Islamist guerrillas. That is one side of an uncertain picture, though on 4 September 2008 the US left no one in doubt: US special forces landed in a Waziristan village and shot dead sleeping inmates of three houses, including women and children. What had happened was that three helicopters dropped US special forces in a village close to the border inside south Waziristan who went into three houses and shot dead all sleeping inmates. Whether they got any high-value target has not been claimed. But some women and children were shot dead. This came out on the eighth day after a secret meeting of Pakistan Army's chief of staff with American forces top brass on an aircraft carrier in the Arabian Sea. Who said what is not known for sure. But the two sides' position subsequently is known. Americans rely on their 'right' of hot pursuit inside Pakistan. They say wherever there is a threat to American security, the US has the right to go and hit. They have shown that Pakistan is an important theatre of war; it houses clear and present threat to US interests and security targets; ergo 'we have the right to go into Pakistan territory and take out the threat'. The US president is supposed to have authorized US forces to go into Pakistan without informing it and 'do what you have to do way back in July 2008.

The 4 September incident had received only a tepid response from government ministers. Next day, the Pakistan Army's chief,

General Ashfaq Kayani laid out a red line: no foreign soldier can come and engage in any military action; Pakistan military will resist and repel it. A day later, the prime minister endorsed his army chief's stand as the government's own. Another day later he clarified his own statement. This PPP-led government took up the matter with the Americans at diplomatic level; the PM said there is no need to fight with the Americans – a complete whitewash of his endorsement of the army and air chiefs' hard-hitting statements. The message to the people is we cannot and will not resist US forces if they intrude and take military action against Pakistanis on Pakistan soil while the military has gone on record to say they would resist and repel any foreign forces that rush in – or invade – and kill Pakistanis. This discrepancy in thinking of the PPP government and the army has explosive possibilities. The army's stance is more patriotic and it is ready to defend Pakistan and Pakistanis, while the civilian government is more cowardly – and obsequious to the Americans. A political turmoil can be looked forward to in future in which other parties will condemn PPP government and praise the army. Some can hear the thump of heavy boots already. Political warfare is sure to ensue that cannot be good for this fledgling democracy.

But what does it say about the Pak–US relations as a whole or at the level of their military-to-military ties? A breach had opened between the two erstwhile allies. The US officials at all levels have made no secret of their distrust and dislike of Pakistan: government, military and its political leaders. They are now openly inimical. American officials, beginning with the president, Robert Gates, the defense secretary, the CIA chief, Admiral Mullen, the top Pentagon offices, have directly put Pakistan on notice that they are certain that al-Qaeda, Taliban and other fighters who are using Pakistan territory as a sanctuary and constitute a 'present and direct' threat to American interests and forces in Afghanistan and elsewhere. This is a blunt warning that direct American action may be under contemplation. Would America take inimical action without the consent of Pakistan, or in other word, invade it? Nobody knows. But it is freely being discussed all over Pakistan. What are the limits of American threat is not known? On the whole, it is a dicey situation in which Pakistan has to chart its courses of action.

There is a valid argument here: the Americans are wrong in thinking that superior firepower or superiority in the quality of armaments would necessarily wipe out the menace they see in the Islamic extremist groups. The fact of the matter is that no gun has been invented that can kill an attractive idea in somebody's brain. You kill that person but other fighters are born. Physical force alone is not enough to fight an ideology. An ideology can be fought with other ideologies. A non-desirable idea can be tackled by flooding the society with new and attractive ideas. All anyone can do is to confront the undesirable elements or groups who are moved by a violence-promoting idea with new and more attractive ideas dealing with the improvement of the society in which they all will be benefitted. The Americans do have grudgingly conceded the relevance of economic development.

It is their first baby steps of the recognition that force alone cannot wipe out any ideology; more is needed in terms of empowering the people. There have to be political reforms of empowering the common people in the target area, viz. tribal areas, and indeed rest of the NWFP where democratic reforms must percolate down into the shape of concrete and enforceable human rights, including massive job creation. Democracy is normally an adequate answer to any violent ideology, provided the issue is not seen as no more than traditional civil liberties.

One fact has to be recognized: there is an essential similarity in the conditions that produce Maoists in India – and more so in Nepal – and which beget Islamic militants in Pakistan. The basic starting point of such guerrilla movements is the stark poverty and loss of hope and prevalence of despair among common people regarding their future. These conditions, in conjunction with the presence of Maoist parties to lead, produce guerrilla movements that are not successfully put down. The Taliban and such like movements have also the same social background: grinding poverty produces loss of hope and creates despair. These are the dominant mind sets in the populace. Such social conditions promote Maoists elsewhere, but they produce Islamist militants in Pakistan and in some other Muslim countries where people are familiar with Islamic idiom.

There is no doubt that Pakistan is the main manufactory of jihadists of all kinds. From the very beginning the people here have been subjected to only one idiom: Islam. They have heard no other idiom or idea from anyone else. Islam's egalitarian creed is over-hyped; in a true Islamic state no one will go to sleep hungry or remain ill without medication. Therefore fight for an Islamic dispensation is a must and jihad is a duty. If you return you are a Ghazi; will have your family's needs looked after; and you will have received some money. But if you die, you will be a shaheed; you will go straight to heaven where many houris will be waiting for you; you will remain young for ever while the ambience will be truly permissive; you will eat what you wish and there will be plenty of everything; you have merely to wish and the thing will be there. Poor semi-starved young lads, with nothing to do, become attracted to jihad for such benefits. It is not that only some mullahs preach this. This is believed about Heaven in all sects and sub-sects everywhere. Since there are no other preachers of other ideologies, Islamic militancy-preaching mullahs become leaders of jihad movements virtually by default. This is what happened in Iran where the mullahs finally captured the leadership of a directionless revolution that was mainly motivated by small shadowy underground leftist groups and liberals without a clear leadership chain. The mullahs are doing the same in Pakistan because there are no left or even true centrist parties here.

In terms of ideological motivation, these new guerrilla fighters are fired-up by an Islamic ideology that promises something good – and bits of social security for the family – as just noted. What the mullahs serve is a powerful brew. The idea of fighting Islamic guerrillas with superior force alone is jejune. It is unlikely to work. What needs to be done is to introduce political reforms of democratic nature plus social and economic development that actually gives jobs to the unemployed, and freedom of expression to all. Tolerance can only come when society makes some social and economic progress in a way that respects democratic norms. Democracy plus social and economic improvements in the lives of the common people is what will fight the Islamic terror. Nothing else will. This was a small digression to intellectually locate Islamic extremism.

However, to return to the actual divergence in the viewpoints of Pakistan Army and Pakistan government, on one side, and the

US and NATO forces, on the other. It is a serious matter. Pakistan becoming another Afghanistan is the minimum of a disaster to be expected, if foreign forces enter Pakistan's tribal areas in some numbers. There is no doubt about the fact that Pakistan is the epicentre of the Islamic militancy, as all say. Wherever a terrorist is arrested, there is some link or connection with Pakistan. The ideological debates, mostly about what Islam enjoins, in Pakistan are sixty years old and have gone on intensely. The fact is that the moderate politicians in Pakistan who are supposed to stand for modernism and democracy are political illiterates and have no concept of how modern societies progress. Most of them take their economic thinking from international financial institutions, because it is these and America which have led Pakistan into whatever development has taken place. The American influence inside Pakistan is immense in its various sectors and facets that sustain support for the US and its ideas.

The most powerful organization in Pakistan is the Pakistan Army. It knows which side of its toast is buttered. American aid has sustained and equipped Pakistan Army for most, if not all, its life. Even lately, it has utilized most of the $ 10 to 15 billion that the Americans have pumped in after 9/11, on army or army-related economic development. The social elites, mostly feudal in character or with that mind set, are basically former toadies of the British and are now America's acolytes. For them, Britain has been replaced with the US. Their thinking is moulded by what the Americans want, either directly or through *Time* or *Newsweek*. The business class is solidly pro-US. But the common people are not. Common Pakistanis are intensely anti-American and one is not even talking of the mullahs. The question is: What will Pakistan military do if US and or NATO forces start operating in earnest inside Pakistan? There are only utter uncertainties and dark apprehensions. Pakistan might then become yet another Afghanistan.

Mullahs have now taken up the mantle of the former left that in Pakistan was destroyed long ago under CENTO's various anti-subversion plans. The Islamists' rhetoric is filling the need of a radical thinking for reshaping of Pakistan because the mullahs claim that not even a dog will sleep hungry along any of the canals in Pakistan if the Islamic ideology is fully enforced. This rhetoric is the mainstay of the Taliban and other Islamist forces.

Another factor has been the work and peculiar role played by the Saudi money and influence. A great deal of money is spent by the Saudis in Pakistan promoting religious consciousness. There is still another factor that may be noted in passing. Pakistan is the only relatively open Muslim society in the entire Middle East where ideological debates are free and intense. There was, and indeed is, a cold war being conducted between the revolutionary Iran and conservative Saudi Arabia, both wanting their influence among the Islamists of the two main sects, that is, the Shias and Sunnis. Iran worked among Shias and Saudis mobilized the Sunnis. Both spend money.

But since free debate does not ultimately hurt, this can go on but the need is for Pakistan in general, and Pushtoon areas in particular, to be flooded with other new ideas and ideals, including those of what the left used to say before the demise of the Soviet Union and China's departure from socialism. It is necessary to emphasize yet again the need of radical political and economic reforms in Pakistan if it has to survive as a free country. What has obtained so far is a dictatorship of the Pakistan Army, sometimes open, sometimes it controls the politics from behind the scenes. One last element to be noted is the abiding nationwide disapproval of America. There is no other Muslim country so anti-American as Pakistan. Anti-American ideas hold sway over most Pakistanis. Given today's intellectual climate, almost automatic benefit of this shallow thinking aimlessness goes to all mullahs who are spearheading anti-Western propaganda. Today there is also a considerable residue of serious misgivings regarding American intentions arising out of inferred US geo-strategic interests and if also juxtaposed with what the American economy demands.

In sum, it is hard to conceive what the US can do to, or in, Pakistan. If there is some good sense it will not be drawn into this fantastically huge quagmire that it can easily become if the American boots are put on the ground, a la the way it has done in Afghanistan. Americans do not seem to be content with the loyal support now mobilized by Western ambassadors in Pakistan from the newly elected victorious PPP? They want to do the job much better, though it can scarcely be a whole lot better. At any rate, it will be cheaper for the American taxpayers if Pakistan Army and its government are relied upon – both are factually willing – by the Americans, because the new government leaders and Pakistan Army are tried and tested pro-Americans. And militant Islam is no friend of this Islamabad. The new government has no other choice but to remain tethered to American chariot. American anger is misplaced.

Disappointments Galore

Benazir's Role, Judge's Restoration and Impeachment of Musharraf

Developments in the country's politics between 3 November 2007 and August 2008 were such that drained all power from the former General-President Musharraf even though he remained in office. On 18 August 2008 he virtually groveled before the nation and resigned, hiding behind the slogan of reconciliation. Earlier, Benazir Bhutto, who arrived on 18 October 2007, was killed on 27 December; she came as a result of a deal she cut with Musharraf with the help of the US, UK, Saudi Arabia and UAE, for the express purpose of keeping and strengthening the hands of President Musharraf.

What went on immediately before haughty Musharraf's surrender needs to be noted. The story has been told in the rest of the book. To recount it here in brief, it began with Lal Masjid affair, if not with Akbar Bugti's killing: Musharraf dilly-dallied for over six months, negotiating with the two fiery heads of the Masjid Complex, with ample talk of mutual concessions while his government propagated that they were linked with Taliban, al-Qaeda and the other militants in the FATA who were using the Mosque complex as a staging post for going into the rest of Pakistan. The government did not contradict the media reports that the complex and the ISI – the headquarters of which was only a mile away – were cooperating for a long time. Then suddenly on 10 July, Musharraf ordered the army commandos to go and flush out all those who were there including students, male and female, the teachers and all those who might be suspected of being Islamic militants, merely using it for a time. The operation was bloody and it shocked the religious sentiments of a large number of people many of whom were, in any case, vaguely supportive of what might be called the Taliban cause itself.

A while earlier, on 9 March, General Musharraf and his cohorts from the army made the first assault on higher judiciary when they called the chief justice of Pakistan, Justice Iftikhar Muhammad Chaudhry, who had been until then on friendly terms with Musharraf, to his Camp Office in Rawalpindi, and was shown a piece of paper that was supposed to be a charge sheet against him and demanded his resignation. The CJP had one look at it and said I will defend myself in an open court of law. The charges had been circulated earlier on the Internet by a Musharraf-supporting advocate. Most media outlets had received it. Musharraf's reaction to CJP's 'No' was sharp. He detained him there and then in his own office; CJP was not allowed to go back to his chambers; he was 'escorted' to his house by apparently the law enforcement agencies in fairly large numbers and locked up in a part of his own house and kept incommunicado for several days. The rest of the story is well known. It gave birth to a lawyers' movement almost instantly. From the day that the chief justice's case was began to be heard in the Supreme Judicial Council which ultimately had to be transferred a larger bench of the Supreme Court itself. That bench eventually reinstated him and fined the government Rs100,000 for scandalizing the court by presenting a silly charge sheet. The rest of the story has also been described.

Throughout the rest of the year, the media, civil society, the lawyers' movement continued to grow. The Western press took serious note of what was happening in Pakistan. It was actually a transformation. Even the common people had been deeply impressed by the chief justice of Pakistan's stand and his saying 'No' to Musharraf's demand for resignation. People from villages came out in their multitudes to have just a look of the chief justice who did not speak before any public gathering; he only made speeches, later, to Bar Councils, associations and similar professional bodies. And he never broached political questions in his speeches; they were all about rule of law, the necessity of a free and fair judiciary that is not afraid of any other pillar of state and so forth.

But the calendar for the year 2007 was a packed one: according to the Musharraf-amended Constitution the requirement was that a general election should take place by mid-November. It was also necessary for Musharraf, according to the requirements of the Constitution he had mangled, that he should get himself re-elected from apparently a similar electoral college that obtains in, say, India. But for Musharraf there was the bugbear: in July, Justice Iftikhar Muhammad Chaudhry had been reinstated. President Musharraf's election and the general election would throw up any number of constitutional issues that many of the litigation-loving Pakistanis were sure to bring before the Supreme Court. A court led by Justice Chaudhry would, other things being equal, give its finding against the executive's case. Musharraf's competence to contest the presidential election was an obvious case that was sure to reach the Supreme Court and it did. The verdict could be foreseen by anyone. He was not even eligible to run for any elective office; the Constitution expressly forbade any government servant from seeking an elective office and Musharraf was a government servant in active service, receiving a salary. Musharraf, determined to stay in power, went further and smashed the whole superior judiciary that had begun to take airs of an independent judiciary and was acting in a manner that diverged from the usual meek role of subservience it played throughout Pakistan's military dictators-studded history. Musharraf said that I will smash them. And he did.

Musharraf's second assault on the higher judiciary began on 3 November 2007 in which he sacked all High and Supreme courts judges and locked up many of them who did not accept the constitutional legitimacy of a number of his actions of 3 November that included imposition of an Emergency, promulgating a new Provisional Constitution Order that enabled the president to make whatever changes he felt like making in the Constitution and gave a slew of orders to discipline the media. There was the predictable uproar in the country; nobody liked it.

It was also a period when Benazir had arrived in Pakistan, and her arrival (and sad demise later) had mirrored the blazing progress of a shooting star across the skies. Her arrival had caused much excitement because she was as the leader of the PPP who came constantly mouthing an uplifting and rousing rhetoric against dictatorship. Although she had actually come as a result of a deal between herself and Musharraf, as noted, that was mediated by the US and British governments. The purpose of the deal was to enable her to come back and participate in the national election that was due in November 2007. The American and British purposes were clear: they only wanted to give a democratic face to Musharraf by requiring the two main political parties to line up behind him to conduct the war on terror more effectively – under a refurbished Musharraf, the leader of an apparently democratic and so-recently-elected system. But the original purpose of the West was to go on using the safe Musharraf, as the leader of the new contrived democracy. War on Terror could thus be fought more efficiently and more vigorously. Over the succeeding weeks, the American perception of Musharraf's abilities changed. The Western media quickly brought Musharraf down many notches in the US estimation. By the turn of the year, the American government had become convinced that Musharraf is no longer the man on whom they should rely. After some confusion, they seem to have fixed on PPP's new leader Asif Ali Zardari who could be their next man to be ably assisted by an equally safe and efficient new army chief. It was under these conditions that 18 February 2008 elections were held. They had been postponed from an earlier date because of the assassination of Benazir Bhutto on 27 December, the year before. But the political situation on the streets on all major cities was that anti-Musharraf slogans were being raised full throatedly and the lawyers' agitation had been joined by many political parties, notably PML (N), and the civil society had become more active in support of the lawyers. The media, both electronic and the press, gave full support to the lawyers' cause.

There were two different streams of thought. On the one hand, the new government had come with the help of the US and British governments with a view to conducting the war on terror, hopefully, more vigorously. This showed the basic realities of Pakistan politics for all to see – there are two power centers: the army and the US. At least Asif Zardari, saw this reality more clearly: there was no way of ignoring the Pakistan Army which did not want its one time chief to be disgraced, tried in a court of law or impeached. President George Bush had a soft corner for Musharraf even after his resignation. Meantime, the party politics between the winners, mainly between the PPP, that had emerged as the largest party in the National Assembly, and the second largest party, PML (N) led by Mian Nawaz Sharif were traditional rivals. They somehow felt compelled to go on manoeuvring for party advantage, especially for the long run. Although Nawaz was not outside the loop because of the Americans having worked on the Saudis who persuaded Musharraf to let Nawaz Sharif participate in the elections and, hopefully, he would also play a sobering role because of Saudi persuasion. By this time, Nawaz has also become a far more sober, calculating and perhaps a little more responsible leader. But keeping an eye on his own party's future, he quickly aligned himself with the lawyers' movement and gained politically.

Although Nawaz later made a very serious compromise with PPP regarding the lawyers' movement and the cause of the judges' restoration by agreeing with the PPP to allow the sacked judges to be reinstated along with those new pliant judges that Musharraf had appointed after 3 November's assault on the superior courts with PPP accepting all Musharraf's wishes and terms. That had much reduced the value of the PML (N)'s support for the lawyers' cause, if it had not negated it. What the PPP government was doing was to give new jobs and not restoring the jobs of the old judges, qua individuals, and that too after taking an oath that had signified allegiance to Musharraf. This was neither the lawyers' purpose or nor did that constitute the judges' cause. These causes required that Musharraf's 3 November 2007 actions should be declared unconstitutional and illegal, and the old judges must be restored as of right while the new pliant ones must be thrown out. Nawaz's PML (N) had accepted the PPP stance that all Musharraf actions – Emergency, Provisional Constitution Order and judges, etc – were constitutional and lawful actions and thus new judges will stay rightfully, while the two major parties, as a humanitarian gesture and as a matter of grace, will accommodate the sacked judges in the courts, provided they accept the constitutional legitimacy of Musharraf's fiat by taking a new oath and accepting that this is their new recruitment. The PPP-led government has broken the back of many of the old judges by offering special incentives or browbeating nearly a third of the sixty-two sacked judges. PML (N)-led provincial government in Punjab has been allowed to continue or PPP did not put the PML (N) leaders into prisons on a decade old charges because of that compromise.

Nawaz was quickly able to prevent much damage by intensifying his support for the CJP and the remaining clutch of judges. In the hurly burly of a movement of rare intensity and Nawaz's even rarer success in mobilizing the people of two cities – Lahore and Gujranwala – he forced the Zardari regime, army and the US to accept all lawyers' terms. As a result, Nawaz emerged larger-than-life politician. Thus the upshot is Nawaz Sharif has managed to add so much to his popularity by his final act of 15 March 2009 in the lawyers' movement – thanks to the rare mobilization of people of Punjab in support of CJP and the lawyers' demand – powers that be were frightened and accepted all demands. By making shrill calls for trying Musharraf for his misdeeds and crimes against democracy, he only added to political height. That more or less meant that while his verbal support for judges' cause seems to remain constant, the damage due to this huge compromise was, for PR purpose, ignored. Nawaz in 2009 is a political colossus.

It was against this general backdrop that the new government is working sans PML (N). Both PPP and PML (N) say they want to see the old coalition survive while being engaged in a fierce power struggle. There seemed to be a strange unity of unexplained higher or overriding purpose between the PPP and PML(N); both seemed to be joined at the hip, although they hate each other. They happily formed a coalition along with everyone else who walked in. And many did walk in; like the Awami National Party in the NWFP and the main religious party alliance, MMA's biggest party, JUI (Fazlur Rehman faction), whose stand on the war on terror has been inconsistent with the British and American purposes – though its leader Maulana Fazlur Rehman has been acceptable, perhaps because of his flexibility and realpolitik. Inside the government there was never much harmony. The PPP government, for PR purposes, continues to support Nawaz Sharif's rhetoric on judges' reinstatement and his verbal call, in August 2009, call for impeaching Musharraf. Nawaz's PML (N)'s protests against Musharraf going to the extent of PML (N) ministers – for a while PML (N) was a part of the government – at first refusing to be sworn in by him (because they did not accept his legitimacy as a president), though later agreeing to be sworn in as a matter of concession with black armbands to show their true feelings. The original PPP–PML (N) government did not last long; the PML (N) component resigned within two months.

The kind of identity of purpose with Musharraf and his obviously (and admitted by himself) illegal actions of 3 November 2007 that PPP leader Asif Zardari has shown is amazing. Indeed after 13 May 2008, when PML (N) ministers walked out, the conduct of the PPP-run government seemed to be as if it was a continuation of the Musharraf regime. The PPP government, to its credit or discredit, has not changed any Musharraf policy in the last 19 months that it has been in office. It owns, rather clumsily, that the war on terror is Pakistan's own war and that it is not fighting America's war. The Taliban is Pakistan's enemy. Before budget-making, Prime Minister Gilani had given his firm assurance to the bureaucracy that there would be no paradigm change and there has been none. Economic policies are the same; foreign policies are the same; all social policies are the same. The only change that the government has made after five months was to impose marginally higher import duties on some luxury goods.

That was less to discourage imports than to earn more revenues from enhanced duties. Such action was needed on day one to discourage imports that are now over twice the size of exports. It is an unsustainable position anyhow. Any responsible government would have either increased the exports to the extent that they would mostly pay for the imports or would cut the imports no matter how or who was displeased. The country cannot continue to import twice as much as it exports without becoming a failed state or insolvency. But the PPP government is soldiering on with Musharraf's old policies. The only recourse it has is to go to Washington every few months and beseech for more help. Washington, no doubt, bails out the Pakistan government in the end with World Bank, ADB and IMF funds. But it is at a cost. The cost will be that Pakistan will eventually have to become a permanent ward of the IMF, implementing its structural adjustments programmes, no matter what the people go through. 'Tough decisions' will continue to be taken then by a PPP-run Islamabad, while it remains wedded to the US-recommended policies.

Pakistanis seem fated to have high hopes one day that are dashed the next day. For instance, look at the case of Benazir's arrival. It was such a fantastic reception when she had arrived on 18 October 2007; at least half a million strong procession had brought her into Karachi. But she was subjected to a bomb attack that she did escape, but only accidentally. But during the period she was in Pakistan her relations with Islamabad, despite the done deal with Musharraf, appeared to deteriorate rather rapidly as her rhetoric adapted itself more and more to the sentiments rampant in the country and she appeared to be becoming more and more anti-dictatorship than anything else. The PPP wallahas, and there are many, are sure, one way or another, General Musharraf himself is somehow involved in the assassination of Benazir. For one thing, it was claimed by the government to be the work of Baitullah Mehsud, a Taliban leader in one of the FATA areas in the NWFP. But the Taliban are not given to denying their responsibility for any particular attacks they make. Baitullah Mehsud flatly denied that he made that attack. Besides, there is no convincing evidence of how she died; there was no autopsy done on the request of Asif Zardari and all forensic evidence were hosed down from the site of the incident within hours. That the PPP adherents remain certain that Musharraf was somehow involved is indicative of public sentiment – no one accepts the government's version – and the worst can be safely attributed to Musharraf. Nothing definite can be said on the subject, of course.

One fine August (2008) morning, Asif Zardari began beating a new drum: Musharraf is a dictator, he has destroyed democracy – he stands for dictatorship while the country needs democracy. A few days later he came out with the charge that Musharraf had committed financial irregularities. Not all the money that the American Army has reimbursed has been accounted for. This was a charge that had actually emanated earlier from Pentagon itself, though it was not pursued for one good American reason or other. Then he suddenly began to call for impeachment of

Musharraf. This was obviously the need to grab public attention and recruit Nawaz's support against Musharraf. Perhaps by that time, the American government, too, had come to the conclusion that Musharraf had in any case to go because his utility had become nil. This new rhetoric and Nawaz's enthusiastic support made the country suddenly excited again. In fact, it wanted the blood of Musharraf. They wanted him to be tried either by the National Assembly for impeachment or in courts of law for specific crimes. That was the long-standing stand of PML (N) that Asif Zardari suddenly adopted and shouted even more loudly. That was by design. That and thanks to Anglo–American opinion, Musharraf's goose was cooked. Musharraf came on TV, talked of his innocence over many things and admitted unspecified mistakes that he made. He just resigned. The excitement lasted a few days. Meantime, Zardari managed to get himself elected as president. Then the reality soon dawned on the people that the PPP government continues to pursue Musharraf's agenda despite his resignation, and the people noted the ease with which the PPP government gave him a 'safe exit' – that he was at least verbally opposed by PML (N) and more stridently by many others.

While there has been so much excitement with high hopes and also with so much fear, the reasons for that are clear. The public is seething with discontent: the economy is in a shambles; the inflation rate is persistently in double digits; the government's and country's accounts are heading toward the country to insolvency: the budget deficit has climbed to 7–8 or so per cent of the GDP. The foreign trade deficit is 100 per cent and more of the export earnings, not counting the rampant smuggling. Current account deficit continues climbing 7 to 8 per cent of the GDP despite increasing amounts of aid. This government has given no relief either in the economic sphere or from the electricity crisis. No major problem has been resolved.

Instead, what is happening is, as noted, the two major parties, PPP and PML (N), are fighting petty partisan wars. The PPP was apparently planning to break the PML (N) government in Punjab by withdrawing PPP from it and preempting PML (N) from gaining the support of independents and PML (Q) in order to survive. That need involved the prestige and resources of the central government which give the PPP a big advantage. The PPP is asking PML (Q) as well as other independents to come and strengthen it. Asif Zardari controls the centre, though Nawaz Sharif too is in a fairly strong position because he controls the Punjab provincial government. PML (N) is also much closer to popular sentiment than PPP, particularly in Punjab which is socially changing fast as a result of the emergence of a new commercial and industrial middle class that wants more political space as well as the freedom of the media, all of which strengthens the civil society. On the whole, it is impossible to say whether in the short-term PPP advantages can eliminate PML (N) government from the Punjab or the PML (N) will ensure that it survives while continuing to oppose the Centre and may possibly capture it after a possible mid-term election. From a long-term point of view, it can be said that no government at the Centre in Pakistan can remain viable for long if the people of Punjab veer against it in political sentiment. However, this partisanship currently presents an unfortunate spectacle.

One fact must be remembered that people's behaviour, particularly in Punjab, is now actually unpredictable. Why? Because of the media and civil society's awareness. These are the major structural factors. But there are also the old facts that have not disappeared. The war in FATA looks like the war against an effective politico–military force in the area. The religious parties are constantly dinning into the ears of tribal people that it is America's war against Islam and that Islamabad's rulers have sold themselves out to the Americans. The writer is not in the business of providing the solution of a problem that is increasingly becoming an international problem – of Muslim countries, at least. The need is to find a proper political system that provides an answer to this problem of Islamic militancy and takes care of economic backwardness of the area.

But a general pointer can be given: since there is no real or doctrinal contradiction between Islam and democracy which involves tolerance and pluralism. The solution may lie in a more free democracy. The tribal areas should be flooded with more politics; all political parties must be allowed to work there; the state must find resources to build the infrastructure: schools and polytechnics and hospitals on a large scale so that the people can find more employment. After all, Muslims live in their millions everywhere without becoming Taliban-like militants. If it can happen elsewhere, it can happen in Pakistan too, provided economic development and political freedoms are fused. The FATA people should have the same liberties and liabilities that ordinary Pakistanis have, except that there should be more economic development in tribal areas on a crash basis.

Today the war on terror is being pursued in a manner in which more civilians are dying than militants and more militants are being recruited as a result of resentment against aerial bombardments by Americans as well as by Pakistanis. This is a shortsighted and suicidal course. Democratic approach has to be applied without needless preference for aerial bombing, strafing and rocketing are not calculated to win the hearts and minds of the people. The Americans have a very narrow vision of minimizing 'their' soldiers' lives; but they also have their long-standing strategic purposes in the area; they are also arrogant and careless about others' feelings or even lives. To this date, no one has found any reason why America should be fighting such a long war in Afghanistan. Given their past friendly approaches to the Taliban government in Kabul, not to mention the rest of the history of America's dealing with Islamic militants, their War on terror makes little sense. Let that be the starting point of a search for solving the problem of extremist Islam.

Prospects

We can only talk meaningfully about the immediate and near future of Pakistan. The future is far too uncertain. A long-term view is hard to take, except in unnecessarily apocalyptic terms. The basic reality after the 18 February election is that a new rainbow coalition government was formed; in less than two months it broke down – the second major partner, PML (N), walked out of the government, though the rest of the coalition still survives. But even after eighteen months, it does not seem to have taken off in any meaningful sense and its moves are already characterized by deadlocks and failures. The basic reason is that there is no unity of purpose among the components of the new coalition. It faced immediate issues that involved painful dilemmas. The first of these was political: the question of what was to be done with Musharraf. If there was one clear verdict of the election, it was the rejection of ex-General Musharraf and all he stood for. But he claimed that he was there as an elected president for the next five years, claiming to be a constitutional entity, and was refusing to go. At long last, the coalition managed to make him resign but, instead of impeaching him, had to give him a safe exit.

Here, a big extraneous factor enters: the US. It is still the only superpower there is. President George W. Bush, the US president, earlier perceived he had big stakes in Pakistan and would like Pakistan to remain a loyal ally of the US and NATO forces in Afghanistan that were fighting Islamic terror there. At the heart of what was an unavowed new crisis in the Pak–US relationship is the fact that the new government's original stated purpose was to fight the war on terror mainly through political means and not through primarily military means, especially inside Pakistan. This was, and is, anathema to the US, other NATO powers and all others who support the US. In point of fact, the US, NATO and ISAF forces were opposed to this central purpose of the new-born government that had, for a while, stood the ground for a few weeks or so with much flexibility that they would tackle Islamic terror in Pakistan through political means; in their view, a purely military approach such as was characterized by US conduct in Afghanistan was going to achieve nothing. The fact has to be faced that Pakistan's economy has received funds of the order of at least $ 12 to 15 billion during the last seven years, mostly from the US. This money has helped achieve the kind of development that Musharraf government used to boast about – with high growth rates of up to 8.4 per cent (if only in one year) and an average 7 per cent GDP growth. This kind of aid to an indigent and satellite regime has created a predilection in America that it has somehow the right to interfere in Pakistan politics and realize its purposes by manipulating various political forces in Pakistan, largely through its influence with: (a) President Pervez Musharraf, and (b) the higher echelons of the Pakistan Army and bigger political parties.

Much of this aid has in fact gone to Pakistan Army for the purposes it fancied or thought were necessary. But the characteristics of the US policies vis-à-vis Asia as an overarching context has to be kept in view:

- The US is a superpower and has many geo-strategic aims in Asia.
- It has to secure the availability of key raw material in Central Asian republics and, if possible, win them over to its side.
- It wants to involve NATO with its geo-strategic purposes in Asia, which is the rationale for NATO's eastward drive and its strange involvement in Asia.
- The immediate preoccupation of the US is Iran and all that involves.

Many think that before too long either the US, or more likely, Israel will make some kind of a military strike against Iran. How that happens does not concern us here. But the fact that it is commonly thought to be a likely purpose that may remain a constant in the near future. This, in US perceptions, requires Pakistan's loyal support to America's larger purposes in Asia. That requires a sympathetic and rather submissive government and for this purpose that the Americans had brokered a political deal between President Musharraf and Pakistan's largest political party, PPP, run by the charismatic Benazir Bhutto and now taken over by Asif Ali Zardari. No other political force is as big and as malleable, or as willing to stay a partner of the US in all it desires or needs. What America would require Pakistan to do in case the push comes to a shove in Iran, is not hard to foresee. The US would have to undertake a range of operations in which the Americans would need new logistical facilities in Pakistan. But it may even require joint intelligence operations in Iran from Pakistani territory; some vague reports have suggested that some of it is already in place. Conceivably, it might even include the use of Pakistani territory by American troops for conceivable open or secret advances into Iran's eastern areas in Iranian Balochistan or on the coast, or even further north on the eastern side of Afghanistan. All such moves will need coordination; which is an important reason why the US wants to see Afghanistan and Pakistan cooperating and remaining yoked to the American chariot. The Pakistan government would be, in one way or another, required to facilitate the US–Israel schemes that might require the use of its territory.

Given the climate of opinion in the country, all this is too tall an order. True, there are elements in the bureaucracy and the army who would welcome such enhanced cooperation with the US for a variety of reasons: their rentier mentality will welcome the chances of enhanced US aid – maybe more strategy-related economic development would enrich their favourite front companies – and as has happened in all Afghanistan-related operations such sub-rosa Pak–American cooperation has enriched Pakistani officers. This is where conspiracy theories crowd in. One does not vouch for any of these. But since they are so insistent, voluminous and apparently plausible, ignoring them may be a mistake.

Thus the US is seen to have designs on lower Sindh areas, particularly Karachi, the port city. Moreover, the PPP is a party that Americans can depend on. Its leadership is expected to be ready to do all that the Americans may want. There is also the MQM that more or less tightly controls the cities of Karachi and Hyderabad in lower Sindh. It is perceived that it would surely need assurances of effectively ruling these areas under whatever constitutional cover is put in place, as the price of their full cooperation. The conspiracy theorists point to the long pow-wows of MQM leaders with fairly senior officials like US deputy secretary of state, John Negroponte, Richard Boucher, the assistant secretary of state and American ambassador. The American ambassador to Pakistan went to London and spent two hours with Altaf Hussain, the MQM boss, while Negroponte and Richard Boucher chose to visit the governor of Sindh (an MQM man) and the city's ruler, the Nazim, also an MQM person. This has been repeated by the Barack Obama administration.

Speculation is rife over what do the Americans want: would it begin by acquiring a naval base in Karachi at a price the PPP and MQM may demand. Earlier, President Musharraf could be depended upon to concede all American demands probably without much questioning. With him was associated the support of the PML (Q) diehards (many of whom have shown interest in cooperating with the new government for usual individual favours or sharing the loaves and fishes of power). However, Musharraf has gone for good. The only party that has so far adopted a hard-line approach is PML (N) of Nawaz Sharif. The PML (N) is also a pro-establishment, right-wing party, though there was personal animosity between Nawaz Sharif and Musharraf which stood in the way of PML (N) cooperating with Musharraf. This barrier has gone. Zardari and PML (N) can still be depended upon to cooperate with the US, though the possibility will be deeply coloured by what PPP does vis-à-vis PML (N).

In theory, the new president, Asif Ali Zardari, has the power to strike down any government by the sword of Article 58 (2) (b) of the still existing Constitution that empowers him to dissolve the recently elected assemblies and dismiss all the governments thus formed. The president who does this can also appoint a caretaker government of his choice and can rule until another election three months later. When the new elections will be held is quite an uncertain category and will probably remain controversial with the president wanting a two- or three-year period to cool down the raw passions. Bangladesh's example of a military-controlled caretaker regime ruling for a long stretch was met with American approval. Why not in Pakistan too? The possibility exists largely because intense political struggles for power between PPP and PML (N), especially over Punjab, are very likely.

In the near future, raw passions can possibly erupt into riots on streets in major cities. The US would still be happy, if not too publicly, if the army's domination can re-emerge (or rather continues) – Zardari's readiness to work with the army is taken for granted by too many. Pakistan Army presumably will not be happy to openly takeover so soon again after such a long stint in running the country under Musharraf and getting a fairly bad name in the bargain. But if the US gives encouragement, it might concur. The entire purpose would be to isolate PML (N) and change the strategy of war on terror, so that it is to be fought mainly through political means, as it understands them. But the possibility of domestic political troubles, may be riots, breaking out is ever present. Pakistan's wholehearted cooperation with the US would cause a lot more upheaval than might otherwise have been the case.

LONGER-TERM PROSPECT

It is time to look for what may impend from a long(er)-term viewpoint. The thing to do is to look at the structure of society and the trends in politics along with the problems. First, let's take structural changes in society. The society remains dominated by feudal values and presence of many large landowners with political influence and traditional connections with the army, on the one hand, and the mullahs, on the other. These two relationships are not equal. The army has an upper hand, though in terms of imposing feudal values, the feudals have the upper hand. In terms of concrete power, there is nothing to match the military. The feudals are the traditional elite groups who have given their values to the whole society, and the lower classes have virtually no stake in anything largely due to their inferiority complexes and actual inferior status that is a part of the feudal mindset, often denoted by the term 'feudal values'. To obey the master and remain personally loyal to him is one of the enforced values meant to keep the lower orders in line. To remain devoted and loyal to the master is regarded a virtue in or for lower social orders. This is the ground norm of feudalism.

In terms of values, feudalism is very much a cognizable fact of political life. They have political influence and social prestige that is not available to mere moneybags that people earn from the services sector, in banks or trade or the export–import businesses. Even bigger industrialists tend to envy the landed gentry who do not have equivalent strength despite much wealth. And they tend to buy land and marry into aristocracy. Among the changes that have taken place and are likely to last are an intermixture or amalgamation of the elite groups. The bigger landlords are also becoming gentlemen farmers over stretches of their own land, while this activity is supplemented with a son or a nephew engaging in business or industry. Those who succeed in industry but did not belong to aristocracy tend to marry into aristocracy or buy land and try to acquire social influence. The kind of upper class that is now emerging is big landowners also engaging in business and industry. A few have become associated with banks, as well.

Having said this, it has to be noted that economic activity did pick up during Musharraf's tenure. There was a notable amount of industrial production. Since population growth has continued and people needed to find some self-employment, either industrial or commercial employment. This has resulted in the emergence of an industry- or commerce-based middle class. Successful professionals and well-educated executives of bigger companies belong to this class. The rise of this middle class is particularly notable in Punjab, though elements of it exist in notable numbers in Karachi, with Hyderabad and Faisalabad coming closely behind. In terms of neat money flows, thanks largely to the narcotics trade, elite groups in NWFP leave others behind. However, the rise of middle class demands and necessities changes. It wants more political space than feudalism (and the army) has ever conceded. They require more democratic freedom and a more organized democratic dispensation to breathe freely and not feel ashamed of their leaders who have had best of things so often and for so long, and still achieved nothing.

Then there is also a virtually new factor: that is the rise of electronic media – the FM radio and satellite channels. The press had been working hard to free itself from constrictions imposed by military or 'civilian democratic' governments that ran bogus democracies. The reality behind them was the domination of the military behind the scenes. Ever since the mid-1980s after the excesses of General Zia-ul-Haq in controlling the press, the journalistic fraternity has struggled hard to acquire ever more freedom. By the time Musharraf assumed charge, the press had become so free that suppressing it and making it sing praises for the military regime had become impossible. And General Musharraf wanted to win brownie points in the West of being more modern, and with the emergence of the middle class he proclaimed that he would promote democratic freedoms. As proof, he allowed a multitude of about 40 to 50 private satellite channels and licenced many private radios, while some emerged in NWFP's tribal areas without any licence.

Although Musharraf has tried to overawe and control the media subsequently, but the outcry against him had become so loud that his success in controlling has not been as complete as he would have desired, though media freedom did suffer, especially after November 2007 when, as noted, he imposed a virtual martial law but called it the state of Emergency, and like any martial law suspended the Constitution with the right to amend it himself – by virtue of being the army chief and not as president. The media did tone down its criticism in general but some parts had become more critical and, after a while, the Musharraf government did retreat a little, though the laws he promulgated in November remain – but their impact on behaviour of the media has decreased. As a result, popular awareness has grown in the country. Secret agencies ensure that criticism is not too loud or radical. The media is still largely free. There used to be a paradox: while the poor and illiterate masses remain scarcely above mere subsistence level with little political awareness in most parts of the country, the small class of landlords are remarkably articulate and politically aware in Sindh, Balochistan and NWFP. The amount of political awareness was always relatively more in NWFP.

But the larger and the most populous (and richest) province of Punjab used to be characterized by political incoherence and lack of political awareness. The landed gentry had a tight grip on much of Punjab and the voting was determined mainly by the aristocracy. The character of the political parties in the country has reflected this structure of society and the kind of industrial and banking growth that has taken place conforms to the broad trends sketched above. All parties are still heavily dominated by landed gentry, and most of the leadership is larger landholders or otherwise rich. The PML (N) stands out as a party that is run by the Sharif brothers who have made their fortune in industry, in which they have grown from what eighteenth century town mechanics were in France into proper industrialists of notable financial strength. This is the only party that is run in part by industrialists, though influence of feudals abounds inside the party in terms of those who get elected on its ticket are mostly aristocrats.

Lower or middle classes are simply absent from leadership posts in most political parties or in the politically dominant professions of bureaucracy, military or learned professions like law, medicine and even journalism. Media barons are rich and conform to feudal mindset. The lower orders have had little exposure to good education. So their entry into these professions, except in a few exceptional cases, remains restricted. In the internal structure of the parties, nearly all parties, including even PML (N), are dominated by landed gentry. Generally, the higher leadership in these parties, often including elected deputies and top leaders, are moved not so much by philosophical ideals as the need for asserting their own importance and acquiring more influence and respect in their constituencies. Along the way, they are open to making a pretty penny when an occasion arises, as the feudals' need for more money is often great. Few of them are idealistic or bound by any strong set of beliefs to ethical principles. Pakistan politics has been politics of power at any cost so as to promote personal, local and regional interests. The main aim is to get into seats of power to enhance their prestige and local power to bestow favours on those whom they wish to impress or favour.

The politics in Pakistan has largely been idealess and too principle-free. It has been purely a politics of power. No doubt, a new trend was set by charismatic Zulfikar Ali Bhutto when he formed his Pakistan Peoples Party. It began with a largely bogus slogan of 'roti, kapra aur makan' that caught the imagination of the masses. In the first election, Bhutto could not get enough feudals as his candidates. He distributed tickets to his lower class party cadres and they were returned. The first in-rush of commoners into parliamentary politics was brought about by the PPP. It projected itself as a left-of-the-centre party. But that was for slogan mongering only.

True, the Peoples Party did implement two measures of land reforms reducing the per head holding of land. But these reforms remained on paper and the landlords, through their local influence managed to keep their lands intact and under their control by transferring excess land to their close relatives or even servants in exchange for IOUs for official record purposes. In order to technically honour the socialistic promises, Z.A. Bhutto did succeed in keeping the industrial wages in line with inflation rates until the end of his rule. In this, the change in Punjab was a determining factor for Pakistan politics. One may say that Punjab today can now opt for modernism and democracy. It has not chosen mullahs in any noticeable numbers. There is now an undercurrent among the middle class in Punjab that is anti-militarist in a blurred sort of way. They want to have free trade with India and are anxious for India's transit trade through Pakistani Punjab to Central Asia. They want democracy and a peace policy.

The old identification of Punjab with the military rule may not survive long, except in numbers; Punjabis are likely to make-up 70 per cent of the army. Even so, this is good news for chances of democracy in Pakistan and the fact is that the amount of popular awareness in Punjab exceeds any other province, and it was in full display throughout the two-year-long lawyers' movement to get the judges restored and have an assertive independent judiciary. This vague anti-militarism and pro-democracy trend in Punjab is not yet dominant in the sense that a party that clearly stands for it will necessarily sweep the next polls. It is not a safe statement to make because of the surviving feudal influence in reserved pockets of the various big landlords and in leadership of parties.

But conditions are propitious for change, if only the political parties were ready for the change. Unfortunately, the conduct of political parties has been less than praiseworthy. Utter absence of idealism and preference for cynical power politics, characteristic of so called pragmatism, make today's parties the unfit instrument to bring democracy to Pakistan. Unless these parties are genuinely idealistic and understand the problems facing the country first, they will not be able to find people-friendly solutions that will work. They have to work for an inclusive politics in which the people are constantly taken along with the leaders, and discussions percolate down to grassroots before major decisions are taken. Such parties are usually left-of-centre parties, committed to the welfare of the common masses rather than for the interests of the upper classes alone.

Among the issues that the new governments will have to face in days to come are the rise and rise of Islamic militancy; it is becoming a cottage industry – anyone with some money to recruit a small lashkar sets out to become a Taliban leader of his own area and tries to concentrate as much power as he can in his hands, while being no less pragmatic or self-centred as any other politician anywhere. Since the discourse in Pakistan has always been in the religious idiom, he now uses that idiom to a telling effect: he claims enforcing the Islamic Shariah. Who can disagree with that formulation? The major elements of the situation from a longer-term viewpoint are that the state of law and order is deteriorating at a dangerous rate. Widespread illiteracy of the people and the prevalence of ill-health, diseases and the poverty of the masses create a condition where the parties that are actually anti-democratic can, by adopting dishonest but catchy or emotional slogans, come to power. There are no popular democratic defences in place in Pakistan: intelligentsia that analyses and explains the implications of different political moves or proposals.

The most important part of the national situation are economic problems. Two stand out: first the inflation rates are now in double digits, led by food items for some years. Unless the various deficits in the budget, trading account, current account and in insufficient savings, investments, and above all over-consumption by both the public and the private sectors (high imports), in comparison with what the country produces and earns will before too long lead to what is an economic meltdown. The government has been running on borrowings, domestic as well as foreign. It is being caught in the debt trap and it may not be able to escape from if the present trends are not reversed. Among the basic causes is running a pointless arms race with India, after it has become clear that there would be no war with India and also after new ideas about Kashmir that were proposed by Pakistan itself that pre-empt the likelihood of any war on Kashmir. Therefore, the quality of the parties and the mountainous problems that people face, particularly because of the unchecked growth of population creates conditions of uncertainty for the future. That is as far as can be foreseen today.

PROSPECTS IN THE NEAR FUTURE

A supposedly new beginning was made with the general elections on 18 February 2008. At the time of this writing, the winning parties are engaged in obscure manoeuvrings to outdo the other and frequently bicker. The question of what are they bickering over is easy to answer, but the issues were more complex than what appeared to be the bone of contention at the initial stages. The easy part of the answer is that there were two questions initially involved: one was what to do with sixty-two odd deposed judges of the High and Supreme courts, including the chief justice of Pakistan. The second largest winning party, the PML (N), was insistent that the first thing to be done by the new Parliament was to not merely release the judges but restoring them to their offices. This was to be achieved by declaring their earlier sacking and incarceration unconstitutional and illegal, by undoing General Musharraf's 3 November 2007 illegal and unconstitutional (executive) orders, by a new executive order of the new prime minister, backed by a parliamentary resolution. That was to ensure a vigorous and independent judiciary. This change was to include sending home the new judges appointed after 3 November's wholesale sacking that amounted to packing all the High and Supreme courts. It did not look easy what to do with the judges who had upheld General Musharraf's 3 November 2007 actions of imposing an Emergency, giving a new Provisional Constitution Order that sacked the old High and Supreme courts including those new pliant judges who were appointed by Musharraf after 3 November 2007 and who accepted all Musharraf's unconstitutional and illegal actions. These Musharraf-appointed pliable judges had no problem taking a new oath of allegiance to thus PCO-amended Constitution. The problem created by General Musharraf was the induction of as many new judges as had been sacked. What to do with them is a problem for those who want to correct what General Musharraf did on 3 November 2007.

Supporters of General Musharraf are still to be found in both houses of the Parliament after the February election and they were insistent that come what may, General Musharraf having been elected by the outgoing Parliament on 6 October 2007, should complete his five years and these deposed judges will, well, have to stay sacked because the newly-reconstituted High and Supreme courts' judges have validated those actions, especially PCO retrospectively in their own interests. These actions were thus constitutional, both directly and by virtue of new judges taking fresh oath of allegiance under PCO and validating Musharraf's actions of 3 November. What these politicians, the third party in Parliament, were saying is that General Musharraf should stay as president and complete his term till 2012, come what may. This has not merely caused much confusion but has occasioned a polarization.

The PPP is the main winner; it had earlier done a secret deal with President Musharraf, with the American and British governments guaranteeing it. Although this agreement came under some strain as a result of tumultuous events after the return of Benazir Bhutto and the compulsions of Pakistan politics made her and other party men indulge in anti-military dictatorship slogans, and take up a more democratic stance for the future of Pakistan. However, she became the victim of dastardly killers who, the government insists, were the Taliban – in fact, Baitullah Mehsud. But the PPP people insisted that the whole thing looked like an inside job in which the high and mighty of Pakistan could not but be involved. For a while it had seemed that PPP will not keep General Musharraf in his place.

But subsequent developments suggested that the agreement between President Musharraf and Benazir Bhutto did not break down despite the PPP seeming to be wary and vague on the question of sacked judges' restoration to their offices. It raised arcane questions about the supposedly complex modalities of how to do it. However, five former chief justices of Pakistan and twenty-two retired Supreme and High courts judges said in a statement that debate on them were quite unnecessary: since they were sacked by illegal and unconstitutional executive action, they can be reinstated by another executive order. PPP continues to hold that the issue could only be solved by constitutional amendments by the Parliament while the leaders of the legal fraternity were, and are, insistent that there are simpler ways of doing that, if only there is political will to do it.

Soon after the formation of the new government, it could do it through a simple executive order; it could also be done by a resolution of the National Assembly. But the PPP, seemed intentionally unclear and vague. It implicitly accepted the validity of those impugned 3 November 2007 actions of General Musharraf having a SC he had thus packed had validated his actions. A part of the Constitution could only be changed by a constitutional amendment. Thus until the Constitution is amended, the judges cannot be reinstated. However, the language and logic of the political stances adopted by all parties in the election campaign that went on to win required the restoration of the sacked judiciary, making Parliament supreme and ensure that the military goes back to the barracks, leaving the political field free for politicians to work.

The PPP could not say so openly that it is opposed to the restoration of the judges; that would have made it too unpopular ab initio and painted it in the same colour as the hitherto King's party: PML (Q) and its allies. The reality, however, is that there was powerful support in PPP for Musharraf's person as the president to begin with the whole range of Western powers – US, NATO powers, India, Japan and Australia – were firmly behind him because he was thought to be an indispensable leader of Pakistan who was a close non-NATO ally of the US in the war on terror. Now it was Musharraf and Musharraf alone who was insistent on throwing out the whole of troublesome top judiciary that was, for the first time in Pakistan's history, spinning out of military's control. He sacked them wholesale on 3 November 2007 as noted and locked up many of them in their houses and also several leading lawyers who were agitating for the judges.

Musharraf is an obstinate man of strong will who was determined to go on ruling Pakistan the way he had done so far.

That left no scope for an assertive and independent judiciary. Hence the insistence of his supporters not to restore those rebellious judges. But the public opinion was so strong in favour of the deposed judges and against Musharraf that, except the rump of PML (Q) and some of its other allies, the PPP dared not speak in favour of Musharraf and against the judges. But it has shown through sustained ambiguity of verbally wanting to restore the deposed judges but it never accepted the view of over a score of retired superior court judges and continues to search for a year for a suitable modality of achieving the supposedly desired purpose of restoring the brave souls.

In action, the PPP accepted for a year the pseudo-legal position of Musharraf loyalists but without openly admitting it. This contradiction can be reduced to a simple proposition: so long as the terms of Musharraf's deal with Benazir continues to be in place there was to be no chance of these judges being restored. An even simpler proposition would be that if the judges are restored, Musharraf's invaluable gift of National Reconciliation Ordinance, under which many top leaders of PPP had corruption charges against them dropped and return to Pakistan along with many other crooks, could be endangered and if the Musharraf understanding stays, the judges cannot be restored. PPP's boss, President Zardari, was only too conscious of his party's role under the agreement that remained the firm recommendation of the Western powers that originally wanted to keep Musharraf still want to protect him from harm or disgrace; and they have such a large leverage over Pakistan's rulers as to ensure that.

The main contentious issue, thus, was not simply the restoration of the judges. There had to be other things: to begin with, the Constitution has to actually change as the PPP's recent proposals of amendments to the Constitution partially show; the military has to be made a subordinate part of government; Pakistan's political, social and economic elites have to end their readiness to willingly accept a military dictator (whom they can easily bribe, coax or even pressurize into adopting policies that benefit mainly them); and somehow the people, the lowly common man, has to get back his sovereignty to change governments at regular intervals and force the government to obey law (the Constitution and democratic conventions). Thus the judges' restoration has been made to hang on a sea change in Islamabad in terms of what the parties have articulated in the election campaign: the Parliament has to be made supreme, judiciary has to be made independent and the Constitution has to be rid of unwanted provisions inserted by successive dictators who have put the whole elected system subject to the will of the president (who, today, is the recently-elected PPP chief). Thus, what still obtains is the military's pre-eminent position in the public life of Pakistan, along with Pakistan Army chief's implicit commitments to America. The latter's substantial aid to Pakistan has given it a large leverage over policy-making in Pakistan. In point of fact, it is hard to imagine that the winning political parties can actually wish to go against American wishes, or not implement their ardently desired objectives.

Few of Pakistan's parties had any substantive differences with Musharraf on either economic policy or other basic questions of Pakistan's polity – the question of Centre-state relations, stance over how to combat Islamic extremists, the Taliban, al-Qaeda and many other groups. There have been no clear differences over foreign policy. This statement is certainly a very broad brush picture; there are relatively minor exceptions, for instance, the Awami National Party, that has won handsomely enough in NWFP, is a declared secular party that has differed with Islamabad over its Afghan policy and the earlier nurturing of Islamic extremism in order to promote its misconceived Afghan and Kashmir policies. On federalism there are many regional nationalist parties that are dead set against an overly centralized system in Pakistan that has reduced provincial governments to glorified municipalities. Religious parties are now against remaining allied with America in the war on terror. But they have suffered serious reverses in the 18 February elections and only one religious party, Jamaat-e-Islami, has escaped the popular verdict by not choosing to fight the elections. Nevertheless, its influence in urban Pakistan is still considerable in the lower middle classes and it ought not to be dismissed as one of the defeated ones, though its importance used to be tom-tommed by military dictators for utilizing its militias for Afghan and Kashmir policies. But on the whole, religious parties were rejected by the voters in NWFP and its tribal areas; a more severe setback was suffered by the main religious party, Jamiate Ulmai Islam (Maulana Fazlur Rehman faction). It is worth repeating that no major party in Pakistan, other than religious parties, wants to part company with the West in its war on terror and JUI (F) also does not seem to seriously oppose America. All the differences are over formal political and constitutional matters. Most parties profess to work for a genuine parliamentary kind of democracy with the president as a nominal head, with the supremacy of Parliament being a given.

Pakistan politics is too volatile to envisage a long-term perspective in any meaningful sense. The reason is that it is encumbered with basic differences over substantive matters of nation building. Most parties are elitist and represent the interests of elite groups in the society. None has any cognizable reform programme. Their real differences can be termed as, very largely, over jobbery. None is against the social and economic status quo in any significant detail. There are so many substantive affinities among major parties and yet parties are usually at one another's throat, leaving few chances of broad-based cooperation. Even during the election campaign when democracy or dictatorship was the question at issue, not all parties could unite: the smaller regional nationalist parties and two lately anti-American parties, Jamaat-e-Islami and Tehrik Insaf, boycotted the election because they refused to believe that election could be free and fair under President Musharraf. Major parties, PPP, PML (N), ANP and MQM, cannot easily remain in the same alignment or government for long, as indeed they could not and effectively ended their coalition within two months; PML (N) shows every sign of saying a final goodbye to the PPP in none too distant a future.

The decisive influencing factors need to be enumerated: it is Pakistan Army, major political parties and the Americans. The reason for Americans' importance is their over fifty year old basic alliance with Pakistan Army and the latter's abject craving for American dollars. The two together have dominated Pakistan politics were since 1953 and few can see the prospect of any departure from this in the near future. It is true that a new factor is emerging: it is the changing face of politics in Punjab's urban centres where an emergent middle class is rebelling against the old political alliance of the feudal aristocracy with the army and

America, with mullahs playing a traditionally junior role. This particular role too has greatly changed since the 1980s when under CIA-ISI tutelage religious parties' importance has grown with the growth of Kalashnikovs and narcotics culture. But this is a relatively new phenomenon. Some compatibility is emerging among the political traditions of NWFP and Karachi's middle class but gives intimation of new factors emerging: different sections of the people are beginning to assert themselves over ethnic and development issues, including the emergence of civil society as a factor. Other factors that would influence the outcome, at least in the near future, are minority provinces' determination to have a more balanced federation in the country so that the smaller provinces can benefit from their own resources. Regional nationalisms in Sindh, Balochistan and NWFP are factors that cannot be trifled with much longer. Who can forget the significance of the ongoing insurgency in Balochistan that clearly aims at establishing the province's control over its considerable resources and through them to the control of the Baloch people? It is in its fourth year and shows no signs of withering away.

Far and away the most important factor that should shape the future is the economic conditions of the masses, given the current high food inflation rates (25 per cent and going up) and the largely man-made shortages of foodstuffs, electricity outages and ever higher user charges of essential utilities. The present conditions cannot continue indefinitely; something has to give way. After an asserted but controversial decline in poverty circa 2004, it seems to be strongly growing again. The disparity of incomes between the rich and the poor is also rapidly growing amidst ever higher price levels. The overall management of the economy has clearly been inefficient and corrupt; the macro-economic indicators are seriously looking downward for the fourth year running. The old worries of an economic meltdown have returned that had disappeared under the initial impact of substantial American aid after 9/11. Although this aid is not likely to disappear quickly, the underlying weaknesses of the economy are moving inexorably toward a Balance of Payments Crisis (on Current Account) that would be difficult to overcome. What is creating persistent pressures is the absence of any programme or plan to correct over-consumption by both the public and private sectors that are seen to result from the WTO rules implemented too soon too fully. True, the US is likely to bail out Pakistan so long as it continues to pursue a course of policy it approves.

But lately, the Americans have become dissatisfied with both the performance of the Pakistan Army in the tribal areas of NWFP and the results of the recent elections in Pakistan: the first result is likely to be an unending tug of war between the PPP president and most politicians in the Parliament. Also, the American media and think tanks have lately (2009) become disenchanted with post-Musharraf government too, though they formally support it while, apparently, grooming the new army chief. However, the Americans have not done too well in their war on terror either in Iraq or in Afghanistan; NATO generals are freely predicting a defeat for American purposes in Afghanistan also, though curiously no Western leader has so far talked of withdrawing from Afghanistan. What the new American administration under Barack H. Obama after Bush would do in 2009 in Iran and also in Afghanistan is basically uncertain. If by any chance the American interest in Afghanistan and the war wanes, its Pakistan policy may also undergo a radical change. The American media, politicians and think tanks were volubly recommending that America should change its Pakistan policy and make it a policy of befriending rather the people of Pakistan. Its earlier US aid policies largely benefited the elite groups in Pakistan and not its people. Obama's answer is the Kerry–Lugar aid bill that will give $ 1.5 billion a year economic aid meant for the people that the Americans will directly spend in Pakistan. The level of distrust of the Islamabad government can scarcely go any further.

In the short run, the Pakistan Army is signalling that it would distance itself from politics as such and would stay neutral in the political games now going on. Since it is not likely that American interest in Pakistan Army would soon decline, and thus their view of its utility can scarcely change; the potential of both army and America to go on determining Pakistan politics looks likely to continue. That effectively dilutes the Pakistan Army's determination to stay away from politics.

But the question has also to be seen in terms of Pakistan's own problems that would continue to intrude on the political situation from time to time and create crises. Few can forget the old question of federalism that has already been dealt with here. Who can forget the country was dismembered in 1971 on this very question when East Pakistan morphed itself into Bangladesh. Then, there is the still growing problem of Islamic Extremism that leads into militancy and insurgency. Hitherto the joint strategy of Pakistan and US military in Afghanistan and also in the Frontier areas have relied on purely military approach: kill or capture them. For Pakistan, a populous and poor Muslim country where far too much of empty Islamic rhetoric has been overused for over sixty years, a rational discussion of this problem is not easy, much less to find a commonly-accepted solution. And yet, it is a major concern of Pakistanis; after all it impinges on their future. Islamic terror, all said and done, is no more than a nuisance for Western powers; but it is a matter that will deeply influence the Pakistani people's safety and well being.

The difficulty is that Pakistan is a man-made state, made only sixty-two years ago amidst much controversy – not only with India as such but among the Muslims themselves. For instance, all Muslim religious parties in India opposed the Pakistan idea including even the Shias; remember M.A. Jinnah had to face Hussainbhai Lalji in his Bombay constituency in 1946 who was then the president of All India Shia Federation. The Deoband seminary never hesitated in its opposition to India's partition. Jamaat-e-Islami changed its line with the fact of partition. All these controversies were inherited and became metamorphosed into Pakistan's first big controversy over its political system: should it be a Western-style democracy or a new pure and Islamic state, a replica of the earliest Islamic Caliphates. That controversy has remained unresolved. That has prevented effective national unity in Pakistan. It distorts politics as well as foreign policy.

SUMMING UP OF THE PROSPECTS

The criteria for prognosticating the immediate future, even quite tentatively, are uncertain interrelationships among several factors. The main among these are:

(a) Success of the governments in keeping law and order amidst rising crime rate, mindless violence, high inflation rates and growing extent of unemployment and poverty.

(b) Growth of political protest as a result of unresolved crises over issues such as:

(i) the clutch of issues created by the judges' restoration, such as the army chief's 3 November 2007 actions of imposing Emergency, giving a new Provisional Constitution Order and a few ordinances for gagging the electronic media and the press;

(ii) extraordinary powers for the president written by various dictators into the Constitution;

(iii) how well does authority tackle the economy's multiple crises, especially the food shortages and high inflation rates as also the deeper problems of poverty and wide-scale unemployment and steady worsening of the macro-economic indicators, indicating an eventual economic meltdown;

(iv) can the Americans be kept in good humour vis-à-vis Pakistan's conduct in the war on terror who have begun intruding into Pakistan territory in active pursuit of, or aerial attacks on, Taliban or al Qaeda-linked Islamic militants that use NWFP's tribal agencies as sanctuary for attacking Western targets or interests in Afghanistan;

(v) since the scope for taking adverse action against Pakistan is indeed wide for the US, it is a matter of immense importance for Islamabad's rulers to manage these relations well because they depend a great deal on the US for vital military and economic aid and the US also gives to, or spends money in, Pakistan that is considerable, any withholding of such aid or facilitation by America can be painful;

(vi) the theoretical possibilities of an angry America (over Pakistan Army wanting to cut separate deals with various Taliban or other Islamic militants as opposed to going on aggressively fighting against them so that the militants do not use Pakistan territory for mounting attacks in Afghanistan) include doing to Pakistan what they did to Cambodia during the Vietnam war, that is, saturation bombing of it because it was thought to be the route Viet Congs took in mounting attacks on South Vietnam. Given America's track record, no Pakistani ruler can discard this possibility off hand.

The assumption being made here is that, made up as Pakistan economy and society are and the way they have been running, it is imperative that Pakistan should keep its relationship with an American-led West in excellent shape. In other words, Pakistan cannot afford to annoy, much less alienate, America. Why? Because its society is so constituted that the economy remains an integral part of the Western economic system and requires a great deal of foreign aid because it has such a large military establishment.that cannot be sustained by the Pakistan economy alone. Pakistan Army is perhaps the world's sixth or seventh largest army. It has to be kept updated in equipment and in training – the US aids it while China also gives a certain amount of military aid. Considering all the current economic factors and the proclivity of the Pakistan elites to consume more than what Pakistan economy can actually provide, this country can scarcely think of changing its basic course of remaining closely aligned with America and the rest of the West. The price of diverging from it would be quite painful for its social and ruling elites. It is impossible for Pakistani elites to do what Iranian rulers do. Iran does not depend on Western aid; it is an oil producer; and has resources of its own, the bulk of which are not appropriated by its social elites; and it prefers to stay self-dependent rather than depending on others.

SCENARIOS TO EXPECT

Scenario One

The first scenario to be expected is that the Pakistani social elites, on the head of which today stands the PPP-led government, followed closely by the Pakistan Army and the so called 'establishment' – basically the bureaucracy that includes the higher echelons of the government, which represents and indeed includes other social elites or at least commands their support – would, other things being equal, do essentially what America dictates, if they are convinced that the Americans mean business and would not allow them off the hook. The issue is whether the Pakistanis will be able to convince the Americans – which is unlikely – of the harsh necessity for them to take a different line from theirs on making peace deals with the Taliban and other Islamic militants in the tribal areas. Otherwise, the Americans have indirectly been threatening Pakistan to do a variant of what they did in Cambodia in the 1970s. It is a moment of truth for the ruling elites in Pakistan. It does look as if things will come to head, sometime during the year 2010. Although Pakistan Army had opted for hard fighting in Swat and Malakand during the spring and summer of 2009, compulsions to making peace agreements with various other militant commanders (or warlords) in various tribal areas, is ever present. Compulsions like the one, in the years after 2004, under which it acted because it has had its nose bloodied. Pakistan Army has suffered far more casualties in the last three or four years than what Western troops have suffered in seven years in Afghanistan – Pakistan may have suffered the loss of approximately 2000 soldiers and paramilitary personnel, since 2004. In this moment of truth, repeating Swat is risky; the decision-makers will have to weigh whether they would risk a possible American aerial bombardment with all they have at one extreme, or would they persuade America away from adopting that extreme course. A via media of some kind is more likely to be evolved to convince the Americans that Pakistanis will do their maximum to prevent the Taliban, al-Qaeda and other Islamic militants from using Pakistani territory as a sanctuary for attacking Afghan or Western targets in Afghanistan. But they have done the hard fighting before. Now, the Americans themselves are trying to cut a deal with the 'moderate' Taliban. Pakistan's campaigns, in the end, strengthened Taliban and other militant groups. Can this recent action achieve any lasting result? Nobody expects that, not even the Americans; they only want Pakistan Army to go on hammering FATA militants to keep them there (and not be able to go out to make armed attacks inside Afghanistan). Damn the longer term cost to Pakistan. What can be expected out of this Afghan war is only barely camouflaged retreat. Pakistan's problem with the Taliban would have been intensified into a grave crisis. The further one looks into the future, the darker is the prospect of a free democratic Pakistan.

The prospect is grim indeed. It begins with the government and the Pakistan Army agreeing to do what the Americans want, but achieve nothing different from what is happening until today. In other words, Pakistan Army continues to alienate not only all the Islamic militant groups in the tribal areas, but also the people of NWFP, by its basically ineffective military actions – with civilian casualties producing yet more militants. Remember a whole armed company of Pakistan Army could be 'abducted' by a score or two of Islamic militants along with their transports. The fact of the matter that has to be faced is: Pakistan Army just cannot go on fighting its own people the way the Americans want – they would desert, they would surrender quickly and all the rest of what a disgruntled soldier in war does. The situation would remain muddy and the Americans and the Pakistanis would continue to bicker. The Americans would continue to make accusations that Pakistan is not fulfilling its part of the bargain, while the Pakistanis will say that they are doing the maximum they can. While the chances of Pakistan's Talibanization will increase, it is also likely to be preceded by a bloody civil war.

Scenario Two

Scenario two would be that the US does punish Pakistan a la the Cambodian model after they despair of the strategy of buying the Pakistani peoples' hearts and minds. But what that would mean is that the whole NWFP and the adjoining areas in Balochistan and Punjab would become even more Talibanized than they are already, and the Americans would have to bring the entire lot of NATO armies into Pakistan in order to quell the big trouble that Pakistan will have become. No kind of victory to the West can be anticipated. They will have produced many more extremists and militants as they kill from the air.

First of all, there are clear limits to what aerial bombardment can achieve anywhere by anyone. Unless there are boots on the ground, no major political objective can be won. If the idea is to destroy the Taliban and other Islamic militants, it would require an army of the size of at least a million or so. But even that cannot achieve victory. It will only involve military occupation. But that will not be of the kind that Britain had imposed on these tribal areas from later nineteenth century till their departure in 1947. The West will be in a far bigger quagmire than Iraq and Afghanistan put together. (It is tempting to dwell on what precisely the Americans are trying to achieve in Afghanistan, and for which reason they would create an unimaginable turmoil in such a populous country as Pakistan that stands at the junction of three regions in Asia). But that is not directly relevant to what to expect in Pakistan in the near future, except to wonder how important the mission is for America and the NATO powers – for which they are spending so much treasure and blood in Afghanistan. Remember, no one is talking about packing up from Afghanistan yet, although the American policy these days is all about withdrawing troops from Iraq – but they are still not putting a date on the withdrawal from Afghanistan. The last question is, can Pakistan escape dire fate?

Scenario Three

The third scenario is far more unlikely. It is one where the Pakistani leadership, army, new president and various governments stick together and decide to resist Islamic zealotry by extending as much modernization, democratic rights and fruits of economic development as they possibly can. This possibly can be their main line of attack. Fighting Islamic extremism may actually involve flooding the area with modern politics, presence of many more contending ideologies and encouraging the people there to begin debating rather than shooting. Promotion of media and forums for discussion will be an inseparable part of this main line of attack. All parties and all democratic rights, jobs and more opportunities and a vigorous and free media should be encouraged there. Military may have to be used as a last resort, with discretion and sparingly in a defensive mode – not as the first choice. Whether this will succeed is uncertain, especially without the amplitude of economic development and jobs. Moreover, all democratic freedoms will anyways be needed. But what the American approach has actually achieved in Afghanistan is that the US is now far more disliked among Arabs, Iranians, Afghans, Pakistanis and others. A mainly political (that is, democratic) approach is what might succeed. Indeed, it is already very late.

Index